D0399841

ifacs

STUDIES IN A CHRISTIAN WORLD VIEW
Sponsored by the Institute for Advanced Christian Studies
Carl F. H. Henry, Editor-in-chief

Titles available

Topics in preparation

The Institute for Advanced Christian Studies is a non-profit corporation dedicated to the development of Christian scholarly writing for our times. Mailing address: Box 95496, Chicago, IL 60694

THE PERSON
IN
PSYCHOLOGY

A Contemporary Christian Appraisal

MARY STEWART VAN LEEUWEN

INTER-VARSITY PRESS
LEICESTER, ENGLAND

WILLIAM B. EERDMANS PUBLISHING COMPANY
GRAND RAPIDS, MICHIGAN

Copyright © 1985 by Wm. B. Eerdmans Publishing Company

Inter-Varsity Press
38 De Montfort Street, Leicester LE1 7GP, England

Wm. B. Eerdmans Publishing Company
255 Jefferson Ave. S.E., Grand Rapids, Michigan 49503

Printed in the United States of America

First Published 1985

British Library Cataloguing in Publication Data
Van Leeuwen, Mary
The person in psychology : a contemporary
christian appraisal.
1. Psychology and religion
I. Title
261.5'15   BF51

ISBN 0-85110-752-4

Library of Congress Cataloging in Publication Data
Van Leeuwen, Mary Stewart, 1943–
The person in psychology.

(Studies in a Christian world view ;
Includes index.
1. Man (Christian theology). 2. Image of God.
3. Christianity—Psychology. 4. Psychology.
I. Title. II. Series.
BT702.V36   1985   261.5'15   85-10181

ISBN 0-8028-0059-9 (pbk.)

Inter-Varsity Press is the publishing division of the Universities and
Colleges Christian Fellowship (formerly the Inter-Varsity Fellowship), a
student movement linking Christian Unions in universities and colleges
throughout the United Kingdom and the Republic of Ireland, and a
member movement of the International Fellowship of Evangelical
Students. For information about local and national activities write to
UCCF, 38 De Montfort Street, Leicester LE1 7GP.

To Raymond, in the spirit of Ecclesiastes 4:9–10

CONTENTS

CONTENTS

CONTENTS

ACKNOWLEDGMENTS

The author and publisher gratefully acknowledge permission to quote material from all the following publications:

Excerpt from "Ethical Issues for Human Services," *Behavior Therapy* 8 (Jan. 1977). Reprinted with permission of the Association for Advancement of Behavior Therapy.

Excerpts from *Christianity Confronts Modernity* © 1981 by Peter Williamson and Kevin Perrotta. Published by Servant Publications, P.O. Box 8617, Ann Arbor, Michigan 48107. Used with permission.

Excerpts from *Our Fragile Brains* by D. Gareth Jones. © 1981 by Inter-Varsity Christian Fellowship of the USA and used by permission of InterVarsity Press, Downers Grove, IL 60515.

Excerpts from *Personality Theories: A Comparative Analysis*, 4th ed., by Salvatore R. Maddi. Copyright © 1968 by Dorsey Press.

Excerpts from *Scripts, Plans, Goals and Understanding* by Roger C. Shank and Robert P. Abelson. Copyright © 1977 by Lawrence Erlbaum Associates, Inc.

Excerpts from *Toward Transformation in Social Knowledge* by Kenneth J. Gergen. Copyright © 1982 by Springer-Verlag.

INTRODUCTION

It is a source of both honor and satisfaction to me to be included among the authors in the IFACS series, Studies in a Christian World View. In light of the positive reception given to Arthur Holmes' *Contours of a World View* and Keith Yandell's *Christianity and Philosophy*, I can only hope that this, the third book of the series, will prove as helpful to its intended readers as the first two volumes have been to theirs.

Although I am an academic social psychologist by training, my target audience for this book includes not only graduate and undergraduate students in psychology but also practicing counselors and clinicians, seminarians and students of theology, and educated laity both within the church and hovering curiously about its fringes. It is intended, in short, for all who have a concern for the content and direction of contemporary psychology and wish to ponder how both might appear when critically observed through the lens of a Christian world view.

Two themes unite the volume—the first theoretical, the second methodological. On the theoretical level, I have concentrated, as the title suggests, on the psychology of personhood and how it relates to the image of God as understood in the broad tradition of Christian theology. Within the various theoretical systems of psychology there is a marked tendency to view the person in either reduced or inflated terms—that is, either as the mere product of natural causes at one extreme, or as the autonomous, self-correcting crown of evolution at the other. Because we as persons are indeed related both downward to the material creation as well as upward to a transcendent creator, there is a moment of truth in each of these extreme positions. But the first (reductionistic) view takes too little account of the image of God in persons, while the second (triumphalistic) view takes too little account of human finitude and sin.

The theoretical task of this volume, then, is the separation of biblical from unbiblical assumptions in several areas of contemporary academic psychology, and the parallel suggestion of theoretical developments that more adequately comport with a Christian psychology of the person. The larger part of this theoretical analysis takes place in the second section of the book, which critically surveys the areas of neuropsychology and behavioral, cognitive, social, and personality psychology. These chapters are deliberately arranged in hierarchical fashion, beginning with an area of psychology closely connected with purely physiological concerns and proceeding to areas in which the problems of biological reductionism shade little by little into the opposite problems of triumphalism and self-deification. In all cases I have tried to give credit where it is due and to capture the richness and excitement, no less than the confusion and implicit ideology, that greet the student of psychology at every turn in this complex human science.

On the methodological level, I have made common cause with much recent philosophy of science in trying to show that the era of "naive realism" in all science—but especially in a human science such as psychology—is being appropriately replaced by what has come to be called "critical realism." Developers of this latter position have shown that scientists' values, interests, and world views— whether implicitly or explicitly embraced—interact with the logic of science at all points, including the construction of theories, the choice and application of methods, and the organization and interpretation of findings. While one cannot and should not press this position to the point of relativizing the entire scientific endeavor, it is still essential to grasp that both natural and social sciences (the latter in even greater degree than the former) have this personal, or interpretive, face interwoven with their better-explicated and more neutral rule-following face. It is in the service of this end that the title of this book is deliberately ambiguous: it is as much concerned with the persons who *do* psychology as it is with the essential nature of the persons about whom they theorize and from whom they regularly gather data.

In coming to appreciate the insights of the critical realist, Christians in psychology acquire two additional mandates: first, to expose the ideology (naturalist, humanist, Marxist, or whatever) in the guise of supposedly neutral science; and second, to clearly articulate their own Christian control beliefs in all phases of their work. If world views inevitably interact with the social-scientific enterprise, I have argued, it is infinitely better to have a world view that is recorded, stated, and subject to ongoing discussion than one that is implicit yet still powerfully influential. This position and its implications for a Christian apprehension of psychology are developed in the first section of the book and used as a critical tool in all chapters of the second section.

As the reader progresses through both of these sections, he or she should bear in mind that although this is an interdisciplinary effort, it is necessarily a work more psychological than theological. While I have done my best to represent accurately the various aspects of the doctrine of persons, the result was never intended to compete with a systematic theological account of the same. In addition, the critical realism that I have urged the reader to focus on psychology should be brought to bear equally on the book itself: it is in no way to be seen as the final, positive word on the relationship between a Christian world view and the psychology of personhood, but rather as one effort among many that I have been encouraged to see emerge in the past decade or so. The Anglo-American Christian community is fortunate to have a growing number of committed and well-trained social scientists addressing their various disciplines through the eyes of Christian belief. Those of us who feel called to such a task generally follow each other's work with interest and appreciation, even when we do not always agree on all points. It has been my wish to present views other than my own in a spirit of fairness and cooperation; for any failure to do so, I accept responsibility and tender sincere apologies.

Many people have aided me in bringing this volume to its final form. The members of the IFACS editorial committee had, from the start, much more confidence in my ability to undertake this project than I had myself. Their unfailing encouragement, gentle criticism, and financial support have made the process of drafting and redrafting chapters much more a pleasure than a burden. Their special consultants for the volume, philosopher Stephen Evans and psychologist Paul Vitz, became very special colleagues as they gave generously of their expertise in reading, criticizing, and improving the style of the manuscript. Neal Plantinga of Calvin Seminary taught me to actually enjoy systematic theology, and Kenneth Gergen of Swarthmore College has confirmed repeatedly that dialogue in a context of mutual respect is eminently possible between Christian and non-Christian reformers in psychology. Various other colleagues at Calvin College, too numerous to mention individually, supplied references, helpful information, and listening ears.

My husband, Ray Van Leeuwen, has been solidly supportive of this project since its inception, and has remained so even when my theoretical and critical analyses have not been as Dutch in character as he might have wished. Our children, Dirk and Neil, seem none the worse for the neglect they may have suffered while I wrote, the latter going cheerfully off to day care as I labored over successive drafts, and the former returning good for ill by helping me to alphabetize the index entries found at the end of the book. To all these persons I extend my heartfelt thanks.

MARY STEWART VAN LEEUWEN

PART ONE
PSYCHOLOGY AND THE STUDY OF PERSONS
From Past to Present

CHAPTER 1

PSYCHOLOGY
IN A
POSTMODERN AGE

Psychology as an academic profession is engaged in by individuals who are part of a microcommunity of scholars. But
these same individuals are part of a larger community—
society at large—and the developing scholar and his ideas,
in part, both reflect and influence the underlying social
structure.

—Allan R. Buss[1]

As I have already noted in my introduction, *The Person in Psychology*
is an ambiguous title, since it might be taken to refer either to the
persons studied *by* psychologists or to persons *in* psychology who are
engaged in the study of others. This ambiguity is quite deliberate, and
reflects my conviction that a Christian treatment of contemporary
psychology must necessarily focus on both aspects. It must evaluate
not only the conclusions that psychologists draw about others but also
those that they draw—explicitly or (more often) implicitly—about
themselves. For the social sciences, unlike most of the natural sciences, are inescapably reflexive: they involve the study of human
activity by human beings who themselves participate in that activity.[2] Consequently, unless social scientists are to regard themselves

1. Buss, "The Emerging Field of the Sociology of Psychological Knowledge," *American Psychologist* 30 (Oct. 1975): 990.
2. For a further development of this theme, see Mary Stewart Van
Leeuwen, "Reflexivity in North American Psychology: Historical Reflections on One Aspect of a Changing Paradigm," *Journal of the American Scientific Affiliation* 35 (Dec. 1982): 193–200.

as a breed totally apart from their human subjects, it is fair to insist that any psychology of persons should also include a consideration of the "psychology of psychologists." This "psychology of psychologists" and its changeable influence on psychology itself are central concerns of the first part of this book.

Yet it is also fair to warn the reader that, in general, Anglo-American psychologists are still not very sensitive to their need to embrace this dual mandate. Psychologists with a disciplinary self-consciousness, like the one represented in our opening quotation, are still a small minority, although one whose work and influence we will have occasion to examine more closely in Chapter Nine. Indeed, for much of this century (the first century of psychology's existence as a formalized discipline) a forceful case was made for eliminating any sort of consciousness—whether the psychologist's or anyone else's—from the list of topics considered appropriate for psychological investigation. As J. B. Watson wrote in 1913,

> Psychology as the behaviorist views it is a purely objective experimental branch of natural science. Introspection forms no essential part of its methods, nor is the scientific value of its data dependent upon the readiness with which they lend themselves to interpretation in terms of consciousness. The behaviorist, in his efforts to get a unitary scheme of animal response, recognizes no dividing line between man and brute—the time seems to have come when psychology must discard all references to consciousness.[3]

Thus began the forceful influence of American behaviorism, a psychology as indifferent to the person of the psychologist as it was to the unique psychology of the persons it studied. In both respects (as Watson readily and proudly professed) it was a psychology that apprenticed itself to the ideals of objectivity then current in the natural sciences, an apprenticeship the history and consequences of which I have traced in more detail elsewhere.[4] Much has changed in psychology since then, although the legacy of behaviorism is still strong (and will receive more detailed treatment in Chapter Seven). But psychol-

3. Watson, "Psychology as the Behaviorist Views It," *Psychological Review* 20 (Mar. 1913): 158.
4. Mary Stewart Van Leeuwen, *The Sorcerer's Apprentice: A Christian Looks at the Changing Face of Psychology* (Downers Grove, Ill.: InterVarsity Press, 1982).

ogy no longer neglects the minds of its human (or even its animal!) subjects. Indeed, it is currently in the midst of what some have labeled a "cognitive revival"—a renewed surge of interest in human thinking that also merits its own separate treatment in Chapter Eight.

Nevertheless, for the purpose of introducing this part of the book, the trends inaugurated by Watson remain important for two reasons. First of all, in writing off consciousness as a legitimate topic for psychology, behaviorists were also retarding the development of a *self*-conscious psychology that could evaluate its institutional existence by any standards other than the narrowly scientific. In other words, although it is now respectable for psychologists to study the minds of people in general, psychologists' reflecting on their own mind-set and the conditions that influence it is still rare. Second, in his eagerness to study the communalities of "man and brute" by a single experimental method, Watson helped to entrench a commitment to evolutionary theory not only with regard to the continuity of animals and people but also with regard to the history of psychology itself. The latter point deserves some elaboration because it furnishes a relevant example of what can happen when the practitioners of a social science fail to study their own implicit assumptions with the same care that they devote to exposing the assumptions and motivations of others.

WHIG HISTORIOGRAPHY, POSITIVISM, AND THEIR AFTERMATH IN PSYCHOLOGY

Due to the remarkable power of the natural sciences and also to the widespread acceptance of evolutionary theory in the biological and social sciences, psychology, from its formal beginnings a century ago, has tended to adhere to a *presentist* view of its own history. According to such a view, psychology (or any other enterprise embracing such a historiography) has progressed in slow but cumulative fashion to its present state, which is considered to be both correct and inevitable. By the efforts of particularly eminent and farsighted individuals— occasionally but unsuccessfully hampered by rearguard conservatives—the scientific discoveries of the discipline have gradually accumulated in a progressive and interlocking way up to the present. Such a view of the past is sometimes called "Whig historiography," after the eighteenth-century English liberals who presumed that their own reformist political views would inevitably succeed those of their conservative opponents.[5] "Whig history," as one critic put it, "is history with a happy ending"[6]—at least for the group interpreting its own past, since it inevitably concludes that the current state of affairs is just what it should be, and that the future will be even better yet.

In the history of science or social science, this type of historiography has tended to be selective about what it has emphasized from the past, placing in a positive light the precursors of present orthodoxy and dismissing almost everything else as prescientific at best or obscurantist at worst. On such an account, current Anglo-American psychology is interpreted as a kind of evolutionary triumph, with the soundest, most correct ideas and approaches emerging victorious from the ongoing intellectual struggle. More than one critic has recently argued that the premier historian of scientific psychology, Edwin G. Boring,[7] was fundamentally a Whig historian who used his considerable prestige as founding chairman of Harvard's psychology department to promulgate a simplistically progressive view of psychology's history that is only now being reexamined.[8]

The presentist historiography that has characterized psychology is linked with a supporting philosophy of science known as *positivism*. As originally conceived by Auguste Comte, a nineteenth-century French philosopher, "positive philosophy" saw human intellectual history in terms of three progressive stages. The first, wrote Comte, was a theological stage in which the world and human destiny were explained in terms of gods and spirits. During the second, or transitional, stage, explanations were in terms of metaphysical (but not religious) essences, final causes, and other abstractions. The third and crowning stage, according to Comte, was the modern "positive" stage, in which absolute explanations of *any* kind were to be abandoned as historically and socially conditioned and therefore unreliable. In their place, he said, humankind should be content to

5. Herbert Butterfield, *The Whig Interpretation of History* (London: Bell, 1951).

6. Barry N. Kelly, "E. G. Boring's Historiography in Relation to the Psychology of His Time" (minor doctoral paper, York University, Toronto, 1980), p. 1.

7. Boring, *A History of Experimental Psychology* (New York: Appleton-Century-Crofts, 1951).

8. See Kelly, "E. G. Boring's Historiography"; and also John M. O'Donnell, "The Crisis of Experimentation in the 1920's: E. G. Boring and His Use of History," *American Psychologist* 34 (Apr. 1979): 289–95.

establish scientific "laws," or regular connections among physical and social phenomena. This limited, testable way of establishing knowledge was all that human beings could be sure of. The positivist attitude that Comte nurtured remains strong in psychology today. (See also Chapter Five.)

In the past few decades, however, the assumptions of Whig historiography and positivism have begun to be questioned. This trend owes much to the work of Karl Popper (1902–   ), a philosopher of science. In his book *The Logic of Scientific Discovery*, published in 1959, Popper argued that even the most current and apparently powerful scientific laws must be regarded only as the "most plausible possibilities" for the present, always open to potential falsification and rejection in light of later and more sophisticated scientific work.[9] But while thus historically relativizing the *results* of science, Popper still maintained that the *logic* of science itself was transtemporally reliable—that is, unaffected by the historical, social, and psychological pressures that surround its practitioners in any given era. It is safe to say that it is the Popperian view of science that has gradually replaced progressivist Whig historiography in psychology since Boring's death in 1968. That is, while showing more modesty about the permanence of its theoretical conclusions, Anglo-American psychology is still essentially a science of persons that neglects or tries to cancel out the personal and group idiosyncrasies of psychologists themselves.[10]

PARADIGMS AND PERSONAL KNOWLEDGE

It has remained for two other scientists turned philosopher-historians to argue that even the actual "logic of science" is other than what Popper would have us conclude. Thomas Kuhn, in his *Structure of Scientific Revolutions*,[11] argued that the very doing of science is itself a

9. Popper, *The Logic of Scientific Discovery* (New York: Basic Books, 1959).
10. For a consciously Popperian view of psychology, see Daniel N. Robinson, *An Intellectual History of Psychology*, rev. ed. (New York: Macmillan, 1981). For works that merely assume this perspective unreflectively, see many of the best-selling introductory texts, including Ernest R. Hilgard, Rita L. Atkinson, and Richard C. Atkinson, *Introduction to Psychology*, 7th ed. (New York: Harcourt Brace Jovanovich, 1979).
11. Kuhn, *The Structure of Scientific Revolutions*, rev. ed. (Chicago: University of Chicago Press, 1971).

subjective and value-laden enterprise. Kuhn's analysis of the history of science revealed that scientists do not proceed solely according to the rules of logic and empirical investigation; they are affected by psychosocial influences within and around them that tend to channel their work in certain directions to the exclusion of others. Moreover, Kuhn suggested, most scientific work is not fearless pioneering into uncharted territory but rather variations on a restricted number of research themes designed to reveal how neatly the scientist can demonstrate what is already well-established. Kuhn used the term "paradigm" to capture what he meant by the matrix of accepted theories, methods, and issues that constrain the work of any group of scientists at any point in history. Such constraints mean that most science is what Kuhn called "normal science"—science more or less unconsciously done within the boundaries of the accepted paradigm: not basic "problem-solving" but mere "puzzle-solving," concerned with the details but not the fundamental substance of that paradigm.[12]

In the doing of such normal science, Kuhn concluded, it is not the brilliant renegade but the cautious conservative hewing to the party line who is most often professionally successful. Scientific revolutions do occur: recall the transition from Newtonian to Einsteinian physics. But they are rare, and they result in changed paradigms only in the face of much well-intentioned (and some merely self-protective) resistance from the current scientific establishment.

Kuhn was concerned to show how the long-standing ideal of modern scientific objectivity was more rhetoric than reality. In doing so, he helped to launch what is often called the postmodern philosophy of science. Yet Kuhn notwithstanding, it seems obvious that scientists, even social scientists, do make coherent advances of a sort, despite the subjective and historical forces that inevitably color their work. As Allan R. Buss put it in the comment that introduced this chapter, they "both reflect *and* influence the underlying social structure" in a dynamic of mutual change (italics mine). Consequently, it has been the aim of a second postmodern philosopher of science, Michael Polanyi, to reconceptualize the nature of scientific discovery following the breakdown of the objectivist ideal. Polanyi's landmark work, *Personal Knowledge*, makes fascinating if challenging reading.[13] In it he makes clear that he believes in and respects the methods of science, but holds them to be largely different from the common

12. Kuhn, *The Structure of Scientific Revolutions*, chap. 4.
13. Polanyi, *Personal Knowledge: Towards a Post-Critical Philosophy*, rev. ed. (Chicago: University of Chicago Press, 1962).

image projected about them. According to him, the truly innovative scientist has undergone rigorous training and works in a sophisticated research setting—but more than that, he or she has the intuitive ability to choose a problem of potential significance before any work has been done on it. In a sense he or she must have a faith that is "the assurance of things hoped for, the conviction of things not seen" (Heb. 11:1). This highly personal process of choosing a fertile starting-point is almost completely neglected in the mainstream philosophy of science. Popper, for example, regarded it as largely irrelevant to the logic of scientific discovery.[14]

Yet Polanyi's own experience as a physical chemist convinced him that the rules of scientific procedure were of secondary importance to the role of creative imagination in choosing a problem and the role of creative perception in extracting new patterns from old facts. As one exponent of Polanyi has put it, "Two scientists could have a perfectly identical understanding of scientific laws and theories, but one may make a great discovery and the other spend his or her life doing ordinary research which conforms to current knowledge. The difference lies in the personal judgment of the scientist."[15]

Polanyi went on to collect numerous case-studies in the history of science that demonstrate the importance of the scientist's intentional and imaginative efforts to find order in reality. Perhaps the most famous of these is the case of Einstein, who in his own autobiography wrote that even as a schoolboy he had begun to think intuitively about the problem of relativity. More specifically, he had begun to wonder what would happen if he were pursuing a beam of light while moving at the speed of light himself.[16] Successful scientific breakthroughs, it seems, are commonly preceded by what appears to be science fiction. Again, this is not to say that a rigorous apprenticeship in science is not necessary—only that, according to Polanyi, it is not a *sufficient* condition for making significant breakthroughs.

POSTMODERN THOUGHT AND THE CHRISTIAN PSYCHOLOGIST

It is certainly accurate to say that most of Anglo-American psychology has not even begun to absorb the impact of Kuhn's and

14. Popper, *The Logic of Scientific Discovery*, chap. 1.
15. Richard Gelwick, *The Way of Discovery: An Introduction to the Thought of Michael Polanyi* (New York: Oxford University Press, 1977), p. 26.
16. Einstein, quoted in Polanyi, *Personal Knowledge*, p. 10.

Polanyi's work. This is somewhat ironic, since both men have explicitly appealed to psychological principles such as social conditioning, defense mechanisms, motivation, and perceptual restructuring to account for both the persistence of normal science and the occurrence of extraordinary scientific discoveries. Yet in my estimation their work is very important both to psychology in general and to the subject matter of this book in particular. I offer the following reasons for such a conviction.

First of all, if their analysis of the scientific enterprise is correct, then we are not obliged to believe that the most currently salient theories and inferences in psychology represent the most accurate statement of the way things really are. We need no longer adhere to a Whig historiography or be intimidated by those who continue to do so. Certainly even Popper would willingly concede this. But Kuhn and Polanyi would go even further and insist that psychologists have, in common with other scientists, vested interests, blind spots, and even individual intuitions that weaken any claim that their methods are somehow transtemporally neutral and totally consistent. Their work is a warning that no scientist, psychologist or otherwise, can absolutize either a particular theory or a particular method of arriving at truth. To do so is at best naive and at worst, for the Christian, bordering on the idolatrous.

To say this, however, is not to endorse methodological anarchy in the sciences or the social sciences, as some extreme postmodern thinkers have done. Paul Feyerabend, for example, insists that even scientific theories from the same domain cannot be logically compared with each other: they are said to be incommensurable, because each necessarily invests the same theoretical constructs with different meanings. Moreover, says Feyerabend—writing from a strongly liberationist perspective—for scientists to claim a single, correct method of doing science is for them to claim a special hold on the truth, an absolutism that is bound to diminish those who are not privy to it. To Feyerabend it is such "experts"—whether theological, political, or scientific—who are the main stumbling-blocks to a liberated society. Against them, he proclaims, "There is no method, and there is no authority."[17] Yet, in the words of Ernan McMullin, a philosopher at Notre Dame, "Surely there may be a reasonable half-way house be-

17. Feyerabend, "Experts in a Free Society," *The Critic* (Nov. 1970): 68. See also his *Against Method: Outline of an Anarchistic Theory* (London: N.L.B. Press, 1975).

tween [positivistic] totalitarianism and well-intentioned anarchy."[18] In other words, it should be possible to incorporate the insights of the postmodern philosophy of science without reducing the conduct of science to mere subjectivism.

McMullin arrives at such a compromise by speaking of the "two faces" of science: its *logical* face and its *interpretive* face. The first of these involves the formal relationships between evidence and hypothesis by an appeal to rules that are formal and applicable to many types of problems. It includes deductive, inductive, and hypothetico-deductive types of argument, often intermingled in complex ways. At the same time that they appeal to the validating rules of logic, however, scientists also attach meanings to and perceive structures in what they study—and this is the *interpretive*, or *patterning*, side of science. This kind of intellectual activity is more difficult to define, more personal, more immediate, and more context-dependent than the application of formal rules—just as Polanyi has shown it to be—yet it is still very much a part of scientific rationality along with the more formal side. Moreover, says McMullin, such interpretive skills are *not* totally idiosyncratic: they are learned skills, dependent on a complex apprenticeship and ultimately validated by pragmatic success. The reading of an X-ray, for example, may be a difficult skill to describe or teach in formal terms. But although dependent on "personal knowledge" kinds of patterning skills, it still has an external criterion of success: did the patient have the disease that was detected in the X-ray or not?[19]

While the logical positivists made the mistake of reducing science to its logical aspects, some postmodern philosophers of science have overcorrected in the other direction and seem to reduce the conduct of science to its interpretive aspect. But both aspects are in fact needed, according to McMullin's analysis. Christians, however, would go a step further still. They are experientially convinced that one particular set of historic documents—the biblical record—has a special status as God's message to humanity. One could liken this experiential conviction to the "personal knowledge" of the scientist

18. McMullin, "Two Faces of Science," *Review of Metaphysics* 27 (June 1974): 655–76. See also his "Philosophy of Science and Its Rational Reconstructions," in *Progress and Rationality in Science*, ed. G. Radnitzky and G. Anderson (Dordrecht, Holland: Reudel Publishers, 1978), pp. 201–32; and also "The Ambiguity of Historicism," in *Current Research in Philosophy of Science* (Philosophy of Science Association, 1978), pp. 55–83.
19. McMullin, "Two Faces of Science," pp. 668–76.

who intuitively knows in advance that a certain area of investigation has significant potential for making discoveries. But it differs from Polanyi's idea of personal knowledge in its claim that what is being tapped is not merely the tacit contents of some ancient Judeo-Christian minds but, by the grace and initiative of God, his own progressive revelation recorded in human, historical terms.

This is not to say that Christians' access to a God-inspired truth creates a totally unbridgeable chasm between themselves and nonbelievers, resulting in consistently different performances in all aspects of life, including the sciences. On the contrary, as Dutch theologian Abraham Kuyper wryly observed, the world often does better than expected and the church, worse.[20] To the extent that all genuinely creative endeavors reflect part of the image of God in human beings, *none* of them can be reduced to the personal knowledge of those involved. Christian or non-Christian, their human vehicles are participating, by God's grace alone, in a small approximation of the transcendent creativity of the Creator himself. Nor does it mean that the doing of theology is somehow specially exempt from the historical, cultural, and psychological influences that affect thinking in other disciplines. This is a point increasingly recognized even by conservative theologians with a high view of Scripture,[21] and a point also made by Polanyi himself to theologians.[22] But Christian convictions should at least mean that the metaphysical assumptions that we now see as permeating all social-science work can be more honestly articulated and more coherently used in theory and research.

This leads us to a second reason for the importance of the postmodern philosophy of science. It is central to a Christian appraisal of contemporary psychology that the work of Kuhn and Polanyi and their followers is slowly undermining the entrenched secularism that has dominated the sciences for so long. For both men have pointed out that scientists are biased, consciously or otherwise, not only by convictions regarding preferred theories and methods but also by what Kuhn calls "prescientific ideas of the order of nature." By these he means essentially metaphysical faith-concepts about the

---

20. Kuyper, quoted in G. C. Berkouwer, *Man: The Image of God*, trans. Dirk W. Jellema, Studies in Dogmatics (Grand Rapids: Eerdmans, 1962), p. 186.

21. See, for example, Clark H. Pinnock, "Getting Our Bias in Perspective," *Christianity Today*, 17 Sept. 1982, p. 58.

22. Polanyi, "Science and Religion: Separate Dimensions or Common Ground?" *Philosophy Today* 7 (Spring 1963): 4–14.

ultimate nature of the universe that condition not only the scientist's preferred research topics and methods but also the interpretation of results and even his or her capacity to communicate with other scientists. Because of such differing ideas about the order of nature, writes Kuhn,

> the proponents of competing paradigms practice their trades in different worlds. . . . Practicing in different worlds, the two groups of scientists see different things when they look from the same point in the same direction. Again, that is not to say that they can see anything they please. Both are looking at the [physical] world, and what they look at has not changed. But in some areas they see different things, and they see them in different relations to each other. That is why a law that cannot even be demonstrated to one group of scientists may occasionally seem intuitively obvious to another. Equally, it is why, before they can hope to communicate fully, one group or the other must experience the conversion that we have been calling a paradigm shift. Just because it is a transition between incommensurables, the transition cannot be made a step at a time, forced by logic and neutral experience. The transfer of allegiance . . . is a conversion experience that cannot be forced.[23]

Now this is something that is of vital significance to Christians. For according to Kuhn, scientific thinking is more like religious thinking than its public image has led us to expect. That is to say, both involve a preliminary faith-commitment to a particular view of the order of nature that is not the same for everyone, and that does not attract adherents solely on the basis of logical argument and empirical evidence, however important these may be. Moreover, even within communities that are committed to a common method of • studying the same "raw material" (nature in the case of science, Scripture in the case of religion), differences of interpretation are unavoidable and sometimes irreconcilable short of the "conversion experience" to which Kuhn likens the scientific paradigm shift.

In short, if Kuhn's analysis is correct, then *everyone*, to use Nicholas Wolterstorff's phrase, "reasons within the bounds of religion," whether they acknowledge it or not.[24] It is not the case (as even many

23. Kuhn, *The Structure of Scientific Revolutions*, pp. 150–51.
24. Wolterstorff, *Reason Within the Bounds of Religion* (Grand Rapids: Eerdmans, 1976).

Christian thinkers have insisted[25]) that one's metaphysical convictions are invoked only in the selection of research topics and the application of results, but otherwise carefully laundered from the actual logical and empirical work of science. Not only do such convictions interact with disciplinary activity, but as Polanyi has tried to document, they are often vital ingredients in making scientific breakthroughs.

* * *

What does all this mean for the Christian student or the Christian observer of psychology? It means, in a sense, that the tables have turned. Christian conviction has long been regarded (even by many Christians) as an impediment to the practice of sound, objective psychology—rather like a personal quirk one must labor to control in polite company. But the postmodern philosophy of science as expressed by Kuhn, Polanyi, and others[26] seems to imply that the reverse is more likely the case. If metaphysical world views affect the scientific practice of even professed atheists, then surely it is an advantage to have a world view that is articulated, recorded, and subject to ongoing discussion rather than one that remains unacknowledged. Not only is this more honest; it is also potentially more beneficial as a scientific catalyst, for it enables psychological thinking and theological thinking to openly cross-fertilize each other, rather than (as in the case of the naturalist or the materialist in psychology) leaving the connection ephemeral and unarticulated yet still powerfully influential.

Thus the scholar attempting a volume such as this needs to acknowledge the special authority of the Bible as it speaks about human nature as God intended it to be, and the very mixed human condition with which we must contend in the wake of the Fall. Moreover (and more difficult still), there is needed a capacity to grasp the thrust of Scripture for a discipline such as psychology in a way that does not, as one theologian has put it, "operate magisterially over the Bible and predetermine what it may authoritatively say to us."[27]

25. For a Catholic example, see Henryk Misiak and Virginia M. Staudt, *Catholics in Psychology: A Historical Survey* (New York: McGraw-Hill, 1956). For various Protestant examples, see Robert W. Smith, ed., *Christ and the Modern Mind* (Downers Grove, Ill.: InterVarsity Press, 1972), especially the essay by Scanzoni on sociology and the essay by Van Daahm on economics.
26. For more recent work in this area, see Frederick Suppe, ed., *The Structure of Scientific Theories*, 2nd ed. (Champaign, Ill.: University of Illinois Press, 1977).
27. Pinnock, "Getting Our Bias in Perspective," p. 58.

It is quite clear to me that in attempting such a task, I, a Christian psychologist (and a nontheologian to boot), risk rushing in where angels fear to tread. Nevertheless, such attempts have been made from time to time, and the results, if expressed cautiously and with appropriate qualifications, have sometimes been fruitful. It is my conviction that a consideration of the past (so often neglected in psychology's adherence to the myth of inevitable scientific progress) is one way to reduce our tunnel vision of the present. Consequently, we will begin (in Chapters Two and Three) with a look at some ancient psychologies of the person as expressed by both non-Western and Western thinkers. This will also give us a historical context with which (in Chapter Four) to contrast the biblical drama of creation, fall, redemption, and future hope, and this in turn will affect our thinking about both psychologists and people they have studied over the years. Finally (in Chapter Five), I will deal with the various ways in which Christians have responded to the challenges of psychology's present-day paradigm, doing so in a way that I hope will give readers a manageable set of issues to carry over into the book's second (and major) section.

CHAPTER 2

NON-WESTERN PSYCHOLOGIES FROM ANCIENT TIMES

> Man, in his quest for an understanding of himself, has at different times seen the problem in different ways, considered different data as relevant, used different methods, and accepted different constructs as explanatory.
> —Robert B. MacLeod[1]

The author of our opening quotation, until his death a well-known psychologist at Cornell University, seems to be confirming a major point of our first chapter: it is unwise to be ahistoric in psychology, because even the most competent and careful scholars inevitably regard the issues of personhood through lenses colored by their own particular times, cultures, and interests. But it was also stated in Chapter One that giving due respect to such a sociology of knowledge should not lead us into the opposite error of concluding that all knowledge is relative, and that the search for truth, in psychology or in any other endeavor, is an exercise in futility. We have been learning, with the help of postmodern philosophers of science, that the doing of science has both an interpretive aspect *and* a logical aspect, the latter involving a stable set of rules even as the former involves what Michael Polanyi called "personal knowledge."

I have already affirmed that this book will examine psychological theories about the person, as well as theories about the persons who do psychology, from the standpoint of a biblical world view. Until the

---

1. MacLeod, "Five Classic Doctrines of Man," in *Historical Conceptions of Psychology*, ed. Mary Henle, Julian Jaynes, and John J. Sullivan (New York: Springer, 1973), p. 149.

advent of the postmodern philosophy of science, such a frank admission of religious allegiance would automatically have limited one's readership to like-minded believers. But the work of scholars such as Polanyi and Thomas Kuhn, in emphasizing the personal and metaphysical aspects of all scientific work, has begun to break down the putative barriers between facts and values, between logic and intuition, and between "objective" science and "subjective" conviction. Consequently, as I also suggested in Chapter One, Christians in psychology need not shrink from using what Nicholas Wolterstorff has called religious "control beliefs"[2] to help them evaluate existing theories of the person and to help them develop, apply, and even disseminate other theories that are more consistent with those beliefs.

This is all the more reasonable when we consider that, in the long reach of history, purely materialist views of the person are the exception. If we go back to a time when social science as we know it was still millennia away, we find that *all* recorded thinking about the nature of persons was religious. Not until the time of the Greeks do we see the beginnings of a separation of psychological questions from religious questions about human nature, and even thereafter, both Christian and Islamic scholars doubted the validity of that separation and labored to find ways to close the gap. But the early, indigenous psychologies of Asia and the ancient Near East were "almost without exception religious psychologies,"[3] concerned to describe the relationship between persons and the forces or deities controlling the world, and to prescribe human behavior in light of these perceived relationships. Even the unwritten testimony of the Stone Age bears witness to the fusion of religious with material concerns: archaeological excavations of both early *Homo sapiens* and their Neanderthal predecessors routinely find ritual burial sites indicating at least a vague conviction that human beings are not limited to purely natural structures and relationships.[4]

The predominance of Whig historiography and the positivist philosophy of science has led to an almost complete disregard for these early "religious psychologies" of Asia and the Near East, and to

2. Wolterstorff, *Reason Within the Bounds of Religion* (Grand Rapids: Eerdmans, 1976). See especially chap. 11.
3. Gardner Murphy and Lois B. Murphy, *Asian Psychology* (New York: Basic Books, 1968), p. xiv.
4. Norman L. Munn, *Evolution and the Growth of Human Behavior* (Boston: Houghton Mifflin, 1955).

the practice of beginning the history of psychology with the more human-centered thinking of the Greeks.[5] But since we have already rejected the view of psychology that uncritically assumes the superiority of the most recent, we have good reason to take at least a brief glance at some ancient conceptions of human nature. For one thing, these will serve as a contrast to the more secular psychologies that emerged in ancient Greece and that have come to dominate modern thought since the scientific revolution. For another, as I have already suggested, they will serve to contextualize the biblical idea of personhood that also emerged and was recorded within the culture of the ancient Near East. In this chapter, then, we will begin with an examination of ancient Mesopotamian ideas about personhood, and then proceed to the Hindu and Buddhist accounts that arose in India and spread to the Far East.

MESOPOTAMIAN PSYCHOLOGY: "WITHOUT HIS PERSONAL GOD, A MAN EATS NOT"

As one of the earliest centers of civilized life, Mesopotamia (literally "the land between the rivers") has yielded archaeological evidence spanning the four millennia before the Christian era. Located between the Tigris and the Euphrates rivers in what is roughly present-day Iraq, Mesopotamia was inhabited first by Sumerians, then later by the Semitic Akkadian peoples, both of whom developed systems of writing that have survived on clay tablets and stone monuments dating as far back as 2000 B.C. From these chiseled cuneiform inscriptions, Near Eastern scholars have gradually put together a fairly coherent account of the historical development, technology, political institutions, and world view of Mesopotamia.

The scientific and technological achievements of the ancient Mesopotamians included sophisticated mathematical and astronomical inquiries, a highly accurate calendar, efficient water-transportation and irrigation systems, and well-designed urban environments. But Near Eastern scholars are generally agreed that the linchpin of the Mesopotamians' existence was a complex religious system that saturated their understanding of every other human un-

5. Murphy and Murphy's *Asian Psychology* is one of the few attempts to appreciate the mingling of psychology with religion in ancient times. A good example of a modern, psychoanalytic attempt to do so is Sudhir Kakar, *Shamans, Mystics, and Doctors* (New York: Knopf, 1982).

dertaking. One scholar has drawn this conclusion: "As the only available intellectual framework that could provide a comprehensive understanding of the forces governing existence, and also guidance for right conduct in life, religion ineluctably conditioned all aspects of ancient Mesopotamian civilization. It yielded the forms in which that civilization's social, economic, legal, political, and military institutions were to be understood, as well as providing the significant symbols for poetry and art."[6]

Although Mesopotamian religion had enduring features such as polytheism, which remained throughout the four-thousand-year span of its civilization, it also seems to have undergone developmental change as well.[7] During the fourth millennium B.C. its basic orientation toward nature worship was laid down. At first it seems that homage was paid directly to the natural forces so vital to human survival, such as fresh water, wind, rain, and sun. Somewhat later these forces were humanized, and we see reference being made to the named gods of various economically important forces and objects. There were gods of marsh life and fish, of bulls and other animals, gods of orchardmen and cowherders and shepherds, goddesses of cows and grains, to name just a few. Nevertheless, this multitude of deities was regarded as (in one writer's terminology) "intransitive"—that is, the deities could not be made to *do* things in response to human petition or sacrifice. Rather, they simply *were*, and as the annual cycle of natural and related economic events ran its course, the relevant deities were each honored in turn.[8] Thus we can infer that the earliest Mesopotamian view of human nature was largely a passive one: human beings simply had to wait upon the timetable of nature to yield them a livelihood, and acknowledge their dependence on the nature deities without entering into any kind of dialogue with them.

Toward the third millennium B.C. this metaphor of gods-in-nature began to change. The civilization was advanced enough to be free of the fear of famine, and politicized enough to have large walled cities the greatest fear of which was enemy attack from without rather than starvation from within. In response to such intermittent attacks, cities began to appoint ad hoc kings to exercise authority during emergencies. Gradually this kingly power was extended to peacetime

6. *Encyclopedia Britannica*, 15th ed., s.v. "Mesopotamian Religions."
7. Thorkild Jacobsen, *The Treasures of Darkness: A History of Mesopotamian Religion* (New Haven: Yale University Press, 1976).
8. Jacobsen, *Treasures of Darkness*, chap. 3.

as well, and kings became more clearly recognized as civil authorities and arbiters of disputes. In parallel with such developments, the kingly metaphor began to be applied as well to the existing gods, who now came to be seen less as personifications of natural forces and more as divine rulers over specific city-based temples and their associated estates. Furthermore, their power was seen as trickling down, in varying degrees, through the ranks of the human overseers of the temples. Yet the sense of total human dependence on the "intransitive" gods remained:

> Since man, as the Sumerians saw him, was weak and could achieve no success in anything without divine assistance, it was fortunate that all these human workers in and outside the temple could invigorate themselves with divine power. Each group of human toilers had human overseers, but above these were the divine officials to direct the work and infuse success into human efforts.[9]

It was through the office of the human city-king that the one-way, intransitive relationship of human beings to deities began to change. The complexities of urban life called for an ever-changing variety of decisions on the part of the human king, and produced an anxious desire to know the mind of the city god before proceeding. Slowly there developed the idea that the king could have access to the divine mind through dreams, visions, and signs, and as a result there developed a detailed technical literature on the practice of divination. Thus, from the total passivity of the fourth-millennial Mesopotamian before the gods, we come to the third-millennial view that at least one person—the king—could converse with the deity (however indirectly) and be his or her agent in the process of ruling the city and its inhabitants.

But it wasn't until the second millennium that the view developed that common people as well as kings could have personal relationships with deities. The surviving tablets from this period and later are particularly fascinating; the Mesopotamians' historical and geographical proximity to ancient Israel led to the Old Testament use of many of the same literary forms that are found in the tablets. The tablets are also of interest to us because the rise of this idea of the

---

9. Jacobsen, *Treasures of Darkness*, p. 81.

"personal god" was accompanied by a religious psychology of the person in the context of his or her relationship to the god. In certain contexts these personal gods were seen in the ambivalent relationship of parent to child: sometimes approachable and forgiving, at other times majestically distant and judgmental (a tension also evident in the psalmist's relationship to the God of the Bible). In other contexts they seem to have been more like the personal saints of traditional Catholicism: favorite mascots from the pantheon who could be expected to use their influence to protect and intercede for their protégés.[10]

In still other contexts these gods were seen almost as personifications of the human beings who professed allegiance to them. A. Leo Oppenheim sees in the several generic terms applied to personal gods an example of the concept of "multiple and external souls"—the idea that different essential aspects of the person are represented by different kinds of supernatural beings.[11] To have an *ilu* spirit, for example, may have meant to possess a kind of general spiritual endowment analogous to a soul. *Ištaru* seems to have been associated with the notion of a personal history or a calling to which the individual was foreordained, as distinct from *lamassu,* which was merely the spiritual form of his or her bodily features. Finally, when addressed as *šēdu,* the god seems to have been personifying the individual's sexual potency and, by extension, *élan vital.* "All four representations," concludes Oppenheim, "are intended to render the experience of the ego"[12]— or the self.

Clearly this Mesopotamian understanding of personhood was inseparable from that culture's pervasive and constantly acknowledged religious underpinnings. Not only were human beings brought into existence by one or another god (the source differed according to various Sumerian and Akkadian creation myths), but their fortunes were so linked to the presence of their personal deities that even mere physical welfare depended on them. "Without his personal god," says a Mesopotamian proverb, "a man eats not."[13]

10. Jacobsen, *Treasures of Darkness,* chap. 5.
11. Oppenheim, *Ancient Mesopotamia: Portrait of a Dead Civilization* (Chicago: University of Chicago Press, 1964). See especially the section on Mesopotamian psychology in chap. 4.
12. Oppenheim, *Ancient Mesopotamia,* p. 206.
13. *Encyclopedia Britannica,* 15th ed., s.v. "Mesopotamian Religions."

HINDU AND BUDDHIST PSYCHOLOGIES OF THE PERSON: "A WAVE TRAVERSING THE OCEAN"

Among the Mesopotamians death seems to have been accepted rather matter-of-factly. It was presumed to be the end of existence and accepted as such to the extent that doctors did not have the high status as life-prolongers that we are prone to give them.[14] But as we move east geographically and closer to the first millennium B.C. historically, we encounter the beginnings of two thought systems in which the self, or soul, is seen as both eternally preexistent and forever resident in a succession of earthly tenements.

Both Buddhism and Hinduism originated in what is today known as India, although Buddhism was largely transplanted from its native soil, taking root in Sri Lanka, Burma, Thailand, and the islands of Southeast Asia and forming one branch (the *Hinayana* or *Theravada*, or "Lesser Vehicle"), and traveling from India via Central Asia to China, Korea, and Japan to form the other branch (the *Mahayana*, or "Greater Vehicle"). What is now integrated and commonly known as Hinduism is the older of the two systems, and represents a pluralistic yet continuous complex of beliefs and practices. Its roots go back to before the Vedic religion of the Aryan peoples, who gradually migrated into northern India about 1500 B.C. and whose beliefs mingled with those of the darker-skinned people they conquered. By contrast, Buddhism originated in the sixth century B.C. with a single founder, Siddhārtha Gautama (the *Buddha*, or "enlightened one"), in the northern region of India. Today Hinduism claims some 350 million followers and Buddhism close to 300 million.[15] Consequently, it is worth our while to examine, however briefly, some of their main assumptions about the nature of human existence and selfhood.

It is admittedly presumptuous to take only a few paragraphs to discuss Hinduism, which has been called "the most complex, the most fascinating, and the most difficult to describe of all the religions of the world."[16] This complexity exists partly because Hinduism

14. Oppenheim, *Ancient Mesopotamia,* chap. 6.
15. Paul K. Meagher, Thomas C. O'Brien, and Consuelo M. Aherne, eds., *Encyclopedic Dictionary of Religion* (Washington, D.C.: Corpus Publications, 1979), pp. 547, 1672.
16. Geoffrey Parrinder, *Asian Religions* (London: Sheldon Press, 1975), p. 31. Other noteworthy works on Indian religion include John B. Carman, *The Theology of Ramanuja: An Essay in Interreligious Understanding* (New Haven: Yale University Press, 1974); William T. DeBary, ed., *Sources of*

represents a historical amalgamation of several influences, and partly because its tolerance for diversity and its caste system have been incompatible with any single, centralized body of doctrines to which all believers are required to adhere. For present purposes we will restrict our attention to the high traditions of Brahmanism as divided into *Advaita Vedanta* ("nondualism") and *Vishishtadvaita Vedanta* ("qualified nondualism").

The roots of Brahmanism can be traced back to the coming of the Aryans into India at least 3500 to 4000 years ago.[17] The earliest and most sacred learned oral texts of the Brahmans, known as *Vedas* (*Veda* means "knowledge"), are compilations of poetic chants, hymns, and other writings to which commentaries, sayings of sages, and philosophical and other bodies of learning have been added. These Vedic scriptures are clearly polytheistic, referring to a diversity of robust nature-gods not unlike the pantheon of early Mesopotamia. Yet although the authority of the *Vedas* was constantly reaffirmed in theory, in practice the more ascetic religion of the priests, or Brahmins, gradually superceded the rather carefree polytheism of the original *Vedas*. Indeed, the Brahmins regarded themselves as a hereditary class of human gods who, according to the *Vedas* themselves, had once taken a sacred drink, or *Soma*, and thereby eclipsed the earlier nature spirits.

The philosophical—and by extension psychological—development of Indian thought was laid down in Brahmanic commentaries known as the *Upanishads*. Brahmanic commentaries on the four original *Vedas*, known as the *Brahmanas*, were followed by the *Aranyakas* ("sayings of the forest sages"), and these in turn were followed by the philosophical and intellectual discourses upon all previous "knowledge" (*veda*). It is these discourses that constitute the *Upanishads*, thought to date from sometime after 800 B.C. In them the cause and ground of all existence is held to be *Brahman*, the Supreme Being, or soul of the universe. Human souls or spirits, on the other hand, are designated by the term *Atman*, and much of the *Upanishads* is devoted to showing that *Brahman* and *Atman* are identical—that is, that the

Indian Tradition, 2 vols. (New York: Columbia University Press, 1958); and Wendy D. O'Flaherty, *The Origins of Evil in Hindu Mythology* (Berkeley: University of California Press, 1976), and *Karma and Rebirth in Classical Indian Traditions* (Berkeley: University of California Press, 1980).
    17. Note that the word *Brahman* is used to denote the Supreme Being, while *Brahmin* denotes the person of the priest.

universal Self is diffused throughout reality yet present in every individual. In the *Upanishads* we read, "He from whom all works, all desires, all sweet odors and tastes proceed, who embraces all this, who never speaks and is never surprised, he, myself within the heart, is the Brahman."[18]

Thus, among the more enlightened and privileged classes, polytheism, with its clear distinction between gods and persons, changed into a pantheistic monism that held that there was only one indescribable Self with whom all other gods and, indeed, all human selves were merged. *Brahman* could be likened to the ocean, all of whose waves—human souls—were inseparable parts. Salvation (in the sense of "escape") came through knowledge of and union with this one supreme self—a union bringing release from the pains and futile desires of earthly life. One body of writings, the *Bhagavad Gita* (actually a post-*Upanishadic* devotional "song" from an epic known as *Mahabharata*) teaches a method of mental training, or *Yoga*, as a means by which one can be freed from earthly desires and so gain pure reunion with Brahman, or the universal Self.

Yet, paradoxically, this totally amoral, intellectual route to salvation is accompanied by another belief—that of reincarnation or rebirth into successive bodies the fortune and status of which is determined by the quality of one's deeds (*karma*) in the preceding existence. This doctrine of rebirth (*samsara*), later developed to a high point in Buddhism, implies a very different route to salvation—namely, through virtuous behavior. According to the *Upanishads*, "Those whose conduct has been good will quickly attain some good birth [—for example,] the birth of a Brahmin. But those whose conduct has been evil, will quickly attain an evil birth, the birth of a dog, or a hog, or an outcaste."[19]

In practice it seems that the doctrine of *karma* softens the moral indifference of Brahmanic monism, since it holds that salvation comes *both* from right thinking and from right behavior, *both* through knowledge of one's unity with Brahman and through self-denial and moral effort. It is the concept of *dharma* (roughly "order, duty, rightness") that governs individual moral and religious conduct according to one's class, station, and status in life. This is a concept that goes

---

18. Excerpt from the *Upanishads*, as quoted in Parrinder, *Asian Religions*, p. 39.
19. Excerpt from the *Upanishads*, as quoted in Nigel McNichol, *Hindu Scriptures* (London: Everyman, 1940), p. 161.

back to early religious manuals (*Dharma-sutras*) that have grown over time into lengthy compilations of law. Yet in Hindu thought, reincarnation—even reincarnation that involves improved status as a result of moral effort—is not seen as a positive thing, since it still ties the person to a material existence that is regarded as illusory at best and evil at worst. The ultimate aim of accumulated *karma* and perfect knowledge is the permanent release of the soul, or *Atman*, from an endless chain of rebirths in this world.

The Buddhist Alternative. The pessimistic orientation of Brahmanic ideology is somewhat tempered in one of its religious offspring, Buddhism. Founded in the sixth century B.C. by Gautama, an Indian of the princely or warrior (*Kshatriya*) caste, its best-attested sources (known as the Pali scriptures) tell of Gautama's renunciation of home and family in a quest for spiritual release from the sorrows of disease, death, and other tragedies. The characteristic yellow robes and shaven heads of today's Buddhist monks are said to date back to Gautama's great renunciation, when, at the age of twenty-nine, he "had the hair of head and face shaved off, donned the saffron robes, and went forth from home to the homeless life."[20]

Being an Indian of Kshatriya origins, Gautama naturally began his search for enlightenment using the methods current in his culture. He became a student of *Yoga*, but he failed to attain the mental tranquility promised by the "three paths" of that discipline. He then resorted to a rigid asceticism, but he found that self-starvation did not lead to enlightenment either. He nourished himself back to health and finally attained the state of *Nirvana* (nothingness, or self-extinction) while contemplating beneath the now-famous Bo-tree, or Tree of Enlightenment: "I did attain unto the utter peace of Nirvana that is free from the impurities, so that . . . the insight came to me thus: Sure is my release. This is my last birth. There is no more birth for me."[21]

It can be seen that Buddhism took over the earlier and already pervasive belief in reincarnation as well as the definition of salvation as release from its cycle. Buddhism also paralleled Brahmanism in neither denying nor affirming the existence of the minor gods to whom its rank-and-file followers remained firmly attached. But it

20. Excerpt from the Pali scriptures, as quoted in Parrinder, *Asian Religions*, pp. 65–66.
21. Gautama, as quoted in Edward J. Thomas, *The Life of Buddha* (London: John Murray, 1969), pp. 63ff.

differed from Hinduism in two important ways. First of all, it rejected extreme self-discipline and mortification as a route to enlightenment. Indeed, Buddha called his "Noble Eightfold Path" of discipline the "middle path," because it combined right thinking with practical advice on right living in the everyday world. It was this "middle way" of moderation in all things that promised to lead its followers to the release or self-extinction of *Nirvana.*

Second and more important from a psychological viewpoint, Buddhist teaching differed from that of the Brahmins in denying the existence of a permanent self, or ego. That is to say, it rejected the doctrine that an eternally preexistent self put on new clothes, as it were, in each incarnation and might eventually be able to strip itself naked for reunion with the one, all-embracing, universal Self. A preferred Buddhist metaphor is that of fire: "Life is like fire; its very nature is to burn its fuel. When one body dies, it is as if one piece of fuel were burned: the vital process passes on and recommences in another . . . so long as there is desire of life."[22] Despite apparent contradictions, orthodox Buddhists insist that this "no-soul" doctrine is still compatible with the doctrine of reincarnation. In fact, for Buddhists the denial of the self is less pertinent to the question about what exists after death than to what the self does *not* consist of during life. In one of his earliest teachings Gautama took pains to insist that the self could *not* be equated with the body, or with the emotions, or with perception, or with consciousness. To be freed from the cycle of rebirth, from what only appears to be selfhood, a person must reject in disgust the mental and emotional as well as the physical aspects of existence.[23]

The Denial of the Person. This denial of the real self has led in later Buddhist teachings to what might finally be called an "antipsychology," which outlines five components (*skandhas*) of life (bodily existence, sensation, perception, motivation, and consciousness), but does so only with the twin goals of showing that none of these (nor even their sum) can be called the metaphysical self, yet that proper reflection on these aspects of "nonself" can contribute much to a person's development by helping him or her to view all things impersonally.[24] Moreover, many Buddhist scriptures teach a

22. Charles E. Eliot, "Hinduism and Buddhism," in Murphy and Murphy, *Asian Psychology,* pp. 20–38.
23. Parrinder, *Asian Religions,* p. 71.
24. *Encyclopedia Britannica,* 15th ed., s.v. "Buddhist Philosophy."

chain of causation (known as "dependent origination") that can be seen as a kind of developmental psychology, but again of a purely negative sort. According to this doctrine, ignorance of the means to enlightenment is what produces earthly suffering, but only through a series of stages prior to actual human incarnation. More specifically, ignorance in the prehuman state produces will; will in turn leads to consciousness, consciousness to perception, perception to the five senses, and these to sensory contact with the outer world. This in turn produces sensations, or feelings, which lead to craving, then to worldly attachments, and finally to actual worldly birth, with its regrettable suffering, decay, death, and reincarnation in the absence of enlightenment.[25]

It can readily be seen that the high Hindu and Buddhist doctrines about reincarnation imply a view of material reality that is very different from that of biblical Christianity. The biblical view holds that the world, although now flawed by sin, was created by God and as such was perfect and good. It was and is affirmed in its intrinsic worth (and that of its inhabitants) by the incarnation of Christ, at whose return the material world, far from disappearing, will be restored to its original, unbroken state, with only a single moral judgment of resurrected (not reincarnated) persons occurring then. In addition, Hindu and Buddhist thinking about the soul (such as it is) is at variance both with the materialistic view of the mind held by most of modern psychology *and* with the traditional Christian view of the person as having both material and nonmaterial aspects that are equally important.

Buddhism in particular seems to have produced a rather sophisticated psychology, but one the sole purpose of which seems to be the transcending of the illusory self, whether physical or mental, to attain a state of self-extinction. As we will see in Chapter Four, this is a view quite at odds with a biblical anthropology, which asserts that persons, while not one with God in the pantheistic sense, are formed in his image in a way that neither sin nor suffering can erase, and that by virtue of this fact human existence is endowed with both dignity and hope. But Buddhism is also a view quite foreign to present-day Western psychology, which routinely equates the mind with its material substrate, the brain, and views both as nothing more than the product of shifting evolutionary pressures. Consequently, psychologists

---

25. *Encyclopedia Britannica*, 15th ed., s.v. "Buddhist Philosophy."

deny—or at least avoid discussing—the possible existence of *any* kind of soul, or eternal self, even as they take for granted the intrinsic as well as the practical worth of the minds and bodies of the people they study. In this respect psychology may be more dependent on the Christian heritage of its surrounding culture than it is prepared to admit.

In contrast to the religious psychologies we have been considering in this chapter are the psychologies that arose during the immediately pre-Christian era of the Greeks. Here we begin to find scholars taking both the human body and the human mind seriously as topics for theoretical discussion apart from their religious significance. In this respect the Greeks are the precursors of modern-day secular psychology as well as the shapers of the culture into which the Christian message was first introduced. It is to some of their deliberations about the nature of personhood that we now turn.

CHAPTER 3

ANCIENT GREEK PSYCHOLOGIES:
Man as the Measure of All Things

> As one of the fathers of atomism, Democritus taught that
> Nature and her subjects were no more than aggregations of
> particles of matter distributed in infinite space. At the time,
> Democritus was considered a skeptic. Today he would, no
> doubt, be judged guilty of a cliché.
> —Daniel N. Robinson[1]

In the last chapter we looked at three ancient cultures with psychologies of the person that were religious at root. However, when we turn to the era of the ancient Greeks (ca. 500 to 200 B.C.), we find a type of thinking about the person that became, like Buddhism, largely atheistic even as it remained metaphysical. Greek thought did not yet reduce persons to the sum of their material parts (Democritus being the notable exception); yet in attempting to understand what it was about persons that was *more* than physical, Greek thought made almost no reference to any kind of supreme deity, or even to the popular pantheon of Greek gods for that matter. In his *Apology* Socrates does speak of the existence of a personal *daimon*, or spirit, something roughly comparable to the Mesopotamian idea of the *ilu*, a godlike entity that personifies some or all of a person's attributes. But in most Greek thought after Socrates, that which metaphysically

---

1. Robinson, *An Intellectual History of Psychology*, rev. ed. (New York: Macmillan, 1981), p. 98.

endures in persons was not assumed to be something externally endowed and therefore mysterious so much as something that could be progressively revealed through the correct use of human reason. In their confidence that reason devoid of revelation could generate an adequate understanding of humanness, the ancient Greeks helped to set the stage for a secularized modern psychology. To examine their thinking more closely, let us consider some of the Greek thinkers—beginning with the pre-Socratics and continuing through Plato and Aristotle—who wrestled with questions we would now term psychological.

THE PRE-SOCRATICS

Up until the time of Socrates (ca. 470–399 B.C.) we have only scattered fragments of manuscript representing the thought of the earliest Greek philosophers. These, plus the references made to them by their intellectual descendants, give us what we know about the pre-Socratics, as they are called. Two of these, Protagoras and Democritus, left behind treatises that included psychological interests.

It was Protagoras (ca. 485–410 B.C.) who wrote that "man is the measure of all things." Although this phrase is often taken to mean that he regarded human beings as the powerful pinnacle of the universe, it was in fact written to express something quite different—namely, the apparent relativity of all knowledge. Each person, Protagoras pointed out, sees the world through his own eyes, and persons looking at the same things do not always see or interpret them in the same way. How then, he asked, can we discover what is real, since each man is his own "measure of all things," and a highly subjective one at that? At best, Protagoras concluded, we can have only opinions, for even if we did stumble upon true knowledge, we would have no means of knowing that it *was* true. "Protagoras," comments one historian of psychology, "presents us with a relativistic philosophy, with man as the inescapable determiner of all relations."[2] The reader can no doubt see that in his skepticism regarding the possibility of reliable knowledge, Protagoras anticipated the more extreme postmodern philosophers of science to whom we made brief reference in Chapter One.

2. Robert B. MacLeod, "Five Classic Doctrines of Man," in *Historical Conceptions of Psychology*, ed. Mary Henle, Julian Jaynes, and John J. Sullivan (New York: Springer, 1973), p. 132.

Democritus (ca. 460–370 B.C.), the other pre-Socratic who claims our attention, had his own answer to Protagoras: a materialist philosophy in which physical matter was seen as the basis of all reality, including the mind. Consequently, said Democritus, it was hardly remarkable that knowledge and perception should be so selective, since "we know nothing accurately in reality, but only as it changes according to the conditions of our body and the things that impinge and press upon it."[3] Rather remarkably, Democritus' materialism anticipated the atomic age, since it postulated a universe composed of an infinite number of tiny, indestructible "atoms," differing from each other only in size, shape, weight, and motion. Democritus thought that those atoms that were smaller, smoother, and livelier than others made up the soul, or the seat of human reason. Perception consisted of the transfer of outer-world atoms through the sense organs to the mind; cognition consisted of the internal agitation of soul atoms already present; and will was the transmission of atomic motion outward from the mind. Democritus thus attempted to resolve the apparent difference between the mental and the physical by concluding that mind was simply a subtler form of matter.[4] He also went on to assign different psychological functions to different parts of the body—thought to the brain, anger to the heart, and appetite to the liver, for example.

We can thank Democritus for recognizing the very intimate, two-way connection that exists between the mind and the body—a connection affirmed by both the Bible and modern research but somewhat underrated by Democritus' immediate successor, Plato. (It is this intimacy of mind and body, particularly as it concerns mind and brain, that we will explore further in Chapter Six.) But in his search for one primary substance to which even mind could be reduced, Democritus was the first of many to suggest that, at root, psychology is merely a branch of physics. In Robert B. MacLeod's words, "To Democritus, man is a part of physical nature, to be explained in terms of physical laws. His psychology is the prototype of a psychology that

---

3. Sextus Empiricus on Democritus' philosophy of infinite atoms and motion, *Adversus Mathematicos*, extracted in *Western Psychology: From the Greeks to William James*, ed. Gardner Murphy and Lois B. Murphy (New York: Basic Books, 1969), p. 26.
4. The doctrines of Democritus as stated by Diogenes Laertius, *Lives of the Philosophers*, in *Western Psychology*, p. 27. See also Robinson, *An Intellectual History of Psychology*, chap. 3.

has been popular for more than two hundred years."[5] Today most of Anglo-American psychology still reduces the mind to the joint product of "nature plus nurture"—that is, of internal physiology and the external environment—to the exclusion of any metaphysical—let alone religious—considerations. These are simply ruled out as inappropriate to a scientific psychology, an assumption that I will challenge in more detail in Chapter Five.

PLATO'S IDEALISM

As modern as Democritus' psychology seems to us, in its time it was actually only a temporary aberration from the mainstream of Greek philosophy, which preferred to transcend Protagoras' relativism not by identifying mind with matter but by doing more or less the opposite. This Greek idealism held that it was not material atoms but eternal forms, intuited through dialectical reflection, that were the fundamental elements of reality. The physical world was regarded as only a partial expression—even a degradation—of this nonmaterial world of perfect forms. A protest against both relativist *and* materialist theories of human nature was already apparent in the ideas of Socrates as recorded by his pupil Plato, and it was in Plato himself (ca. 428–347 B.C.) that Greek idealism attained its zenith.

For our purposes Plato's idealism is of interest not only for its view of the mind and its relationship to matter but also for its related conclusions about the nature of scientific inquiry. For Socrates as well as for Plato, the most irreducible feature of human beings was their power to think. In addition, both held that through clear and disciplined thinking a person could increasingly discern the ultimate truth that was masked by mere appearances. Correct and logically precise thinking in abstraction from any empirical observations was thus held to be the sole means of scientific discovery. Mere observation of the material world was, in line with Protagoras, considered to be too unreliable. Moreover, the pinnacle of scientific thought was considered to be mathematics, for while mathematicians might compromise with appearances by using algebraic signs and imperfect geometric drawings, their ultimate goal (at least in idealistic thought) was to conceive of abstract, pure "triangularity" or "circularity" devoid of any sensory representations. Although this apprehension of pure

5. MacLeod, "Five Classic Doctrines of Man," p. 135.

mathematical ideas could never be complete (given the variety and complexity of reality), the idealists nevertheless held that the logical consistency of mathematical thought was an assurance that the thinker was going in the right direction. The fact that mathematics could be used to uncover what was logically premised in an argument made it a powerful and respected intellectual tool.

By this criterion science is more or less a "bootstrap" enterprise: the true understanding of reality is potentially present in the mind, and if correctly trained the mind will gradually be able to discern it. In one of the dialogues attributed to Socrates by Plato, Socrates demonstrates this doctrine of innate ideas, as it has come to be called, by taking an illiterate slave-boy and, through judicious questioning (the famed "Socratic method"), eliciting from him a version of the Pythagorean theorem concerning right-angled triangles.[6]

This, of course, is not a view of the scientific method advocated by many people today—least of all by mainstream psychologists. On the other hand, Plato's doctrine of human nature has more staying power among modern psychologists than most are prepared to admit. His doctrine of innate ideas, for example, suggested that concepts such as space, time, number, and causality were waiting within the human mind to be unfolded, a view that still finds expression in the work of developmental psychologist Jean Piaget and his followers. Moreover, the cognitive unfolding of the idea of justice (also held by Plato to be innate) is the subject of Lawrence Kohlberg's well-known but controversial work on moral development.

It is in his treatment of justice that Plato's theory of human nature and its specifically psychological implications can be seen most clearly. In The Republic[7] he is primarily concerned with the problem of social ethics, but in the process of discussing this he reveals to us his psychology. In essence, says Plato, the nature of the well-run state parallels that of the harmonious individual. Plato's ideal Greek city-state has a class-based division of labor corresponding to the innate talents of each of three groups of people. At the bottom of the class structure are the workers (e.g., farmers, craftsmen, and traders), who

6. Plato, The Meno, in The Dialogues of Plato, trans. Benjamin Jowett (New York: Random House, 1937).
7. Plato, The Republic, trans. F. M. Cornford (New York: Oxford University Press, 1955). For a precise list of the pertinent passages regarding Plato's theory of human nature, see Leslie Stevenson, Seven Theories of Human Nature (New York: Oxford University Press, 1974), chap. 3.

produce the material necessities of life and are thus characterized by a preoccupation with the satisfaction of physical *appetites*. Next, serving as a species of middle-level executives, are the soldiers, whose job is the defense of the state and whose innate virtue is thus *courage*, or spirited self-assertion. At the top, however, is the ruling class of "philosopher-kings," who must make all the decisions and whose virtue, honed to perfection by years of education, is to be *wisdom*.

How does this tripartite division of the state parallel the nature of the individual in Plato's scheme? The *appetitive* inclinations make up the lowest part of human nature, not unlike what modern psychology characterizes as instincts, primary drives, or basic needs. The *spirited* part is somewhat harder to pinpoint, but Plato seems to identify it with ambition and tenacity of purpose—rather akin to the motives some personality theorists call the need for achievement and the need for power.[8] This "middle virtue" can be enlisted on the side of appetite or, more ideally, on the side of the highest virtue, reason. For it is only through humankind's highest endowment, rationality, that Plato says persons can attain truth, recognize beauty, and guarantee a peaceful social existence. For Plato, reason is the highest faculty of an immaterial and immortal soul that is eternally preexistent and takes up only temporary residence in a human body. Although hampered and even degraded by this association with the physical, through reason the soul can progress back to the ideal world of pure and perfect ideas. Moreover, says Plato, because it is the philosophers who love wisdom the most and whose self-discipline and courage protect them from yielding to self-interest and mere appetitiveness, it is they who are the best and most trustworthy rulers in the ideal city-state.

To modern Western ears, Plato's theory of the just state often seems repugnant and undemocratic, based as it is on a system of classes to which people are assigned without opportunity for inter-class mobility. Yet, both psychologically and socially, we have a mind-set more like Plato's than we usually admit. For example, Freud's tripartite division of the human psyche into *id, ego,* and *superego* has some similarities to Plato's threefold division of the human faculties, especially in Freud's later writings, where he warned that the progress of civilization depended on the tempering of the

---

8. See, for example, David C. McClelland, *The Achieving Society* (New York: The Free Press, 1961), and *Power: The Inner Experience* (New York: Irvington, 1975).

id-based appetites by the more rational *ego.* "The platonic doctrine," writes one historian of psychology, "is still with us. Whenever, in our judgments of ourselves and others, we distinguish between rational and irrational, between higher and lower, we are speaking the language of Plato."[9] This is true not only of Western thinking generally but often of Christian theologizing throughout history (the results of which have often been less than fully biblical, as I will try to show in the next chapter). For whenever we assume that the mind is somehow more "spiritual" than the body or that the educated pastor is a higher-class Christian than the farmer or the factory worker, we too are speaking the language of Plato more than that of biblical Christianity.

Furthermore, on the societal level, "whenever anyone asserts that the cure for our problems is that we should be ruled by those who really know what's best, then he is asserting the essence of Plato's theory [of human nature and society]."[10] This too has an enduring heritage in modern psychology. For example, behaviorist B. F. Skinner has contended that a well-designed, cooperative society—one in which negative emotions and conduct would cease to exist—would be a society run by social science experts, particularly those trained in behavioral engineering.[11] To assume, as Skinner implicitly does, that technical and intellectual expertise are sufficient to qualify a person for almost absolute authority is a mistake made by Christians and non-Christians alike; it is as if to say that clever and well-educated people are invariably the most moral and dependable people as well. But such an attitude is in fact a debasement of Plato. For him reason *included* a knowledge of the good; he did not reduce it to mere logical and technical skills as we tend to do today.

Moreover, in science generally and in Anglo-American psychology particularly, there persists the rarely articulated assumption that since scientists and social scientists are a "breed apart" (itself an unconsciously Platonic assumption), they are exempt from many of the moral and ethical rules that apply to society generally. One glaring example of such thinking in psychology (and also in much medical research) is the assumption that it is perfectly legitimate to lie to human research subjects in the interests of furthering scientific inquiry. Yet it is considered morally incumbent upon the research

9. MacLeod, "Five Classic Doctrines of Man," p. 137.
10. Stevenson, *Seven Theories of Human Nature,* p. 23.
11. Skinner, *Walden Two* (New York: Macmillan, 1948).

subjects themselves to be unwaveringly honest with the scientific experts.[12] (See also Chapter Nine.)

It seems to me that there are at least two aspects of Plato's legacy that are of enduring and positive significance to the Christian student of psychology. First of all, we can sympathize with Plato's rejection of a simplistic materialism, and its associated relativism, as an explanation of human mind and conduct. We may argue against his identification of the human soul with only the rational capacities, and Christian theologians have traditionally rejected his idea that souls are eternally preexistent rather than individually brought into existence by God through the medium of human procreation. But these qualifiers should not blind us to the fact that modern psychology is much more the descendant of Democritus than it is of Plato, and that it has scant resources, so far, for any analysis of human experience that is not cast in purely material and amoral terms. In those few theorists like Piaget who have dared to look at the human mind in terms not reduced to the material, we encounter a richness that is absent from much modern psychology and for which we owe Plato a continuing debt.

Second, as Christians we can identify with Plato's assumptions about the uniqueness of human beings in contrast to animals and nonliving things even as we reject his assumption that it is uniquely the human *mind* that partakes of the divine. This too is in contrast with the prevailing mood of evolutionism in modern psychology, with its marked tendency to overemphasize the biological continuity of human and nonhuman species. Thus, in their rejection of extreme relativism, materialism, and biological reductionism, Christians can at least partially share in the world view of the author of *The Republic*.

ARISTOTLE: THE FATHER OF MODERN PSYCHOLOGY

If in terms of amount of influence Democritus and Protagoras can be considered grandparents of modern psychology, and Plato perhaps a great-grandparent, Plato's pupil Aristotle (384–322 B.C.) can be con-

---

12. For a more detailed treatment of this and related issues, see Mary Stewart Van Leeuwen, *The Sorcerer's Apprentice: A Christian Looks at the Changing Face of Psychology* (Downers Grove, Ill.: InterVarsity Press, 1982), especially chap. 2. See also Van Leeuwen, "Social Science Issues and the Christian Liberal Arts College," *Center Journal* 2 (Spring 1983): 95–113.

sidered an even closer relative. As the de facto founder of the fields that psychology now labels sensation, perception, and cognition, he is virtually a parent of modern psychology. Many of the basic assumptions of these fields trace their heritage directly back to Aristotle, whose thinking (revived in the sixteenth century) had so much to do with the emergence of modern science generally.

Aristotle concurred with Plato in rejecting a simplistic materialism as the ultimate explanation of reality, but he rejected his teacher's insistence that a true understanding of that reality could be achieved only through the use of a priori reason. Rather, said Aristotle, ideas are the abstracted forms of real, material entities, and consequently matter and abstract form are always tied together in the only world to which we have direct access. Rejecting a view of science based on either purely innate or purely empirical knowledge, Aristotle instead combined the two. What he called a "demonstrative proof" in science, although syllogistic in character, included as its minor premise an empirical observation from nature. For Aristotle, then, the tool of science was not reason alone but rather a combination of empirical observation *plus* reason—or, more specifically, the four-step method of observation, classification, intuitive abstraction, and finally deduction. [13] It is these aspects of Aristotle's philosophy of science, resurrected almost two millennia later, that helped to launch the scientific revolution in Europe and that continue to hold an important place in the methodological assumptions of science even today.

Although scholars see varying degrees of continuity between Plato's and Aristotle's writings, they are generally agreed that one central Aristotelian doctrine concerning man is almost totally his own. This is the so-called "teleological principle," according to which the understanding of human beings is to be sought in an implicit purpose that gradually reveals itself in their development. At first hearing this seems like a religious—even a quasi-Christian—doctrine: "Thou has made us for Thyself," wrote Saint Augustine some seven centuries later, "and our hearts are restless till they find their rest in Thee." In these words he expressed the Christian convic-

13. The basic source for psychologists is Aristotle's *De Anima*, although his psychological theorizing also appears in his *Logic, Ethics, Poetics,* and *Rhetoric.* His theory of science appears particularly in the *Posterior Analytics.* Pertinent parts of these have been extracted and arranged by Richard P. McKeon in *Western Psychology,* pp. 47–67.

tion that human purpose is best summarized as reconciliation with God, and praise and enjoyment of him thereafter. But like Plato, Aristotle was largely indifferent to the place of any deity in human affairs, even though he postulated a supreme being who alone was Pure Form and no part material. Aristotle's teleology held rather that there was an inherent purposiveness in nature itself and in every process and organism that partook of nature. In his emphasis on the course of human unfolding toward innately predetermined adult goals, Aristotle provided an organizing principle for the developmental psychology that emerged as a formal part of psychology in the twentieth century.

In his *De Anima* ("About the Soul"), Aristotle developed his interpretation of human nature. Persons as such are indeed a part of the physical world, but their essences, or souls, belong to the category of pure form. Moreover, in keeping with the teleological principle, the soul's true purpose can be seen to unfold more and more during the course of a lifetime. That purpose, in line with Plato's thinking, was that human conduct should be guided by reason. In *De Anima* Aristotle sees psychology as the discipline that explores not only the formal (i.e., rational) essence of the soul but also its various earthbound attributes. The former, wrote Aristotle, can be understood only by the use of reason itself. But the latter, he maintained, could be ascertained by systematic observation of real human behavior—an anticipation of modern psychology's commitment to empiricism.

What, then, did Aristotle conclude from his observations about the attributes of human beings in their earthly existence? Essentially that they were animals—but *rational* animals. That is, like other animals they were seen to possess the appetites and physical structures essential to growth and reproduction as well as the sensory and motor equipment necessary to monitor and move about in their environment. But in addition, Aristotle maintained, through their uniquely human powers of reasoning, persons could transcend their animal limitations and understand the laws of pure reason as found in the discipline of logic. Nevertheless, they must still do this by relying upon their bodies, which must contend with the limitations as well as the assets of functions like perception, memory, and imagination. Accordingly, Aristotle devoted much attention to each of these topics.

It was Aristotle who first suggested that the five senses are the "gateways to the mind," and his theory that these five senses are coordinated by a higher-order "common sense" is one basis of psychology's present-day distinction between sensation and perception. He referred to memory as the capacity that enables us to retain the impressions of the senses, and imagination as that which permits us to recombine these impressions into new ideas. He also postulated certain principles of association—such as similarity, contrast, and closeness in time and space—to account for the fact that one idea can suggest another. It should be noted that Aristotle did not equate these simple mental functions with transcendent human reason but rather saw them as natural phenomena that were amenable to systematic empirical inquiry. In studying them he made his most lasting contribution to the systematic psychology that is taken for granted today.

In anticipation of the following chapter, two further points may be made concerning Aristotle's influence on psychology. The first is that his distinction between peripheral senses and higher-order central reasoning continues to play an important role in cognitive psychology, which still assumes that the raw input of the senses is reworked and organized in the mind, even though the latter is still usually held to be a purely material entity. But psychologists continue to debate the question (which is as old as Aristotle) about how *closely* what we call thinking depends on mere sensory input and how much is the result of independent activity in the brain. For example, B. F. Skinner, who is a staunch materialist, ties thinking very closely to input from the empirical world that feeds into it via the senses, whereas Piaget, who is more of a rationalist, attributes much more creative independence to the mind itself. It is often an Aristotelian identification of the independently rational mind with the image of God in persons that makes theorists like Piaget seem more acceptable to Christians than someone like Skinner. But this is an assumption that has its own limitations, as we will see in the next chapter and also in Chapter Eight.

A related point concerns Aristotle's teleological principle and his suggestion that human beings best reflect their inherent purpose in the final unfolding of adult rationality. I have already pointed out that developmental psychology follows this assumption of a natural unfolding of behavior toward a mature ideal, and that abstract reasoning is often considered the best expression of that ideal. But Aristotle's concept of mature rationality (like Plato's) included *wisdom* and *virtue* in addition to the capacity for theoretical abstraction—something that cognitive-developmental psychologists easily forget. It is possible, then, that in our continuing reverence for the mind, we are overlooking aspects of human purpose that are at least as important. How might the developmental drama of the Bible regarding creation, fall, redemption, and the final goal of history alter our perspective toward the idea that reason and the material benefits that it brings in its wake represent the developmental goal of human existence? Let us explore some possible responses to that question now.

CHAPTER 4

THE BIBLICAL DRAMA AND THE MEANING OF PERSONHOOD

The concept of the exceptional position of man is to be derived less certainly from the "principal passages" . . . than from the overall impression made by the entire OT [Old Testament], where God's precepts and commands apply only to man, where the divine revelation is given only to man, where man alone is responsible for his decisions, and where man alone can be sinner or "righteous."

—Fritz Maass[1]

The emergence of Christianity must be counted as an occurrence whose importance to psychology is matched, if at all, only by the Hellenic epoch.

—Daniel N. Robinson[2]

Let us review briefly what has been said in Chapters Two and Three about ancient conceptions of the person and their implications for psychology. We saw in Chapter Two that the ancient Mesopotamians had developed a clear sense of both the *power* and the *personal nature* of their gods. In some contexts the powers of these gods were considered available, upon petition, to their loyal followers; in other con-

1. Maass, "Ādhām," in *Theological Dictionary of the Old Testament,* ed. G. Johannes Botterweck and Helmer Ringgren, trans. John T. Willis (Grand Rapids: Eerdmans, 1974), 1:85.
2. Robinson, *An Intellectual History of Psychology* (New York: Macmillan, 1981), p. 111.

texts the gods were actually considered to be spiritual expressions of the different aspects of human functioning. But either way it was understood that the gods were personal beings, willing under the right circumstances to engage in dialogue with human underlings who were in some respects like them.

By contrast, both Hinduism and Buddhism have insisted on the *impersonal* nature of a single, metaphysical force and hence the illusory nature of human personality and the desirability of transcending it to attain unity with this impersonal "soul of the universe." The result has been an implicitly "abnormal" psychology, focusing on human existence and thought processes largely as indicators of various levels of bondage to an undesirable worldly life.

When we come to post-Socratic Greek thought, we find Plato locating the bridge between human and divine realms within human reason itself, best developed in an elite class of "philosopher-kings" who strive to transcend the deceptive world of appearances in order to explore the eternal and stable world of pure ideas. To Plato this meant that all of scholarship, including psychology, was to be a rational enterprise, little concerned with empirical observation, the results of which were considered idiosyncratic and hence largely unreliable. To Aristotle, however, human beings were more clearly creatures of two legitimate realms, one material and the other immaterial. While the human soul's ultimate nature and purpose centered on pure reason, and had to be studied by abstraction from the empirical, much else that was human—including many psychological functions—could be regarded as natural and could be essentially understood through empirical observation subsequently refined by rational classification and deduction aimed at ascertaining what teleological principles were at work.

The reader should by now understand that a particular culture's *anthropology*, or theory of human nature, intimately determines its psychological *epistemology*—that is, its assumptions as to how the details about human beings and their unique functions can best be studied. Democritus believed that the universe and the human beings within it were reducible to a common set of atomic elements. We should not be surprised, then, that he and his intellectual heirs have thought of psychology as ultimately being a branch of the natural sciences, and have insisted that the only valid way to study human thought and behavior is to look for causal laws of a deterministic sort. By contrast, Plato (and to some extent Aristotle) regarded the human psyche as transcending the physical and thus requiring for its under-standing a very different approach than the one recommended by Democritus—requiring, for instance, an approach based on the un-derstanding and application of the rules of logic that were themselves regarded as metaphysical ideals.

EVOLUTIONISM IN MODERN PSYCHOLOGY

In the last chapter I suggested that modern psychology seems to vacillate somewhat uneasily between these two positions—between a view of human thought and behavior as ultimately material in nature and hence reducible to causal laws, and a more rationalistic position that seems to accord the human mind a greater degree of indepen-dence from the physical order and appeals to a set of logical rules for its understanding. It might be more accurate, however, to say that naturalism in psychology has tended to swallow up the rationalist position by appealing to a third and more recent tradition—namely, evolutionism. Rooted in the eighteenth-century idea of progress and refined by Darwin's work in the nineteenth century, this point of view asserts that all human structures and functions—including those that seem the most mentally creative and independent—are the result of natural selection acting on genetic diversity.

Briefly summarized, evolutionism holds that members of any species of animal living in a state of nature will show great genetic diversity in their makeup, a diversity that makes it likely that some individuals will have characteristics enabling them to adapt in a superior way to their environment. Such individuals are consequently the most likely to survive and produce offspring—that is, their genes are most likely to be naturally selected. When invoked as a total anthropology by psychologists, evolutionism concludes that "the characteristics and abilities that make us *Homo sapiens* have been shaped by natural selection. We are what we are because we have survival value—not just as individuals, but as a species. . . . We are the largely accidental result of particular environmental pressures acting on the available genetic material."[3] By such an account there is nothing mysterious or metaphysical about our possession of extraor-dinary abilities that seem to separate us from other species: we would

3. Gardner Lindzey, Calvin S. Hall, and Richard F. Thompson, *Psy-chology* (New York: Worth, 1975), p. 31.

not have survived, multiplied, and altered our world so successfully if the chance genetic mutations underlying such abilities had not been sufficient to compensate in intelligence, linguistic ability, and social tendencies for what we lack in mere brute strength. As expressed by another psychologist, "We are Homo sapiens, the self-named wise one, due to a large degree to our well-developed brains, our opposable thumbs, the fact that we walk upright, and our ability to communicate through the use of arbitrary symbols."[4]

Such an anthropology need not be naively optimistic about human nature. On the contrary, most contemporary adherents of evolutionism conclude that we carry many compromises and even defects as part of our random genetic inheritance, and that these will persist provided only that they do not reduce our fitness to have offspring.[5] Moreover, the occasional writer of a psychology text will be a self-conscious enough Popperian to concede that evolutionary theory, especially as applied to human abilities and institutions, is open to falsification like any other scientific theory and therefore should not be taken as dogma.[6] For the most part, however, evolutionism has become the basic anthropology of Anglo-American psychology. "In Genesis we read that God created the world, including man," runs an opening chapter in a highly respected psychology text. "But the creation of man and woman, their idyllic life in the Garden of Eden, and their banishment from this paradise for eating the forbidden fruit are regarded by most people today as lovely myths, rich in symbolic and moral significance." By contrast, the writer continues, "Darwin's theory of evolution is quite rightly called the greatest unifying theory in biology. It provides a framework for the relatedness of all living creatures . . . [and accounts for] the countless ways in which man's genetic make-up affects his behavior."[7]

THE CHRISTIAN RESPONSE

How is the Christian student or Christian observer of psychology to react to the claims of rationalism, naturalism, or evolutionism within

4. Guy R. LeFrançois, *Psychology* (Belmont, Calif.: Wadsworth, 1980), p. 37.
5. See, for example, Edward O. Wilson, *Sociobiology: The New Synthesis* (Cambridge: Harvard University Press, 1975), and *On Human Nature* (Cambridge: Harvard University Press, 1978).
6. See, for example, LeFrançois, *Psychology*, p. 37.
7. Lindzey, Hall, and Thompson, *Psychology*, p. 29.

the discipline? By way of an introductory summary, the following should be noted. First of all, over against naturalism and evolutionism, Christianity points to the possibility of an *immaterial* part of ourselves that survives death. Relatively little is said about this in Scripture, however, because much more emphasis is placed on the final resurrection of *whole persons*, including their bodies. Second, this points to a biblical emphasis on the unitary nature of the self in opposition to the atomism that began with Democritus and continues in psychology even today. For although souls may be "separable" from bodies during an intermediate state (after death but prior to the resurrection), this is perhaps best seen as a temporary aberration: both at creation and at the final resurrection the norm is clearly an embodied soul, functioning as a whole person rather than as an uneasy alliance between material and immaterial functions. This, of course, puts the Christian view of persons at odds with Platonic dualism as well. Third, the biblical view of persons sees them as irreducibly *in relationship*—first with God, then with the physical world and with other persons. Human freedom and individuality are important because they are God-endowed; indeed, these are grounds for asserting that the very concept of the individual person arose only with Christianity.[8] Yet human freedom is not absolute or unqualified but rather is exercised in the context of our inborn dependence on God and the physical world he upholds, and of our equally inborn interdependence on each other. This Christian notion of irreducible interrelationship contrasts with all movements in psychology that rest on individualistic assumptions. (See especially Chapter Ten.)

But within this network of relationships, finally, the Bible sees persons as *accountable stewards* over the rest of creation, answerable to God for their activity in all spheres of life—natural, social, artistic, political, and so on. Although qualified, our freedom enables us to act intentionally and purposefully, at least much of the time; yet this very freedom is accompanied by moral responsibilities that are unique to persons. With these anticipations of what the Bible means when it speaks of persons—immortality, unity, relationality, and responsibility—let us look in more detail at the biblical world view of which personhood is the central feature. The reader should, of course, bear

8. See, for example, Robinson, *An Intellectual History of Psychology*, chap. 4; and Max Muller and Alois Halder, "Person Concept," in *Sacramentum Mundi*, ed. Karl Rahner (New York: Herder and Herder, 1969), 4: 404–19.

in mind that I make this examination not as a systematic theologian but as a psychologist looking for the biblical themes that are most pertinent to a contemporary appraisal of psychology.

THE BIBLICAL WORLD VIEW: BOTH A THEORY AND A DRAMA

In a little book entitled *Seven Theories of Human Nature,* philosopher Leslie Stevenson suggests a set of useful guidelines for understanding past and present attempts to answer the question, What is Man? Implicitly or explicitly, says Stevenson, a complete theory of human nature will include four features: a background theory about the nature of the universe, a theory about the essential nature of human beings, a diagnosis of the present human condition, and a prescription for the ills diagnosed.[9] Let us begin our review by using Stevenson's fourfold classification.

A biblical view of the universe begins with the assertion of the opening lines of Genesis: "In the beginning God created the heavens and the earth." That is to say, the God whom Christians acknowledge is not just one of many objects in the universe but rather the originator of the entire enterprise. Neither is he to be identified with "everything that exists," after the manner of pantheistic religions such as Hinduism and Buddhism. For "although in some sense present everywhere and all the time, He is also beyond or outside the world of things in space and time."[10] But if the God of the Bible is thus inaccessible by any of the empirical methods of science, this does not mean that he is a mere abstraction or a totally impersonal entity. As the creator of the universe he is all-powerful, and yet at the same time he is a personal being who loves his creation, and especially his human creatures, with an intense and intimate concern.

In addition, and also in opposition to the thinking of much of the ancient world, God is portrayed in Scripture as having a high view of his material creation. Matter and organic processes are not to be despised as being of a lower order than intellectual and spiritual concerns, but rather used with thanks and careful stewardship as gifts from him. Finally, to say that "God created the heavens and the

9. Stevenson, *Seven Theories of Human Nature* (New York: Oxford University Press, 1974). The seven theories surveyed by Stevenson are those of Plato, Freud, Lorenz, Sartre, Skinner, Marx, and Christianity.
10. Stevenson, *Seven Theories of Human Nature,* p. 36.

earth" does not mean that he wound up the universe like a clock and then withdrew to let it run—and run down—on its own, as the deist of the eighteenth and nineteenth centuries supposed. On the contrary, the world and its inhabitants are dependent on him moment by moment for their continued existence. Christ "reflects the glory of God . . . , upholding the universe by his word of power," says the writer to the Hebrews at the opening of that epistle, and Christians confess that nothing in the universe exists except by God's continuing purpose, or at least by his permission.

But having affirmed that God himself is no mere impersonal entity but a personal being involved with his creation, it is perhaps wise to balance this abstract doctrine with a picture that captures his personal nature and involvement somewhat more completely. Let me suggest, in keeping with a number of other Christian scholars, that Christianity is not only a theory but also an unfolding historical drama with a definite beginning, climax, and ending. Of this ongoing drama God is the author, director, and producer all at once, and consequently no less involved for seeming to be offstage for most of the performance. Paul Tournier's image of God as both composer and conductor of a symphony may also be helpful, because it captures the idea of a director continually in contact with the players before him.[11]

The Original Human Creation. The images of God as author and director of a play or composer and conductor of a symphony also help us to understand the contours of a Christian doctrine of persons. For it is said that we are "made in God's image," and therefore like him in ways not shared by the rest of the material and organic world. Clearly the players on the stage or in the orchestra pit are much more like their director than they are like the props they handle or the instruments they play. But what is the nature of this similarity? What does it mean to say that we are "in God's image," especially when this phrase occurs only rarely in the Bible and receives very little elaboration?[12] Are *all* persons "made in God's image" in some way that

11. Tournier, *The Meaning of Persons* (London: SCM Press, 1957).
12. Aside from the Genesis 1:27 passage, only three others refer specifically to the concept of persons as made "in the image of God": Genesis 9:6 ("Whoever sheds the blood of man, by man shall his blood be shed; for God made man in his own image"); 1 Corinthians 11:7 ("For a man ought not to cover his head, since he is the image and glory of God"); and James 3:9 ("With [the tongue] we bless the Lord and Father, and with it we curse men, who are made in the likeness of God").

distinguishes them from, say, animals, or is the image confined to those who acknowledge God through Jesus Christ? Or are even Christians only incomplete imagers of God, still "seeing through a glass darkly," as Paul put it in his letter to the Corinthians. Is it even possible that some non-Christians are better imagers of God than some Christians in certain ways, and if so, how?

Such questions have been debated by theologians for many years now, and their importance to Christians in psychology would seem obvious. But despite persistent controversy over the fine details, this much seems both scripturally clear and historically consistent in Christian theology: God's original will and achievement was the creation of male and female human beings who occupied an intermediate place in the creation. Formed of "dust from the ground," they were as fragile and earthbound as their animal neighbors, needing food, sleep, air, and self-propagation as much as any other living thing. Yet human beings were apparently made to be more than merely complex living *things*, for we are told in the creation accounts of Genesis 1 and 2 that God himself bestowed upon them "the breath of life," making them living *beings* in a way not accorded to other creatures. These beings, physically vulnerable while on earth, were nonetheless meant to live forever in relationship with God and each other. Moreover, both creation accounts speak of God as giving human beings a special kind of control over the rest of creation: to name its animals; to "fill the earth and subdue it"; to "till . . . and keep" the Garden; to "have dominion . . . over every living thing that moves upon the earth." Thus it seems that a significant way in which persons originally "imaged" God was as accountable overseers of his creation, endowed with the capacities, the curiosity, and the relative freedom to carry out that mandate.

Human beings, then, were created to be both continuous and discontinuous with the rest of creation, and the tension between these two states must clearly be reflected in any Christian appraisal of contemporary psychology. Given that we are indeed creatures of flesh and blood, such an appraisal cannot exclude *some* examination of human behavior that appeals to the theories and methods used to study nonhuman entities. Nor does it preclude the possibility, as many "theistic evolutionists" have suggested, that human beings, by God's *fiat*, did evolve from lower species but at a particular point in this process were set apart as God's special "imagers," or representatives. [13] But it does mean that neither naturalism nor evolutionism will suffice as the foundational anthropology for the Christian psychologist.

Central to the Christian's understanding of human nature is a conviction regarding the person's ongoing relationship with God, a relationship that was intended to be of both a providential and a covenantal sort. That is to say, any temptation to human arrogance was precluded by a sense of continuing dependence on God (shared with the lowest of creatures and inanimate objects) as the very source of life and meaning. Human self-debasement—the opposite error—was precluded by the fact that God had called men and women into partnership with him, and thus endowed them with dignity and purpose. But it was a partnership, a covenant, sealed with a condition: eternal, satisfying fellowship with the Creator in return for a modest behavioral token of their dependence upon his ultimate authority. While the exact historical details may be debated by biblical scholars, this much seems clear from the biblical record: men and women were not to use their autonomy and dominion to legislate the nature of good and evil; this prerogative belonged to God alone.

We know this much, then, about our original relationship to God: first, he stamped us with the "seal" or "image" of accountable dominion over the earth; and second, we were to exercise this stewardship as his covenant partners according to norms set by him alone. In all of this, the most critical feature—what one personality theorist would call the "core tendency" of human beings[14]—seems to be our openness, our responsivity to God. By nature we were made to be in touch with him, and by voluntary obedience to serve him.

The Diagnosis. I have sketched the essentials of a biblical view of the universe and of human beings within it. But I pointed out earlier, with Leslie Stevenson, that no fully orbed theory of human nature has ever stopped there. On the contrary, all acknowledge that something is not ideal about the present human condition, and all attempt to

13. See, for example, the following: Bernard Ramm, *The Christian View of Science and Scripture* (Grand Rapids: Eerdmans, 1954); Edmund J. Ambrose, *The Nature and Origin of the Biological World* (New York: John Wiley, 1982); and Robert B. Fischer, *God Did It, But How?* (La Mirada, Calif.: CalMedia, 1981).

14. Salvatore R. Maddi, *Personality Theories: A Comparative Analysis*, 4th ed. (Homewood, Ill.: Dorsey Press, 1980).

explain what that "something" is. In Chapter Two we saw the ancient Mesopotamians concluding that their offenses against natural and political deities were the source of human unhappiness. In Hindu and Buddhist thought, outlined in Chapter Three, overattachment to material and temporal modes of existence was seen to be the cause of human woe. To Plato it was disharmony among the three parts of the soul and a refusal to put reason before ambition and appetite that brought trouble to individuals and societies alike. So what is the Bible's response to the question "Where did things go wrong?"

The heart of the matter, according to Scripture, lay in the willful misuse of the very freedom and dominion that God gave to human beings as his stewards. Not willing to leave "the knowledge of good and evil" to God alone, our first ancestors preferred to violate the modest behavioral code, the keeping of which had been a token of their voluntary acknowledgment of God's lordship. The result was an immediate and permanent distortion of the *shalom*—the right and peaceful ordering—of the original creation. Self-consciousness of a shameful and defensive sort invaded the human mind. The formerly natural fellowship with God was replaced with a sense of guilt and fear toward him. The harmonious relationship between husband and wife took on highly ambivalent overtones. From that time on, neither earth nor the human womb would yield its fruit without hard work. Most tragic of all, the inevitability of death descended upon humanity: "In the sweat of your face you shall eat bread till you return to the ground, for out of it you were taken; you are dust, and to dust you shall return" (Gen. 3:19).

To return to our dramatic metaphor, the human fall represents a tragedy. For to be a tragic hero, a person must originally have been of some importance—a man or woman of substance, tempted by circumstances, to be sure, yet still personally responsible for choosing evil. "Our tragedy," wrote Pascal in the seventeenth century, "is that of a fallen nobleman." And yet one must not ignore the circumstances that made that disobedience possible. I do not agree with Stevenson that "it is not necessary for Christians to postulate some kind of personal devil to express the idea of a cosmic fall."[15] C. S. Lewis seemed to be much closer to the mark when he wrote,

> One of the things that surprised me when I first read the New Testament seriously was that it talked so much about a Dark

15. Stevenson, *Seven Theories of Human Nature*, p. 41.

Power in the universe—a mighty spirit who was held to be the Power behind death, disease and sin. The difference is that Christianity thinks that this Dark Power was created by God, and was good when he was created, and went wrong. Christianity [says] that this universe is at war. But it does not think this is a war between independent powers. It thinks it is a civil war, a rebellion, and that we are living in a part of the universe occupied by the rebel.[16]

And so the plot of the biblical drama intensifies. We are indeed willful, accountable rebels against the God who made us—but at the same time we are naive, addicted followers of an archrebel, the origin of whose own sin in the cosmic realm remains a baffling mystery. We are free actors on the stage of life, able to hear yet choosing to ignore the promptings of the author-director of the drama. Instead, we share with our primal ancestors the determination to let ourselves be strung up and manipulated like marionettes by a "dark power" who has, as it were, stolen the author's copyright and reinterpreted the script. Our wills, as Luther put it, are in bondage, and the results of this voluntary self-incarceration show up both in human character ("None is righteous, no, not one"; Rom. 3:10) and in the imperfect state of the natural world, which is continually "groaning in travail" and "bondage to decay" (Rom. 8:22,21).

Seen in this light, it is true on one level to say that all psychology is "abnormal" psychology, if what we mean is that none of us functions as God originally intended us to. Indeed, when I quoted historian Daniel Robinson (at the beginning of the chapter) as saying that the emergence of Christianity may have surpassed the Greek epoch in its importance for psychology, I took this from a passage commenting on the efforts of the early church fathers—and in particular Augustine—to understand how the human will, paradoxically free yet bound, both apprehends and resists the voice of God. Robinson concludes that although Plato's dialogues "assert the existence of extrasensory, immaterial truths of a finer quality and graver meaning than any accessible to earthbound human beings," Christianity went even further:

[Christianity] required not a philosophical life, but a religious one which, if neglected, led not to ignorance and its attendant unhappiness, but to sin and the ultimate retribution. It replaced

16. Lewis, *Mere Christianity* (London: Collins-Fontana, 1955), p. 47.

[Plato's] true forms with the all-seeing vision of the timeless architect of all truth, an architect whose infinite love was carefully balanced against infinite justice. . . . This shift in emphasis provided early Christian scholarship with a decidedly psychological cast. The early Christian's problem about knowledge was not one of uncovering the truth, but of transmitting it, of readying the pagan mind for the light of faith. The problem thus conceived, Christian scholars inquired more deeply into the psychological, as opposed to the purely rational factors governing human conduct. [17]

Robinson goes on to point out that Augustine's *Confessions* were particularly indicative of this shift in orientation away from Greek metaphysics: "Where Socrates merely counselled against the rule of passion over reason, Augustine laid bare the genuinely personal and psychological dimensions of the conflict."[18] Herein lies the reason that Augustine has often been called "the first psychologist" and Freud "the godless Augustine." What both shared was a conviction about the passionate, irrational nature—however disguised and rationalized—of much human conduct, reduced to biological and interpersonal dynamics by Freud but interpreted by Augustine "in an unblushing, otherworldly idiom."[19]

The Prescription. We have said, in effect, that a "dark power" put into the minds of our remote ancestors the notion that they could be their own masters and invent for themselves some kind of dependable happiness outside of fellowship with God. Throughout history this inherent determination to run ourselves on the wrong fuel, as it were, has been the cause of human misery. What, according to the Bible, was God's response to this act of human rebellion? Did he merely withdraw in a fit of pique, leaving us to flounder in the consequences of our own disobedience? Not at all. Right away, in several different ways, he began preparing us for the solution.

First of all, into the now distorted and co-opted human drama he inserted what theologians have often called "common grace"—that disposition or act of God that holds the spread of corruption in check, as Calvin defined it.[20] Or in C. S. Lewis's more modern idiom, "He

17. Robinson, *An Intellectual History of Psychology*, p. 123.
18. Robinson, *An Intellectual History of Psychology*, p. 123.
19. Robinson, *An Intellectual History of Psychology*, pp. 123–24.
20. Calvin, *The Institutes of the Christian Religion*, trans. Henry Beveridge (Grand Rapids: Eerdmans, 1957), 2.3.3.

left us with conscience, the sense of right and wrong; and all through history there have been people trying (some of them very hard) to obey it."[21] Although not sufficient to reverse the consequences of the Fall, this sense of right and wrong served and still serves to maintain a degree of order in human life, and also (if not totally crushed or ignored) to prepare men and women for a decisive and more complete return to God.

Second (Lewis intriguingly suggests), even in our puppet-like state as Satan's minions, God got through to us with "good dreams": "those queer stories scattered all through the heathen religions about a god who dies and comes to life again and who, by his death, has somehow given new life to men."[22] Thus both human conscience and human legend were allowed to grope back toward God's original intention and forward toward his final solution for human sin. Then, to cap it all off, he set up a species of "pilot plant," an experimental community. He selected one particular group of people, the Jews, and progressively revealed his ways to them over the centuries—not so that they might regard themselves as intrinsically superior to others or exempt from the fallenness common to all, but so that they might be the vehicle through which, at the right time, the Author himself would appear onstage and reorient the entire human drama. And this was the climax of the entire sweep of history: "Among these Jews there suddenly turns up a man who goes about talking as if he was God. He claims to forgive sins. He says that he has always existed. He says He is coming to judge the world at the end of time. . . . [And] the claim to forgive sins makes sense only if he really was the God whose laws were broken and whose love is wounded in every sense."[23]

It is as if the Author of the play suddenly joined the players onstage and began to add new lines conveying the true meaning of the script, which until then had been interpreted at best incompletely and at worst with deliberate distortion. Yet even then they misunderstood: they assumed that his agenda was a purely local one, aimed at restoring the Jewish nation to its former independence and military might. But in fact his aim was to break the spell of the original fall, giving to all persons—Jews and Gentiles alike —the possibility of a

21. Lewis, *Mere Christianity*, p. 51.
22. Lewis, *Mere Christianity*, p. 51. The only modern psychologist to suggest the existence of such a "racial memory" (although he gives it different content) is Carl G. Jung. (See Chapter Ten.)
23. Lewis, *Mere Christianity*, pp. 51–52.

second chance. "We are told that Christ was killed for us, that his death has washed out our sins, and that by dying he disabled death itself. That is the formula. That is Christianity."[24] Or, as the Gospel of John puts it, "To all who received him, who believed in his name, he gave power to become children of God; who were born, not of blood nor of the will of the flesh nor of the will of man, but of God" (John 1:12–13).

The Prognosis. But what does all this mean for present, ongoing existence? Is Christ's atonement, once appropriated, merely an abstract assurance of freedom from ultimate judgment after death, or does it have practical implications for life on earth? Christian commitment claims to carry with it the power to enact its own prescription in individual and corporate life. "By this all men will know that you are my disciples, if you have love for one another," Christ said (John 13:35). Although it was a commandment, it was also a promise, delivered to the early Christians in the coming of the Holy Spirit at Pentecost—delivered so radically that it prompted non-Christian observers to marvel at the transformation that had taken place in such ordinary people (Acts 2–5 passim).

So the Christian prescription for the human condition indeed carries with it a powerfully positive prognosis. As persons appropriate Christ's salvation, both individual and corporate restoration begin to take place, with consequences spilling over into all areas of life. But even as Christians confess this in faith and affirm it in experience, they add some essential qualifiers.

First of all, conversion brings with it the seed, not the full fruit, of restoration. To this end the quality of the human soil is relevant. The New Testament makes it clear that the inherent talents and burdens of individuals will condition their progress in the new life. In this sense at least, God is the supreme relativist: he judges persons not by standards of perfection (although without Christ this would indeed be the case) but rather by the quality of a person's efforts relative to innate and acquired gifts and struggles (Matt. 25: 14–30). To put it another way, individual differences matter to God. Although persons share a common heritage both as an earthly species and as God's recovered rebels, there is a wide variety of both special gifts and special limitations—a variety that ensures that the Christian life can never be reduced to a mere formula.

24. Lewis, *Mere Christianity*, p. 55.

Second, whatever the nature of the soil, the motivations of the cultivator also influence the outcome of the harvest. God does not force sanctification on persons any more than he forces sin on them, and Scripture warns that there will be imposters within the church and even some who may deliberately reject the new life after they have tasted it (Heb. 10:23–31). Third, it seems that God puts limits on human progress in order to keep persons mindful of their continuing dependence on him. "We have this treasure in earthen vessels," Paul wrote to the early church, "to show that the transcendent power belongs to God and not to us" (2 Cor. 4:7). In other words, the building of the new heaven and the new earth is still in God's hands; Christians are not able to pull themselves up by their own bootstraps, however progressively strengthened they are becoming in Christ.

Finally, as Luther put it in a famous hymn, "Still our ancient foe / Doth seek to work us woe." To borrow Lewis's picture of the biblical drama as a cosmic battle, Christians live, as it were, between D-Day and V-Day. "Enemy-occupied territory: that is what the world is," wrote Lewis. "Christianity is the story of how the rightful king has landed, you might say landed in disguise, and is calling us all to take part in a great campaign of sabotage."[25] In other words, the decisive invasion, which marks the turning point of the war and of all history, has occurred. But there is still fighting to be done—with attendant casualties—before "the author walks onto the stage [and] the play is over."[26] And this too limits Christian progress in the new life, at least for the duration of earthly existence. There will be—indeed, there must be—substantial healing, for this is the mark of the Christian church, without which the rest of the world will understandably give it no more attention than it will give any other theory of human nature. Yet, as preachers in the Reformed tradition so aptly put it, Christians live in the era of "the already, and the not yet." The turning point has occurred, but the strife is not yet completely over.

*　　*　　*

This chapter has focused on the Judeo-Christian concept of the person, especially those aspects of it that contrast significantly with prevailing assumptions in psychology. I have noted that the biblical drama speaks of the immortality of persons in their entire, embodied selves, even though a period of immateriality of the soul may inter-

25. Lewis, *Mere Christianity*, p. 47.
26. Lewis, *Mere Christianity*, p. 64.

vene between death and the final resurrection. I have also noted that the biblical view of persons sees them as unitary (not fragmented), relational (not purely individual), and capable of responsible dominion within the limits imposed by their finitude and sinfulness. Moreover, the person who becomes a Christian makes the claim of being— and continually becoming—a "new creation," capable of exercising progressively more of the "freedom within form" that was intended before the fall of humankind. Although this process is conditional (many other factors come into play), it is nevertheless real.

It is possible to use this outline of the biblical drama as the basis for a more fully developed theory of personality than has been suggested here. I will attempt this development in Chapter Ten, in the context of a general consideration of personality theory. In the meantime, recalling the earlier statement that anthropology and epistemology go hand in hand in psychology, we need to look at the significance of a biblical view of persons for the way in which they are currently studied in psychology. This will be the task of the following chapter.

CHAPTER 5

PSYCHOLOGISTS
AND PSYCHOLOGY'S PARADIGM

No science can be more secure than the metaphysics which
tacitly it presupposes.
                                —Alfred North Whitehead[1]

In the past chapter I attempted to cover the essentials of a biblical
view of persons. By speaking of "essentials," I am acknowledging the
fact that although Scripture says a fair amount about human nature
(much more than it does about other parts of creation that are the
concern of scientists), it does not supply us with a fully detailed
anthropology in the way that, for instance, a personality theorist
might set out to do. The Bible seems to tell us as much as we need to
know for our salvation and sanctification, given that our eyes are
opened to its truth by the working of the Holy Spirit. It is the ongoing
task of Christian theologians, psychologists, and other scholars to
meet the challenge of filling in the details, to go beyond biblical
truths but to keep them consistently in mind as control beliefs.

I am going to suggest three areas in which I think the basic
biblical drama needs further elaboration for Christians in psychology.
First, our commitment to the contours of the biblical drama raises the
question about whether or not a single psychology of persons is even
possible. If the Fall has distorted our humanness and if restoration in
Christ applies only to some, then we might be led to conclude that we

---

1. Whitehead, as quoted in James E. Martin, "Presentationalism: Towards a Self-Reflexive Psychological Theory," in *Cognition and the Symbolic
Processes*, ed. Walter B. Weimar and David Palermo (Hillsdale, N.J.: Lawrence Erlbaum, 1981), 2:69.

need two separate psychologies, one for Christians and one for non-Christians. Second, even if it is concluded that a common psychology of persons is valid (as I believe it is), we still need to ask whether psychology as we now know it is covering all the essentials in its implicit anthropology. Third, given the intimate connection that we have found to exist between a social science's anthropology and its epistemology, or philosophy of science, we need to examine in more detail the current paradigm held by mainstream psychologists and decide whether or not it needs some qualification in light of a biblical anthropology.

IS A COMMON PSYCHOLOGY POSSIBLE?

In the previous chapter we anticipated some of the knotty questions facing the Christian student of psychology. Just what is the nature of God's image in persons? Do all persons, Christian or otherwise, share this image? Can we say that all Christians share it equally? Is it even possible that some non-Christians might surpass some Christians in manifesting certain aspects of this image? With regard to the actual nature of the *imago Dei*, I made a case for a human "core tendency," which I called responsivity to God, and for the peripheral capacities needed to control creation as his regents in a way such that we are morally accountable to him. But the question regarding the degree of communality between Christians and non-Christians has still to be considered, and it is to this that we turn now.

To the question regarding the continuity of God's image in human beings after the Fall, theologians have usually given an equivocal answer. Yes, the image persists in the "broad" sense (meaning that human beings retain the peripheral properties, or capacities, that mark them as uniquely human in distinction from other species). But in the "narrow" sense (by which theologians mean the core *tendency* or *motivation* to direct our human capacities in accordance with God's norms), we did indeed lose—and willfully so—an essential aspect of that image, the restoration of which is possible only through Christ. Some theologians have even objected to this broad-versus-narrow distinction, seeing in it the danger of underrating the radical antithesis between the unregenerate life and the redeemed life in Christ. In addition, they see in the preoccupation with essential properties an insufficient emphasis on the importance of obedient *behavior* as the mark of a sanctified life.[2] But although perhaps in need of qualification, the distinction between a "broad" (capacity-defined) image shared by all and a "narrow" (motivationally defined) image shared only by some seems to me to be a good starting point, for at least two reasons.

First of all, the notion of a common, "broad" image captures the vital point that even fallen human beings are still human. Despite our willing collaboration with the Evil One, we have not become devils, and despite the inevitability of bodily death and decay in the wake of the Fall, we have not become mere things or animals. With this I think even the most cautious theologians would agree, especially because it is implied by those few passages in Scripture that do refer to a post-Fall image. "Whoever sheds the blood of man, by man shall his blood be shed; for God made man in his own image," announces God to Noah after the flood (Gen. 9:6). While such a passage does not elaborate on the actual properties implied by the *imago Dei*, the universal character of the proscription (*"Whoever* sheds the blood of man . . . "*) certainly implies that something of God's image persists in everyone. Then, lamenting the intractable nature of the human tongue, the apostle James points out that "with it we bless the Lord and Father, and with it we curse men, who are made in the likeness of God" (Jas. 3:8-9). Again, the general nature of the pronouncement (*"No* human being can tame the tongue . . . "*) suggests that what it says applies to everyone.

Second, the distinction between "broad" and "narrow" images, with its insistence on a commonly shared set of human properties, is surely in keeping with our own everyday experience. There exist Christian traditions that insist that the new life in Christ leads its possessors to do *everything* in a radically different way from non-Christians, including the most mundane and routine of activities. But this conclusion, while containing a vital element of truth, seems to me to be too simple. Its truth lies in its desire to avoid what might be called "religious dualism," the idea that only certain human activities (such as worship and personal morality) are affected by Christian commitment, whereas others (such as work and art and scholarship) are religiously neutral. The reader was alerted to this kind of un-

2. See, for example, G. C. Berkouwer, *Man: The Image of God*, trans. Dirk W. Jellema, Studies in Dogmatics (Grand Rapids: Eerdmans, 1962), chap. 2.

biblical dualism in Chapter Three; in contrast to it, the Bible clearly seems to claim all aspects of life for God's concern and lordship. "The earth is the Lord's and the fulness thereof," proclaims the psalmist (Ps. 24:1), and with theologian Abraham Kuyper we must surely confess that "there is not one square inch of creation which Christ has not claimed as his own."[3]

But pushed to its extreme, such a position suggests that Christians and non-Christians share no common ground at all—that they will (or should) do all things differently all the time. This is a position that simply cannot stand up to the test of practical experience. The fact is that Christians and non-Christians in any culture share dozens of assumptions, skills, and behaviors. Any attempt to deny this can only lead to an unbiblical (as well as an unpractical) separatism that shuns contact, even for evangelistic purposes, on the grounds that Christians and non-Christians are such totally different species. Thus, while rightly rejecting one form of unbiblical dualism, such a position easily lapses into another that is just as serious.

Thus we may assume that at least in terms of the "broad" image, Christians and non-Christians share certain common properties that make possible a common psychology. But even in terms of the "narrow" image, referring to the God-ordained *use* of those properties, we must be careful not to oversimplify. I have already referred to the existence of God's common grace, which limits the evil human beings can do, signals something of God's existence and nature to everyone, and causes godly fruit to be produced, at times, even in unbelievers. (Scripture's classic and much-repeated example is that of the Persian king Cyrus, who although not a believer in Israel's God was "stirred up" by him to help the Jews rebuild the temple in Jerusalem—Ezra 1:1–5; 2 Chron. 36:22–23; Isa. 44:28.) We have also been reminded that even in committed Christians, the new life is only partially realized during this era of "the already, but the not yet." Practically speaking, then, it may be impossible at times to distinguish between a struggling, incompletely sanctified Christian and an unbeliever in whom God's common grace is hard at work!

Finally, despite the biblical metaphor of the sheep and the goats, it is possible to overdraw the division of humankind into clearly Christian and non-Christian camps. "The world does not consist

3. Kuyper, paraphrased in John Cooper, "Dualism and the Biblical View of Human Beings," part 2 *Reformed Journal* 32 (Oct. 1982): 16.

only of 100 per cent Christians and 100 per cent non-Christians," observed C. S. Lewis. "There are people (a great many of them) who are slowly ceasing to be Christians; some of them are even clergymen. There are other people who are slowly becoming Christians although they do not call themselves so."[4] No doubt God can recognize his own among these apparently equivocal cases, but we are forbidden to judge—probably in part precisely because behavior and self-report can be so very ambiguous. This is a further reason to affirm a common psychology for all persons.

I conclude, then, that notwithstanding the radical cleavage between those who want to follow Christ and those who reject him, our common humanness, God's common grace, and our common frailties make possible and necessary a single psychology of persons. But that is not to say that no work remains to be done and that we should be content as Christians just to accept the existing theories and methods of psychology. In Chapter One I suggested that Christians should pay special attention to Thomas Kuhn's exposure of the metaphysical side of scientific paradigms. For if, as both Kuhn and Michael Polanyi argue, extrascientific beliefs about the "order of nature" permeate all scientific work, then we have a responsibility to expose such assumptions in psychology and compare them with our understanding of the biblical world view. Moreover, if we find such assumptions wanting, it is both scientifically and Christianly legitimate to argue for changes, provided that such changes lead to fruitful theory and research of a sort that the current paradigm cannot generate. To begin such a task, we need to look at the ruling paradigm in psychology regarding both the *nature* and the *study* of persons. We need, in other words, to look more closely at psychology's anthropology and epistemology.

PSYCHOLOGY'S CURRENT PARADIGM

A paradigm—a discipline's particular blend of preferred theories, methods, and critically acclaimed studies—can also be likened to a discipline's corporate self-image. One way to understand that self-image as it exists in psychology is by reading the opening chapters of its best-selling introductory texts. For in the opening chapters of such volumes students are normally introduced to "what psychology is,"

4. Lewis, *Mere Christianity* (London: Collins-Fontana, 1955), p. 173.

and the answers given in the best-selling texts would seem to reflect what most teachers of psychology want their students to hear. When we look at such texts—the durability of which is reflected in the fact that they are published in new editions every few years—we almost always find two repeated and interconnected themes.

The first theme is that psychologists should use the scientific method wherever possible, and the second, that they should do so with the aim of predicting and controlling human behavior. The meaning of the term "behavior" has broadened considerably since J. B. Watson's insistence that it refers only to outwardly observable movements; nowadays, as one pair of reviewers has conceded, it "includes behavioral processes that are observable, such as gestures, speech, and physiological changes, and processes that can only be inferred, such as thoughts and dreams."[5] Nevertheless, the majority of the most-used introductory texts hold that whatever psychologists choose to study, they should study according to a *causal model*. Thus, according to one text, psychologists may differ in emphasizing either the *historical* causes of present behavior (such as genetic endowment, childhood emotional climate, and past learning experiences) or *current* influences (such as immediate motives, perceptions, and environmental constraints). But what both must share is a search for explanations of a certain type: they must "attempt to identify the relevant psychological variables and use them to predict and control behavior."[6] According to such an approach, to explain a behavior is to reduce it to its component causes—past and present, innate and acquired, biological and social. Thus, as I have already noted in Chapter Four, the anthropology of the paradigm of current psychology tends to be thoroughly naturalistic.

Moreover, whenever possible, the controlled *experiment* is the preferred method for isolating these causes. According to another popular text, "One can have a science without doing experiments— this is more or less the case with astronomy and geology—but the inability to experiment entails a certain loss of status. [For] among the advantages of the experiment are the investigator's ability to control

5. Kenneth E. Clark and George A. Miller, eds., *Psychology: Behavioral and Social Sciences Survey Committee* (Englewood Cliffs, N.J.: Prentice-Hall, 1970), p. 12.
6. Ernest R. Hilgard, Rita L. Atkinson, and Richard C. Atkinson, *Introduction to Psychology*, 7th ed. (New York: Harcourt Brace Jovanovich, 1979), p. 16.

when and where observations are made, to repeat his studies or have others repeat them [and to] approach his problem in a systematic manner in which all of the steps are explicitly set forth."[7] Elsewhere I have explored the logic and conduction of a typical psychology experiment in which human beings are the subjects, and this need not be repeated here.[8] More significant for present purposes is the point that the philosophy of science behind this approach is distinctly Popperian.

In Chapter One I referred to Karl Popper as the person who argued that no scientific law is fixed and irreplaceable. Indeed, Popper insisted, true scientists are always ready to *falsify* their most cherished theories—to say, in effect, "If my theory is right, then it can be provisionally retained if such-and-such happens in thus-and-so test situation. If it doesn't happen, then my theory will be abandoned." What is enduring in Popperian science, then, is not any specific set of theories themselves (however durable under experimental tests) but rather the supposed *logic* of scientific discovery—the procedures used in phrasing one's claim and in tying it to the domain of observable events to which it refers. Few psychologists know enough about the philosophy of science to label their approach distinctly Popperian, or "falsificationist." But the most respected intellectual surveys of the field are quite explicit about this allegiance. According to Daniel Robinson, for example, Kuhn's claim that most scientific theories rise or fall according to *extra*-logical factors (sociological, interpersonal, metaphysical, etc.) merely describes science (including psychology) as it often regrettably *is*, whereas Popper describes it at its situationally transcendent best. Much of the history of psychology, says Robinson, may be "Kuhnian in orientation, but this is not to say that science itself is. [My own] bias is decidedly Popperian."[9]

---

7. Gardner Lindzey, Calvin S. Hall, and Richard F. Thompson, *Psychology* (New York: Worth, 1975), p. 13.

8. See Mary Stewart Van Leeuwen, *The Sorcerer's Apprentice: A Christian Looks at the Changing Face of Psychology* (Downers Grove, Ill.: InterVarsity Press, 1982), chap. 2.

9. Robinson, *An Intellectual History of Psychology* (New York: Macmillan, 1981), p. 28. It is somewhat ironic that although Robinson is correct in identifying himself and most other psychologists as Popperians in the sense I have indicated, Popper himself now insists that the "Popper legend," portraying him as a falsificationist type of positivist, is far too simple. See, for example, his *Realism and the Aim of Science* (Totowa, N.J.: Rowman and Littlefield, 1983), pp. 176–77; and also James Farr, "Popper's Hermeneutics," *Philosophy of the Social Sciences* 13 (1983): 157–76.

We might summarize the preceding by saying that in contemporary psychology, the dominant anthropology is a naturalistic one, and the dominant philosophy of science is falsificationist. Or, to put it another way, persons are studied by psychologists mostly "as if" they were somewhat "larger rats or slower computers,"[10] while persons who also happen to be psychologists are rarely studied at all, since their personal characteristics and values are held to be largely irrelevant to the way they conduct themselves as scientists. It is psychology's enduring commitment to a methodology based on natural science, a methodology that stresses causal explanation, that interacts with and maintains its naturalistic anthropology in a mutually reinforcing way. Moreover, it is psychology's firm commitment to a falsificationist view of science that leads it, for the most part, to ignore the "psychology of psychologists." For in this Popperian view, if the rules for doing science are carefully followed then factors that are personal to scientists themselves will be laundered out, and the pure logic of scientific discovery will be left to do its work. By contrast, in the view of scholars like Kuhn and Polanyi, those same personal factors that Popper would exorcise from the scientific enterprise are in fact intrinsic and even essential to it.

CHRISTIAN RESPONSES TO PSYCHOLOGY'S PARADIGM

I have said that any Christian evaluation of psychology's paradigm needs to take into account both its naturalistic anthropology and its falsificationist epistemology. But such an exercise is complicated by the fact that Christians often differ from *one another* in their evaluations of each of these aspects of psychology. Some concede that psychology's naturalistic metaphor is vastly overdrawn but still regard its philosophy of science as beyond question. Others, including myself, believe that since psychology's naturalistic anthropology and its prevailing philosophy of science are intimately interdependent, both are in need of revision. But since both positions are defended by sincere appeals to a biblical world view, it would seem wise to try to understand the contours of each.

Helpful to us at this point is C. Stephen Evans' thoughtful vol-

10. James F. T. Bugenthal, ed., *Challenges of Humanistic Psychology* (New York: McGraw-Hill, 1967), p. vii.

ume entitled *Preserving the Person.* [11] Writing as a Christian philosopher interested in the social sciences, Evans explores ways in which Christians have wrestled with the naturalistic anthropology that has dominated not only psychology but the other social sciences as well. And wrestle with it they surely must. For the thrust of Scripture is that persons are God's accountable stewards, endowed with the capacities needed to subdue the earth and hence transcend their downward connections with it. By contrast, a naturalistic anthropology sees in human beings only a more complex version of animal or machine—and who among us would hold either an animal or a machine morally accountable for its performance?[12] In his book Evans analyzes no fewer than six ways in which Christians might approach this dilemma while still trying sincerely to maintain the authority of Scripture. But since these six ways are also grouped into three broader categories that are quite sufficient for present purposes, we will content ourselves with an examination of these.

Reinterpreting the Personal. First of all, writes Evans, it is possible to evade the "mechanistic-personalistic dilemma" entirely if one simply identifies the causal, naturalistic account of persons with the scriptural account. To do this, one must lean very heavily on those passages that stress the sovereignty of God—passages, that is, that seem to picture God as controlling and determining all things for his own purposes, including people and all their activities. When Calvinist theologians stress that it is God who chooses who will be saved and who will not, and further emphasize that any good done by human beings is totally the result of God's Spirit working in them, this does indeed seem to reduce to a species of "theological determinism," with God as the first cause from which the many secondary causes described by science are seen to derive.

But as Evans himself rightly points out, the dilemma cannot be resolved quite so neatly. For even the most committed Calvinist will not deny (indeed, will staunchly affirm) that human beings are morally accountable to God and to each other for their wrong actions, even if they can take no credit for their right ones. And, says Evans, "When we hold a person morally responsible, do we not say to him, 'You could have done otherwise, *even given* your past and present

11. Evans, *Preserving the Person: A Look at the Human Sciences* (Downers Grove, Ill.: InterVarsity Press, 1977).
12. But see also those parts of Chapters Six and Eight concerning the growing field of artificial intelligence.

[causal influences]'?"[13] This is something we do not say of even the most sophisticated robot or animal.

Perspectivalism: The Preferred Resolution. In the end Evans cannot cite any contemporary Christians who actually have rationalized acceptance of psychology's paradigm by an appeal to the nature of God's sovereignty (although earlier theologians such as Jonathan Edwards seem to have tried this route to resolution). For even those with the most developed view of God's sovereignty still see Scripture holding that sovereignty in paradoxical tension with a degree of human accountability that cannot be explained away. Nor does Evans himself recommend this way of resolving the tension between naturalistic and biblical anthropologies.

But the second part of Evans' typology is far from hypothetical. Indeed, it is the route to resolution most preferred by evangelical social scientists in the Anglo-American tradition.

Those in Evans' second group do not try to reduce the biblical account of persons to a naturalistic or mechanistic one; they are "limiters of science"—persons who state that the scientific method is fine in its proper place but that it cannot tell us everything we need to know about ourselves and the world. Evans' first type of limiters, whom he calls "territorialists," will be discussed more fully in Chapter Six, as they adhere to a mind-brain dualism that questions the appropriateness of ever using a causal model to study the mind. But for present purposes the type of limiters whom Evans calls "perspectivalists" are of most interest, since they advocate what is in fact the preferred stance of many Christians regarding the nature and scope of psychology, and indeed of science in general.

According to perspectivalists, the sciences, including psychology, are indeed Popperian, and rightly so. That is to say, scientists may draw theoretical inspiration from any source they wish, but all such theories must finally be falsifiable through certain empirical steps that are logically bound together. Put somewhat differently, we could say that perspectivalists adhere to what is called the "unity of science" thesis. This holds that there is only one method employed by all genuine sciences, and this method consists of giving deterministic, causal explanations that are empirically testable.[14]

This extremely high view of science, classically understood, is usually justified by an appeal to the historical participation of Christians in the scientific revolution itself. Perspectivalists point out that

13. Evans, *Preserving the Person*, p. 99.
14. Evans, *Preserving the Person*, chap. 7.

many pioneers of modern science were professing Christians, including most of the founding members of Britain's elite Royal Society. Furthermore, many were devout Puritans whose reading of Scripture led them to conclude that since God valued his creation and had made it orderly, part of the human mandate was to explore it with a view to exposing these orderly functions. As psychologist David Myers summarizes it,

> Their obedience to the Source of truth motivated them to explore the material world, not disdain it, and to accept humbly whatever facts creation should offer. They believed that whatever they discovered was ultimately God's, and that they owed no ultimate allegiance to any human authority. Here, then, were grounds for celebrating science, not villifying it. [15]

But despite their belief in the unity and importance of science, perspectivalists draw the line at calling any scientific account complete or ultimate. Scientific explanations, they say, give us only one "perspective" on reality, the perspective that specializes in causal explanations tied to an empirical base. Thus Christian psychologists may freely explore what seem to be the causal bases of any human activities, including mental ones, but they must not thereby conclude that they have told the whole story any more than one has told all there is to know about a poem by describing the composition of the ink in which it is written. Thus, for example, Christian psychologists may freely study the way in which religious beliefs result from childhood socialization, provided that they do not *reduce* religious beliefs to "nothing but" the effects of parental training. Or they can legitimately study the environmental factors that promote altruistic behavior among people without thereby denying that those same people still are responsible for choosing whether or not they will act altruistically. Among Christians in the Anglo-American, Protestant tradition, Malcolm Jeeves, Donald MacKay, and David Myers represent some articulate spokespersons for the perspectivalist resolution between the biblical world view and psychology's paradigm. [16] Myers summarizes the perspectivalist position as follows:

15. Myers, *The Human Puzzle: Psychological Research and Christian Belief* (San Francisco: Harper and Row, 1978), p. 6.
16. See Jeeves, *Psychology and Christianity: The View Both Ways* (Leicester, U.K.: Inter-Varsity Press, 1976); MacKay, *The Clockwork Image: A Christian Perspective on Science* (London: Inter-Varsity Press, 1974); and *Human Science and Human Dignity* (London: Hodder and Stoughton, 1979); and Myers, *The Human Puzzle.*

If we are to understand why scientific and religious explanations need not be considered mutually exclusive, we must recognize that there are a variety of possible ways by which one might explain a given event, all of which can be simultaneously true in their own terms. An exhaustive description at one level does not invalidate explanation at some other level. . . . We may affirm, at its own level, the completeness and accuracy of the naturalistic description of the person without retreating for a moment from a conviction that this person is also the noblest work of God's creation. . . . Once we recognize the complementary nature of various levels of explanation, we are liberated from all the useless argument over whether human nature should be studied scientifically or introspectively and humanistically. It is not an either/or matter. Both methods are valuable for their own purposes. [17]

What can be said about the perspectivalist's desire to maintain psychology as a causally oriented science while at the same time containing it within limits? That it is an improvement over uncritical attempts to collapse scriptural and mechanistic accounts of the person seems obvious. In a sense, perspectivalism captures the tension of humankind's intermediate position in creation. Inasmuch as persons are related "downward" to other animal and material forms, they can be studied in their earthbound aspects by methods originally developed for the study of those lower forms. But inasmuch as they are related "upward" to God, in their accountability to him and in their capacities to be his agents, the sieve of science is too coarse to capture all the essentials. Nor is there any question of perspectivalism falling into an unbiblical dualism of values that denigrates the merely material and biological side of human nature in comparison with the so-called "higher" capacities, such as thinking, creating, and worshiping. Like their Puritan forebears, perspectivalists have a high view of God's material creation and of humankind's calling to study it as closely and as honestly as possible.

Yet, despite these encouraging qualities, it seems to me that perspectivalism leaves too many unanswered questions to be the final word on the relationship between Christianity and psychology. To begin with, perspectivalism is not unique to Christians. It is safe to say that almost all Anglo-American psychologists are becoming "token" perspectivalists, inasmuch as they are beginning to acknowledge that science cannot give a complete account of personhood but must be

17. Myers, *The Human Puzzle*, pp. 11, 13–14.

supplemented by literary, artistic, and other perspectives as well. Indeed, the most-used introductory texts referred to earlier often acknowledge this at some point in their opening chapters. But among both Christian and non-Christian perspectivalists this acknowledgment still reduces to *only* a token one. That is, it does not go so far as to concede that the paradigm of *psychology itself* should be adjusted to better capture the nonmechanical aspects of its subject matter. To the perspectivalist the perspective of psychology must stay firmly within the paradigm of natural science, leaving to the humanities any consideration of ways to explore the accountable, transcendent aspects of persons. A perusal of the course requirements for psychology in any college—Christian or otherwise—only confirms the strength of this basic commitment.

Such a stance, however, leads to problems for Christian and non-Christian psychologists alike. For one thing, it has produced an awkward schizophrenia in psychology itself. Many readers will recall C. P. Snow's *The Two Cultures and the Scientific Revolution*, in which he described the apparently unbridgeable gap between the vision of personhood assumed by the humanities and the contrasting, mechanistic one assumed by the natural sciences and many of the social sciences.[18] It is not inaccurate to say that within psychology as a single discipline these same "two cultures" exist in uneasy tension. For although the paradigm and the training requirements are largely borrowed from the natural sciences, close to half of all persons holding doctoral degrees (and even more of those with only one postgraduate degree) are actually in clinical and counseling psychology, where accountability, choice, and the power of commitment are simply *assumed* to be key ingredients of personhood and are built right into most types of therapist-client interaction.[19] Should we then be surprised that most Christians, if they can succeed in running the gauntlet of their undergraduate requirements, opt to turn their backs on psychology's official paradigm and train to be clinicians or counselors?[20]

18. Snow, *The Two Cultures and the Scientific Revolution* (Cambridge: Cambridge University Press, 1959).
19. American Psychological Association, *A Career in Psychology* (Washington, D.C.: APA, 1978).
20. My source for this conclusion is not systematic. However, when it is realized that the one North American organization for Christians in psychology (The Christian Association for Psychological Studies) is made up overwhelmingly of counseling and clinical psychologists, the conclusion does not seem unwarranted.

In addition, the perspectivalist's insistence that psychology remain unified around a naturalistic anthropology and an experimental methodology creates awkward tensions within psychologists themselves. I have described these tensions in more detail in *The Sorcerer's Apprentice;* they can be summarized by being referred to as "the reflexivity problem" and "the ethical problem."

The first of these phrases refers to the difficulties that arise when psychologists apply to human beings with as little qualification as possible those methods originally developed for use with subhuman entities. In particular, when psychologists use controlled experimentation to determine cause-effect sequences in human behavior, they have to reckon with the undeniable fact that, merely by *thinking* about the experimental conditions of which they are a part, human beings (unlike animals and material objects) are able to change themselves and hence the experimental situation as a whole. "Reflexivity" refers to this self-transcending cognitive capacity, which is clearly operative in a great many human situations and which, moreover, would seem to be an essential endowment for being accountable overseers of the creation. The Christian can, I believe, agree with Rom Harré and Paul Secord (see also Chapter Nine) that one of the significant features of human personhood is "the capacity to *monitor* control of one's actions. . . . The person is not only an agent, but a watcher, commentator and critic as well."[21]

Yet, far from adjusting the research paradigm to take this vital human capacity into account, it is standard practice for both Christian and non-Christian psychologists to do their best to *cancel it out*— that is, to reduce its influence in the experimental situation by simply deceiving the participants about the nature of the research. The experimenters hope that, thus deceived, the participants will be unable to monitor and adjust their reactions in any way that will significantly interfere with the experimenters' *actual* manipulations. What the reflexivity problem exposes is an implicit double standard at work in psychology: a cognitive capacity on which the very doing of science depends is routinely assumed to be present in psychologists them-

---

21. Harré and Secord, *The Explanation of Social Behavior* (Oxford: Basil Blackwell, 1972), p. 6. See also Martin, "Presentationalism"; Mary Stewart Van Leeuwen, "Reflexivity in North American Psychology: Historical Reflections on One Aspect of a Changing Paradigm," *Journal of the American Scientific Affiliation* 35 (Sept. 1983): 162–67; and David Lyon, Clifton Orlebeke, and Mary Stewart Van Leeuwen, *Knowing Ourselves: Reflexivity in the Social Sciences* (forthcoming).

selves yet ignored or circumvented in the persons they study. As one critic has phrased this contradiction,

> At the heart of most psychological theories is a fundamental distinction between "scientist" and "organism." They provide different languages for the two, and imply that the "scientist" is a very different kettle of fish from the "subject." Thus, for example, in learning theory terms, the subject is being [passively] "conditioned," while the experimental psychologist is [actively and freely] "testing" hypotheses. [22]

For a minority of psychologists this double standard does not appear to be a problem. If, as we mentioned in Chapter Three, one invokes the assumption that social scientists are a breed of "philosopher-kings" quite different from the rank and file of humanity, then it is perfectly acceptable to have a "psychology of psychologists" quite different from that which is applied to ordinary mortals. But I have already argued against this double standard as a Christian, pleading instead that we need a common psychology for a common humanity. Moreover, this double standard is one that most psychologists seem to reject on the level of their nonprofessional commitments, since some seventy percent of them (in America) consistently vote Democrat. [23]

The reflexivity problem in turn highlights an ethical problem or contradiction that perspectivalism seems ill-equipped to handle. The practice of trying to neutralize reflexivity by deceiving participants in experiments has inevitably forced psychologists to ponder the morality of such a technique and to articulate professional guidelines for its regulation. How elaborate can such deception be? Who has the right to arbitrate when there is disagreement about the use of deception in a given study? What are the relative rights of researchers and participants in such cases?[24] The dilemma implicit in such questions should be obvious: if psychologists adhere consistently to a paradigm that regards persons only in terms of amoral structures and functions and regards science as the value-free pursuit of value-free knowledge, where are they to turn for the wisdom to answer such challenges right

---

22. Donald Bannister, "Personal Construct Theory and Research Method," in *Human Inquiry: A Sourcebook of New Paradigm Research*, ed. Peter Reason and John Rowan (New York: John Wiley, 1981), p. 194.

23. Charles G. McClintock, Charles B. Spaulding, and Henry A. Turner, "Political Orientations of Academically Affiliated Psychologists," *American Psychologist* 20 (Mar. 1965): 211–21.

24. See also Chapter Nine.

within their own laboratories? Moreover, how can Christian perspectivalists limit the mandate of psychology to the purely technical task of specifying mechanical relationships when the very process of studying these relationships confronts them with their research subjects' freely reflexive processes and their own moral accountability in deciding whether or not to counteract it with the use of deception?

"Questions of moral obligation, of purpose and direction, of ultimate meaning are not directly addressed by a science of behavior," writes perspectivalist David Myers, and asks that we let psychology "[contribute] its insights to one level of discourse, humble and unpretentious enough to recognize that many of the deeply significant questions of life are *not* psychological questions, and that we ought not to talk of them as if they were."[25] But I have argued, with Kuhn and Polanyi, that such a neat compartmentalization of scientific and value questions simply does not and should not take place in psychology. Moreover, it seems to me that Christians should be the last persons to insist otherwise. For if we believe that accountability is at the heart of personhood, and if we confess with Augustine and Luther that the effects of the Fall permeate all aspects of human life, then there is no way that we can declare *any* human endeavor epistemologically "clean" or morally neutral, even in principle—and this includes science. When perspectivalists argue for a "humble and unpretentious" confinement of psychology to the specification of mechanical relationships, they are in danger of asking that scientists qua scientists be considered "the exception"—to be seen as somehow exempt from what is fundamentally and inescapably human. For the Christian to grant such an exemption is at best naive and at worst idolatrous.

The Humanizer's Option. The perspectivalist, I have said, is faithful to the thrust of Scripture in refusing to reduce personhood to its mechanical aspects, but mistaken in his or her insistence that psychology can and should study only those mechanical aspects, using only natural-science methods. Does this mean that psychology should totally abandon its mechanistic, Popperian paradigm and look for something that is more adequate to its human character and subject matter?

This is, in fact, the position of those whom Evans calls the "humanizers of science." Such persons maintain that the discon-

25. Myers, *The Human Puzzle*, p. 37.

tinuity between human beings and lower forms is so great as to require an entirely different approach to the study of persons within the social sciences.[26] Such humanizers draw on the work of social scientists and philosophers in both the European and the Anglo-American traditions. In Europe the methodological writings of Wilhelm Dilthey, Eduard Spranger, and Maurice Merleau-Ponty are pertinent.[27] In Britain those of R. G. Collingwood and Peter Winch could be cited.[28] In North America the entire "third force," or humanistic psychology movement, stands in opposition to the dominant paradigm.[29] And, as we will see in Chapter Nine, there is a similar but more rigorous reform movement gaining momentum among American social psychologists.

All of these "humanizing" reform movements seem to be united by at least three general concerns. First of all, in one way or another each is concerned to eliminate the double standard that presently separates human researchers from their human subjects. If reflexivity is a taken-for-granted feature of social scientists, then it must not be a neglected or circumscribed capacity in their research subjects. If ordinary persons are prey to conditioning forces of which they are largely unaware, then so must social scientists be, even in the very doing of their science. Furthermore, this inevitable interaction of values with the conduct of science must be exposed and clarified—but not necessarily exorcised, since human-science advocates generally acknowledge that the valuing process (the need to search for and attribute meaning to all our activities) is an irreducible feature of personhood.

This leads to a second area of agreement among human-science reformers. Human actions, they say, cannot be understood merely by observation and description from an outsider's point of view. Indeed, most cannot be adequately understood until the observer finds out what those actions *mean to the actor*. Consequently, methods are needed that will enable the scientist to understand, in active coopera-

26. Evans, *Preserving the Person*, chap. 10.
27. *Wilhelm Dilthey: An Introduction*, ed. Herbert A. Hodges (London: Routledge, 1944); Spranger, *Types of Men*, trans. P. J. W. Pigors (Halle: Niemeyer, 1928); and Merleau-Ponty, *The Structure of Behavior*, trans. Alden L. Fisher (Boston: Beacon Press, 1963).
28. See Collingwood, *The Idea of History* (Oxford: Clarendon Press, 1946); and Winch, *The Idea of a Social Science and Its Relation to Philosophy* (New York: Humanities Press, 1958).
29. See Henryk Misiak and Virginia S. Sexton, *Phenomenological, Existential and Humanistic Psychologies: A Historical Survey* (New York: Grune and Stratton, 1973).

tion with the subjects, how the subjects see their particular situation. This is something that is rarely done under the current psychological paradigm. Instead, the researcher observes behavior or asks for self-reports from subjects on a series of verbal items, and only after analyzing these does he or she proceed to *infer*—without reference back to the subjects themselves—what the collective responses can be presumed to mean. (See also Chapter Nine.)

A third and final feature uniting the would-be humanizers of science is their concern to do justice to the whole, integrated person—to develop, one might say, a "psychology of the self." For it is "selves" who choose and are accountable, "selves" who provide the continuity of identity across human time, "selves" who must, for better or for worse, coordinate and interpret the bodily states, perceptions, habits, and environmental stimuli that are presently studied in such fragmented fashion by psychologists. And finally, it is selves who do science and attribute meaning to the individual and corporate results thereof.[30]

Readers of *The Sorcerer's Apprentice* will know that the humanizer's position is one for which I have quite a lot of sympathy, and one the three main concerns of which I consider scripturally defensible.[31] Yet I would hesitate to reform psychology simply by substituting the humanizer's agenda for the current paradigm. For in its extreme form, which rejects *any* natural-science analysis of human behavior, it is just as questionable as a mechanically reduced conception of persons and a value-free image of science. That is to say, our desire to free psychology from the confines of an amoral and deterministic paradigm must not make us revert to an idealistic monism that rejects our "downward" relationship with the rest of creation. Moreover, if psychology's current paradigm places too *little* stress on reflexivity, meaning, and the wholeness and integrity of the self, it is also possible for a "humanized" psychology to stress these three things too *much*.

Let us recall that Augustine was called the "first psychologist" and Freud his secular successor because both recognized that human beings are at least some of the time defensive, and consequently *cannot* always give an accurate account of their own motives and behavior. Augustine thought that our legacy from the Fall makes us resist awareness of many of our own motives; Freud thought that the

30. See C. Stephen Evans, "The Concept of the Self as the Key to Integration," *Journal of Psychology and Christianity* (in press).
31. Van Leeuwen, *The Sorcerer's Apprentice*, chap. 3.

explanation lay in the child's unfolding biosocial nature within the dynamics of family life. Both recognized, however, that no human being is totally the captain of his or her own ship.

Thus an important, twofold question confronts us as Christians in psychology. Under what conditions should we study human behavior (including our own) by indirect means, not relying on the direct testimony and self-interpretation of those being studied? And under what conditions can we invoke the capacity—and the right—of persons to account for their own thoughts, motives, and actions rather than debunking such human capacities and their God-given origin and function? These are complex questions for which I claim no easy or final answers, although some possible answers will be developed in the second section of this volume. At this point in psychology's history, however, I would say this much: Christians and others in psychology must abandon their insistence that psychology's paradigm remain unified around a mechanistic, Popperian ideal, and must begin to support, use, and teach approaches based on the human-science agenda as well.

What this means is that perspectivalism must invade *psychology itself* in a self-conscious and coordinated fashion. Rather than insisting on a cross-disciplinary division of labor, with science and the social sciences focusing on the naturalistic side of persons while the humanities study their more transcendent functions, psychology is in need of a more equitable division of labor *within*. The approaches of psychologists with a natural-science orientation and those of psychologists with a human-science orientation must be given more equal place, and more active coordination of the two must be encouraged.

In this latter function it may be that Christians have an especially crucial role to play. For what other world view is so acutely aware of humanity as both "dust" and "a little lower than the angels"? What other world view is so aware of the pull—and the value—of our material side as well as the transcendence of the reflexive, accountable self over the merely material? What other world view is so sensitive to the inevitable misuse of all our capacities—a misuse that we are so prone to deny or rationalize whenever we can get away with it? To bring these confessed convictions to bear on our presently one-sided psychology will not be easy. But as we continue our selective tour through the landscape of the discipline, they are convictions that will inform our vision of what is possible for the future as well as what is retainable from the past.

PART TWO
PSYCHOLOGY AS A MODERN ENTERPRISE

Contemporary Debates About the Person

CHAPTER 6

PSYCHOLOGY
AND THE
BRAIN-MIND DEBATE

A prudent investigator knows very well that the fact of his having penetrated a little way into the intricate process of nature gives him no right, not a scintilla more than any other man, to pronounce dogmatically on the nature of the soul.

—Hermann von Helmholtz[1]

The brain is so organized that it is simply impossible to separate any of its functions according to their social implications. The brain is not nearly so simple as some of our cherished ideas.

—D. Gareth Jones[2]

In the first part of this book I tried to set the stage for this, the second and longer portion of it, which deals with several specific areas of concern to Christians as they focus on the person in psychology. As promised in the Introduction, we will deal with these topics in a roughly hierarchical fashion, beginning in this chapter with a topic in psychology that is very closely connected to purely medical and physiological concerns—namely, the relationship of the mind to the brain and the extent to which the one can be identified with the other. In

---

1. Von Helmholtz in a letter to his father, 4 March 1857, as quoted in Leon Konigsberger, *Hermann von Helmholtz* (Braunschweig, Germany: 1902), 1:291–92.
2. Jones, *Our Fragile Brains: A Christian Perspective on Brain Research* (Downers Grove, Ill.: InterVarsity Press, 1981), p. 128.

subsequent chapters, as we deal with behavioral, cognitive, social, and personality psychology, we will find not only that there is progressively less talk of identifying persons with purely natural structures and functions, but also that there is correspondingly more uneasiness about the appropriateness of using methods based on natural science to explore these levels of personhood. This being the case, I hope that the reader will be able to understand, by way of progressively more concrete examples, the argument that I made in Chapter Five concerning the need for a more self-consciously pluralized paradigm in psychology.

Let us begin our exploration of the brain-mind debate by referring to the two quotations with which this chapter opened. Written almost 125 years apart, each has come from the pen of a prominent neuroscientist deeply concerned with the study of the human nervous system. Hermann von Helmholtz (1821–1894) was one of the pioneers of experimental psychology. Trained to do research in physics and physiology, he later developed an interest in the psychology of vision and hearing, and to this day his theories about these processes are cited in textbooks on perception. D. Gareth Jones is presently a professor of anatomy and human biology in Western Australia, and his book, *Our Fragile Brains*, is one that I will refer to a number of times throughout this chapter.

These opening quotations highlight a feature common to both scientists. Despite the prominence that each has enjoyed as a neuroscientist, neither has been able to resolve the perennial mystery about how our material brains— "two handfuls of pinkish-grey matter"[3]— underlie and relate to our essential selfhood. Because the brain is so intimately implicated in all of our mental and behavioral functions, it has for centuries been the locus of the philosophical "mind-body debate" and its theological counterpart: the question about how the soul, or self, can interact with a living and materially finite body.

The debate concerning what Wilder Penfield called "the mystery of the mind"[4] has thus been a perennial one, and my treatment of it is divided into four sections. First of all, I will point out the ambivalence that Christians have historically shown toward investigating any part of the human body, including the brain. Then I will summarize the Cartesian origins of mind-body dualism and one present-day ex-

3. Jones, *Our Fragile Brains*, p. 13.
4. Penfield, *The Mystery of the Mind* (Princeton: Princeton University Press, 1975).

pression of it. Next I will present dualism's major competitor among Christian psychologists and neuroscientists, which is a form of the perspectivalist approach to which we were introduced in Chapter Five. Finally, I will try to summarize the strengths and weaknesses of both dualist and perspectivalist positions and suggest a third alternative in keeping with the reforms suggested at the end of Chapter Five.

CHRISTIAN AMBIVALENCE ABOUT EXPLORING THE BODY

Throughout history Christians have intuitively known and behaviorally acknowledged that persons are intimately one with their bodies yet somehow also more than the sum of their biological parts. Prior to the medieval era the church affirmed the importance of the body to the essential self in the founding and running of hospitals. Throughout the Middle Ages in Europe (and until even later in the New World), Christians continued to be leaders in the establishment of hospitals and the development and practice of medicine. As the major guardian of scholarship during the Middle Ages, the church preserved and transcribed classical Greek treatises on medicine that would otherwise have vanished. In all of these activities the church was acknowledging the importance of earthly, biological existence in God's sight and the fact that its optimal expression depended on the structures and functions of a healthy body.[5]

But it is also claimed that the early Christian church sometimes had an adverse effect on the development of medicine. In some of its hospitals disease was regarded primarily as a punishment for sin, and prayer and repentance were emphasized more than bodily therapy. In addition, the human body was held to be so sacred that dissection of cadavers, even for the sake of medical progress, was forbidden. Inferences about human anatomy and physiology were permitted from only two sources. One was animal dissections, the results of which were often wrongly generalized to apply to human beings. Then there were the classical writings of Galen, a Greek physician who practiced in second-century Rome and whose experiences as a surgeon in the gladiatorial arenas gave him some incidental—but very flawed—knowledge of human anatomy.

5. *Encyclopedia Britannica*, 15th ed., s.v. "Hospitals, history of."

Yet it was a devout Christian physician from Brussels, Andreas Vesalius (1514–1564), who did the most to break the taboo against the dissection of the human body and its consequent anatomical mapping. Not only did he attend a progressive university where dissection was practiced, but in later years he insisted on doing his own dissections rather than following current practice and leaving them to laboratory assistants. As a result, his seven-volume work on the human body, published in 1543, was more extensive and accurate than anything that had previously appeared on the subject. "After Vesalius," writes one of his biographers, "anatomy became a scientific discipline [and] medicine became a learned profession."[6]

Historically, then, Christians have been understandably uneasy about making flippant invasions into the human body and treating it as if it were just a more complex animal or machine. At the same time, the history of Christians in medicine and the neurosciences shows a religiously motivated desire to study the body's structures and functions, not only with the aim of understanding that part of God's creation but also with the goal of preventing or alleviating human suffering. And of all parts of the body, the brain and the spinal cord are certainly the most complex and the most radically affected by damage. Our central nervous systems, as Jones stresses from the title through the closing sentences of his book, are exceedingly fragile.

MONISM VERSUS DUALISM: A PERENNIAL DEBATE

What is the central issue reflected in this enduring Christian ambivalence toward the exploration and manipulation of the body? Expressed in twentieth-century terms, it seems to be as follows: How can we do justice to our biological embodiment as earth-bound creatures of God (with all that this implies regarding respect and concern for the human body) without at the same time becoming biological reductionists (with all that this implies regarding the loss of human uniqueness and the possibility of arbitrarily interfering with people's minds through the use of drugs, psychosurgery, or other techniques)? Expressed in more traditional terms, we are dealing with the mind-body problem, which concerns the relationship of human thoughts,

6. *Encyclopedia Britannica*, 15th ed., s.v. "Vesalius, Andreas."

feelings, beliefs, and actions to that physical organ, the brain, on which they depend for their expression. Or, as Jones articulates it, "[How do we] hold together the *obvious* characteristics of people and their external behavior, and the not-so-obvious characteristics such as their internal mental states[?] Often the dilemma is expressed as the tension between the material and the immaterial, between brain and mind, between body and soul."[7] Let us begin our consideration of this question by referring back to René Descartes, the devout Catholic thinker who first saw the implications of the scientific revolution for the brain-mind debate.

Cartesian Dualism. René Descartes (1596–1650) was in many ways a philosopher torn between two worlds. His life span overlapped the period in which the scientific revolution was taking place, and no scholar of that era had a greater vision than he for the development of a unified science—based on mathematics, empirical observation, and deductive logic—that would apply to all aspects of the material world. At the same time, he was profoundly aware of the unreliability of human observation, and of the convolutions and self-contradictions of which human thought was capable. How was he to resolve this tension between total skepticism on the one hand and his desire for a reliable, unified scientific method on the other?

For Descartes the answer was summed up in his famous phrase *Cogito, ergo sum*—"I think, therefore I am." That is to say, even when the uncertain evidence of the senses is rejected, even when the existence of one's own body is doubted as a possible illusion, the very process of doubting implies the existence of a doubter, of someone who can think. On the cornerstone of this "self-evident certainty" Descartes was to build his entire philosophical edifice.

In affirming the indubitable existence of the *mind* in contrast to the doubts and distortions to which *matter* is prey, Descartes concluded that the mind must be a fundamentally different entity from the material body that it inhabits. For him the universe consisted of two basic and totally contrasting substances: matter (including the brain), which is explicable in scientific laws and mathematical formulae; and mind (including logical thought but also moral and religious thought), which is ephemeral, qualitative, and totally unamenable to scientific analysis. And because Descartes located moral

7. Jones, *Our Fragile Brains*, p. 249.

moral and religious thinking in the mind along with rational thought, it became standard practice for theologians to see the mind-body debate as being one with the body-soul debate.

Yet despite the autonomy Descartes accorded the mind, he went much further than his predecessors in limiting its scope and physicalizing everything else. Medieval thought had seen the mind-brain relationship as essentially a one-way process. The mind was likened to an autonomous puppeteer, pulling on the passively responsive strings of the body and totally controlling not only logical thought but also perception, movement, and even reproduction. While Descartes agreed that mind influenced body, he also suggested that the reverse might also be true, and that many functions once attributed purely to the immaterial mind (such as perception) might really be mostly physical in nature.

Because of his dualistic outlook, Descartes holds an ambiguous place in most histories of modern psychology. He is praised for mechanizing human functions to the extent that he did, but he is also seen as having religious convictions that intellectually hampered him from going any further. "His dualism was his way of resolving the conflict between religion and science," writes E. G. Boring in his *History of Experimental Psychology*. "He resolved to find the right way to justify both the Pope and Copernicus, an ambition never wholly fulfilled."[8] By contrast, Boring's own position accurately reflected the naturalism of twentieth-century psychology. "The ideal would be ultimately to get away from conscious dimensions to the happy monism of the scientific heaven," he proclaimed. "Salvation [is] to be found through a physicalism formulated, whenever possible, in physiological terms."[9]

Yet, as I pointed out in Chapter Five, the conflicts over which Descartes agonized have not vanished with the secularization of psy-

---

8. Boring, A *History of Experimental Psychology* (New York: Appleton-Century-Crofts, 1957), pp. 161, 632. See also, for example, Duane Schultz, *A History of Modern Psychology*, 3rd ed. (New York: Academic Press, 1981); and Henryk Misiak and Virginia S. Sexton, *History of Psychology: An Overview* (New York: Grune and Stratton, 1966). It should also be noted that the Catholic church of Descartes' time did not appreciate his efforts to resolve the rise of modern science with the classical conception of the soul; the church saw him as verging on heresy and at times restricted discussion of his works.

9. Boring, *The Physical Dimensions of Consciousness* (New York: Dover Publications). The first sentence is taken from p. v of the preface of the 1963 edition; the second sentence from p. xiii of the preface of the 1933 edition.

chology. Rather, they have resurfaced in twentieth-century clothing—in the form of the ethical problem and the reflexivity problem,
for example. By what criterion can psychologists (and others), if they
are wholly material entities, make valid and nonrelative moral judgments about their own actions and those of others? Or through what
mechanisms can such machines study themselves, altering the state of
their brains and consequently their existential situations simply by
thinking about the latter? It is with such enduring problems as well as
more specifically theological ones that Christians in the neurosciences continue to wrestle, and it is to some of their contemporary
reflections that we now turn.

   Stanley Jaki: A Contemporary Christian Dualist. Stanley Jaki is a
Hungarian-born physicist, historian of science, and Benedictine
priest who now lives in America. His considerable knowledge of the
history and philosophy of science has led to a number of distinguished
books, lectureships, and awards. Although he is not a neuroscientist
in the professional sense, the close attention that he pays to the fields
of physics, physiology, and psychology makes him an able commentator on the brain-mind debate.[10]

   Jaki is very aware that much of the history of science with materialist leanings is also the history of Christian apostasy. As he amply
documents in his book *The Road of Science and the Ways to God,* far too
many major figures in the history of science have regarded Christianity, "with its commitment to a transcendent, personal God [as]
the hotbed of fanaticism, the fountainhead of debasing asceticism,
and the mainspring of the enslavement of the mind."[11] The quotations by E. G. Boring cited in the previous section of this chapter are
but one case in point. Against such an attitude, with its attendant
scientism, Jaki is concerned to preserve a sense of humanity's finite-
ness before the elusive mystery of God, the fear of whom, as the
psalmist reminds us, is the beginning of wisdom. In company with Sir
John Eccles, a neurophysiologist with whom he shares his dualistic
position, Jaki "wishes to put forward a worldview incorporating the
mystery of our existence, its supernatural meaning, and the fact that

   10. See, for example, *Brain, Mind, and Computers,* which received the
Lecomte du Noüy Prize for 1970 (South Bend, Ind.: Gateway Editions,
1969); *The Road of Science and the Ways to God,* originally presented as the
Gifford Lectures of 1975–76 (Chicago: University of Chicago Press, 1978);
and *The Origin of Science and the Science of its Origin,* originally presented as
the Fremantle Lectures of 1977 (South Bend, Ind.: Gateway Editions, 1978).
   11. Jaki, *The Road of Science and the Ways to God,* p. 102.

we are part of some great design."[12] To that end he uses much of his expertise as a scientist, philosopher, and historian to argue for the fundamental *inability* of physical science to reduce the mind to the brain, despite more than three centuries of work devoted to that purpose.

In the history of natural science, Jaki contends, there has always been an eagerness to reduce the human mind to a variation of whatever mechanical device is currently in vogue, whether that be a robot, a hydraulic pump, a gasoline engine, a telecommunications system, or a computer. But, he maintains, the attempt to confirm any of these models through empirical research invariably turns into an embarrassment, and he goes on to cite a long list of scientists whose initial claims to have found the key to mind-brain identity later deteriorated into a sense of bafflement. [13]

One such person was Karl Lashley (1890–1958), one of America's early and most productive psychobiologists, who is best remembered for his work concerning the effects of brain lesions on the learning ability of rats. Like his behaviorist predecessor and teacher, J. B. Watson, Lashley expected to demonstrate simple, point-to-point connections between observable behavioral reflexes and parts of the brain, with the latter serving as a kind of switchboard that transferred incoming sensory impulses into outgoing motor messages to the muscles. "The faith to which we all subscribe," he reminded colleagues in 1948, "[is] that the phenomena of behavior and mind are ultimately describable in the concepts of the mathematical and physical sciences."[14] Yet, after thirty years of trying to pin down the cerebral location of memory traces in animal brains, he made the following half-humorous, half-cynical comment about his own work: "I sometimes feel, in reviewing the evidence on the localization of the memory trace, that the necessary conclusion is that learning is just not possible!"[15]

Another example of materialist monism modified by scientific experience can be seen in Wilder Penfield (1891–1976), a Canadian

12. Jones, *Our Fragile Brains*, p. 256.
13. See especially Jaki's *Brain, Mind, and Computers* for examples.
14. Lashley, "The Problem of Serial Order in Behavior," as quoted in Jaki, *Brain, Mind, and Computers*, p. 72.
15. Lashley, "In Search of the Engram," in *The Neuropsychology of Karl Lashley: Selected Papers*, ed. Frank A. Beach et al. (New York: McGraw-Hill, 1960), p. 501.

neurosurgeon who pioneered studies of the temporal lobes of human beings during operations to correct epilepsy and other brain disorders. Near the end of his productive career he surprised the neuroscientific community with the following statement:

> I worked as a scientist trying to prove that the brain accounted for the mind, and demonstrating as many brain-mechanisms as possible, hoping to show *how* the brain did so. . . . In the end, I conclude that there is no good evidence, in spite of new methods (such as the employment of stimulating electrodes, the study of conscious patients, and the analysis of epileptic attacks) that the brain alone can carry out the work that the mind does. I conclude that it is easier to rationalize man's being on the basis of two elements than on the basis of one.[16]

The conclusions of Lashley and Penfield are typical of examples cited by Jaki of the enduring resistance of the mind to a completely natural analysis, despite the continuous efforts of many erudite scientists to forge such an identity. In cataloguing such a trail of failures, Jaki is clearly concerned to defend a classic Cartesian dualism. "Undoubtedly," he insists, "those who believe in a personal God would reject out of hand the notion that machines think. For them, thinking is the exclusive feature and function of an immortal soul which in turn can be created only by God and is united by him to no other system of matter but the one known as the human body."[17]

I find myself sharing the company of those who admire Jaki's determination to preserve the uniqueness of both God and persons via such an analysis. Even D. Gareth Jones, who is anything but a professing dualist, applauds with utmost sincerity the "exemplary Christian motives" of his colleagues who lean toward dualism. "They are intent on viewing human beings as ends in themselves," he writes, "with meaning, values, purpose, and responsibility. In starting from the self-consciousness of individuals, they insure that individuals will not be reduced to partial materialistic components and thereby lose their personhood. For such strong premises we are grateful."[18]

Besides what Jones rightly affirms, there is a second advantage for Christians in this classically dualist position. In addition to preserving the awesome "otherness" of God and the mystery of his image in us,

16. Penfield, *The Mystery of the Mind*, pp. 113–14.
17. Jaki, *Brain, Mind, and Computers*, p. 228.
18. Jones, *Our Fragile Brains*, p. 256.

dualism is able to account for what theologians call "the intermediate state" that characterizes believers after death and before the resurrection. According to philosopher John Cooper (another scholar who now believes dualism should be given a renewed hearing),

> Any doctrine of the future life—except the theory that we cease to exist from death until the resurrection, traditionally rejected as heretical—requires a dualistic anthropology. Whether we exist consciously or unconsciously in an "intermediate state" with the Lord until the resurrection, or even if we are given resurrection bodies at the instant of death, there is an irreducible difference between a person and his or her [earthly] body. And that amounts to dualism.[19]

One can, of course, argue that since Christian psychologists are concerned only with the embodied minds of here-and-now persons, they need not trouble themselves professionally with problems regarding the intermediate state. But as I will try to show a little later, the issue cannot be dismissed quite so easily.

From the perspective of the postmodern philosophy of science, there is a third strength to a carefully thought-out dualism. Because of their acute awareness of the materialist bias of much modern science, dualists such as Jaki have a keen appreciation for the sociocultural baggage that inevitably accompanies the putative objectivity of scientists. "Their readiness to ignore both lack of evidence, and evidence to the contrary, provides a graphic proof of the fact that scientific work or reasoning depends not only on the sober weighing of experimental evidence," he reminds us. "Scientific work has to rely also on what is usually called scientific faith, which, like its religious counterpart, can be enlightened as well as obscurantist."[20] As I have stressed in earlier chapters, such critical self-awareness is long overdue in a scientific enterprise that too often assumes that its methods somehow guarantee immunity from the influence of its practitioners' world views.

Dualism has often been rejected on the grounds that it is an obscurantist position bent on preventing science from penetrating the remaining frontiers of the mind. But in fact there is little evidence that this is really the case. The dualism of Eccles and Penfield has

19. Cooper, "Dualism and the Biblical View of Human Beings," part 1, *Reformed Journal* 32 (Sept. 1982): 13.
20. Jaki, *Brain, Mind, and Computers*, p. 72.

hardly prevented them from becoming frontrunners among neuroscientists. Moreover, in reading Jaki's works one is constantly struck by his ability and passion for painstaking scientific detective work. Over against the comfortable assumptions of mainstream materialist neuroscience, he constantly says, in effect, "Look again! It's not so simple. Don't forget this-and-that contradictory evidence. Remember this-and-that lesson from the history of science." In short, he tells physical and biological scientists to proceed very cautiously in their theorizing, and only as fast as rigorously collected and verified evidence will permit.

He also tells them very bluntly to respect their professional limits, and not to use their scientific prestige to make facile theological (or antitheological) pronouncements about the ultimate nature of persons and the universe. "Focus only on the material world to which you have legitimate professional access," he seems to be saying. "But do it well, and do not trespass on mysteries of the mind about which you are not qualified to make pronouncements. In so limiting your scope, you will be a better mapmaker of your authorized territory than if you try to violate its boundaries."

On the other hand, there is some evidence that Jaki's dualism may not be quite as strict as he himself makes it out to be. I have already quoted his concession that souls, or minds, are united to God *through* the system of matter known as the human body. Elsewhere he writes that "the mind's essential *dependence* on the body" is just as important a theme as "the mind's ability to reach . . . *beyond* its own body." He then adds, "For the conceptualization of such a view of the mind, no single word, be it 'soul' or something else, can do full justice. It can only be grasped by an unreserved commitment to that very richness which nature displays in man alone."[21] When he writes thus, Jaki almost seems to be flirting with a perspectivalist rather than a strictly dualist position—that is, with the notion that there are different but equally valid levels of description for human existence, with the desire to attempt an exhaustive description at one level in no way precluding an equally valid description on another level, be it artistic, economic, religious, or the like.

In addition, it is hard to be a rigid dualist and an honest follower and supporter of clinical neuroscience. It is true, as Jones concedes, that "the extreme complexity of the human brain daunts many peo-

---

21. Jaki, *The Road of Science and the Ways to God*, p. 260 (italics mine).

ple, and sometimes proves too much even for neuroscientists."[22] Yet it is equally true that certain surgical and chemical interventions in the brain have proved helpful to people who, because of epilepsy, chronic depression, or other problems, have apparently *lost* much of that capacity for responsible freedom that we associate with full personhood. Often neuroscientists do not understand the exact mechanisms at work in such interventions, or why they seem to help some people while they simply worsen the state of others.[23] But the fact remains that material intervention in the body often has impressive effects—for good or for ill—on what has traditionally been called the mind or the self. Yet if the mind is as "off limits" to the physical scientist as a strict dualism implies, it is hard to see how neuroscientists—and even many experimental psychologists—can receive anything but condemnation for the work that they do, no matter how compassionate their motivation. This is a problem that Jaki never directly addresses, although he does concede that, for all its philosophical problems and antireligious motives, materialist science has made human life easier in many ways, and that such blessings are not to be scorned or rejected. From this we may conclude that Jaki's dualism is not quite as unbending as it seems on first reading.

PERSPECTIVALISM: ANOTHER CHALLENGE TO DUALISM

While Catholics such as Jaki lean toward dualism as a way of preserving the uniqueness of persons, most of their Protestant evangelical colleagues have opted for what was earlier called the perspectivalist position.[24] In the previous chapter I defined perspectivalism as that view which, unlike dualism, does not declare any part of human functioning "off limits" to a natural-science analysis. At the same time, perspectivalists are not materialist monists, since they assert

22. Jones, *Our Fragile Brains*, p. 241.
23. See Jones, *Our Fragile Brains*, chaps. 3–5, for a balanced account of such interventions.
24. Although I have chosen MacKay and Jones as representative of Christian perspectivalists, there are many others in psychology and related fields who adopt this same position, as I pointed out in Chapter Five. See, for example, David G. Myers, *The Human Puzzle: Psychological Research and Christian Belief* (San Francisco: Harper and Row, 1978); Malcolm A. Jeeves, *Psychology and Christianity: The View Both Ways* (Leicester, U.K.: Inter-Varsity Press, 1976); and also Ronald L. Kotesky, *Psychology from a Christian Perspective* (Nashville: Abingdon Press, 1980).

that while scientists can legitimately explore *all* aspects of reality, they cannot claim that science can give an exhaustive or metaphysically ultimate explanation of *any* of it.

MacKay's Perspectivalism. Donald MacKay, a British neuroscientist who works in the areas of perception, cognition, and artificial intelligence, suggests numerous examples to capture the nature of the perspectivalist position. The phenomenon of a printed word, for example, cannot be wholly captured by an exhaustive analysis of the ink and paper that compose its material expression; its social, grammatical, and literary meanings (to name only a few other kinds of meaning) must also be analyzed at their particular levels, or from their particular disciplinary "perspectives." The word EXIT printed over a door is amenable to thorough physical analysis in terms of its cardboard and ink—but socially it also indicates a means of quick and orderly access to the outside; grammatically it is a Latin verb that has become an English noun. And modern literature scholars recognize *No Exit* as the name of a play by Sartre, a title that signifies the pessimistic despair of the existentialist who is forced to look for meaning only within himself or herself. The choice of analytic tool, MacKay points out, depends on one's "viewing distance," which is just another way of saying that the same phenomenon can be seen from a number of perspectives, or in terms of multiple "categories," or "levels of description."[25]

And so it is with persons, argues MacKay. They can be thoroughly analyzed as mechanical, chemical, organic, psychological, sociological, economic, or religious beings (again, to name only a few possibilities) without insistence that any single analysis is capable of doing the entire job. But there is an added complication in MacKay's scheme: all of these "perspectives," or analytic levels, are various ways of looking at persons *in the abstract,* or *in general.* They are, as MacKay puts it, different aspects of the "O-story"—that is, the "objective" or "outside" story as seen by scientists, historians, artists, theologians, and so on. But in addition to this multifaceted "O-story," each individual also has an "I-story"—that is, an "inside" story, represented by a subjective consciousness that is just as multifaceted. The "I-story" consists of a multitude of experienced states,

25. Donald M. MacKay, *Brains, Machines and Persons* (Grand Rapids: Eerdmans, 1980), chap. 2. See also his *Clockwork Image* (London: Inter-Varsity Press, 1974); and *Human Science and Human Dignity* (London: Hodder and Stoughton, 1979).

both present and remembered, such as perceiving, hoping, imagining, enjoying, problem-solving, fearing, believing, and so on.

Thus, concludes MacKay, we can study persons in general through a variety of "O-stories"; moreover, we can—and should—try to understand individuals using both "O-story" and "I-story" resources. Yet despite these multiple levels of analysis, MacKay insists, "Man emerges as a unity—a single theatre of complex and mysterious events—but a unity with many complementary aspects, each needing to be reckoned with at a different logical level, and all interdependent."[26]

Fortified by these numerous qualifiers, MacKay feels free as a Christian to push the mechanistic analysis of brain functions to its farthest possible limits. Does the dualist claim that logical processes are uniquely human? Not any more, replies MacKay, since any thinking task that can be specified according to consistent rules is within the capacity of a general-purpose computer that can manipulate logical symbols. Does the dualist then argue (as Jaki, in fact, does) that more subtle and ambiguous kinds of thinking are still beyond the reach of such logically programmed digital computers? So they are, at this point in time, concedes MacKay. But then he goes on to say that "there is no reason why an automaton could not be built [using analog rather than digital processes] to digest information in ways that neither it nor we could reduce to a sequence of precise and discrete logical steps. . . . [We cannot] dispose of the possibility that our brains, viewed at the information-engineering level, may themselves be automata, albeit of a rather special kind."[27]

Does the dualist finally argue that computers and other automata, however complex, can never have a reflexive self-consciousness—that they can have only an "O-story" and not an "I-story," as human beings do? Even here MacKay does not shrink from contemplating the possible realization of what for the moment he concedes is "sheer science fiction." He writes, "If some of the workings of my brain as a physical system are correlated with the conscious experience that is mine as a personal agent, is there any reason why some of the physical workings of an artificial computing mechanism should not be similarly correlated with the experience of a conscious

26. MacKay, *Brains, Machines and Persons*, p. 80.
27. MacKay, *Brains, Machines and Persons*, pp. 61–62. See also Chapter Eight of this book.

agent?"[28] How we could be *sure* that we were in the presence of such a subjectively conscious agent is, he admits, both a technical and a philosophical problem—much debated in a slightly different arena by those who follow the experimental attempts to teach chimpanzees the rudiments of a language for communicating with human beings. Nevertheless, writes MacKay,

> I believe that the Bible at least provides no justification for ruling out such possibilities *a priori*. . . . The fact is that on this question (not unnaturally) the Bible is simply silent. . . . From the biblical point of view the extent to which consciousness could be sustained in artificially constructed organisms is left an open question—entirely up to the Creator. He has not told us; and we would do well to avoid the impertinence, however well meant, of telling Him the answer in advance.[29]

Because MacKay's confidence regarding the future of artificial intelligence has implications for our later chapter on cognition, I will delay a detailed consideration of it until then. For the moment, however, the reader can discern that his is a powerful rhetoric regarding *both* the power of science *and* the dependence of every mental act on its physical and mechanical embodiment in the brain—or even, in MacKay's speculations, in an automaton. As I pointed out in Chapter One, it is not unheard-of for scientific and technical breakthroughs to begin in such "sheer science fiction"; consequently, MacKay can hardly be faulted for his imaginative boldness, especially when it is accompanied by a well-run interdisciplinary research program such as the one he has established at the University of Keele.

In addition, his perspectivalism seems to guard against repeating an error that most Christians in the sciences have come to dread: that of deciding in advance what science can or cannot discover and making related theological pronouncements that one (or one's descendants) might live to regret. That was what happened when the church announced that Galileo could not possibly have established that the earth moved around the sun. It was also what happened when geologists began to challenge the idea that the earth was only a few thousand years old, as some Christian thinkers maintained. And perspectivalists seem determined that such blunders will not occur again if they can help it. This does not mean that they feel compelled

28. MacKay, *Brains, Machines and Persons*, p. 62.
29. MacKay, *Brains, Machines and Persons*, pp. 63, 64.

to climb onto every scientific bandwagon that happens to pass by; but it does mean that they feel no uneasiness about exploring current scientific theories to the limit, fortified by their claim that even an exhaustive physical analysis of mental functions would in no way preclude the necessity of other "O-story" and "I-story" accounts.

However, given the rather speculative nature of MacKay's conclusions, which are tied to his work with artificial models of perception and cognition, we should also consider the work of a perspectivalist who works more directly with the brain before we evaluate the relative claims of perspectivalism and dualism. For although the use of such theoretical models is both common and essential in mind research, we would also do well to heed the conclusion of Karl Lashley, who, as one of psychology's premier learning theorists and neurophysiologists, finally had this to say about mechanical models of the brain:

> Descartes was impressed by the hydraulic figures in the royal gardens and developed a hydraulic theory of the action of the brain. We have since had telephone theories, electrical field theories, and now theories based on the computing machine and automatic rudders. I suggest that we are more likely to find out how the brain works by studying the brain itself and the phenomena of behavior than by indulging in farfetched physical analogies. The similarities in such comparisons are the product of an oversimplification of the problems of behavior.[30]

And indeed, when we turn to the work of neuroanatomist D. Gareth Jones, a perspectivalist who has studied the brain and its associated functions more directly, we seem to find more qualifiers of and fewer clear-cut answers to the age-old debate about brain and mind.

D. Gareth Jones: A Neuroanatomist's Perspective. That Jones shares the basic elements of the perspectivalist resolution is made clear throughout his book, *Our Fragile Brains.* "[We must not overlook] the contribution that can be made by adopting more than one perspective to the wholeness of the human person," he writes. "For certain purposes a person can usefully be compared to a machine. But he is simultaneously and equally a person created by God. . . . The two complementary descriptions are intimately interwoven aspects of what being human is all about."[31]

---

30. Lashley, as quoted in *The Neuropsychology of Karl Lashley,* p. xix.
31. Jones, *Our Fragile Brains,* pp. 265, 271–72.

Like MacKay, Jones sees perspectivalism as allowing him to describe human beings as exhaustively as possible in physical and biological terms. But as his book makes clear, this is a task of overwhelming proportions—and one barely begun—when it comes to the complexity of the brain. And unlike MacKay, Jones rarely speculates about the religious implications of remote but hypothetical scenarios, such as the status of conscious automata or the implications of a completely material analysis of persons for the concept of human freedom. Preferring to tie his analysis more closely to the current state of brain research, Jones finds therein more than enough questions to challenge a thoughtful Christian.

One of his more thought-provoking chapters deals with the relationship of "damaged brains" to "diseased personalities." As Christians, he affirms, we believe in the integrity and continuity of the self as a responsible moral agent. Yet clinical studies of brain-injured persons show that such damage seems to alter their personalities in profound ways—usually for the worse:

> Their behavioral changes may include a lessening of responsibility and consideration for others, and an inability to plan ahead and think in abstract terms. Their lack of foresight and inability to appreciate the rewards or punishments consequent on a given line of conduct will likely lead to unacceptable social behavior. . . . Can people be so radically transformed that they become unrecognizable as themselves?[32]

Jones' thoughtful treatment of this question deserves to be read in its entirety, but for present purposes his three main points can be summarized. On the one hand, he suggests, we may simply have to regard brain damage as a kind of harbinger of human death, which is the way we now regard major illnesses such as cancer. But whereas with the latter the body usually deteriorates much faster than the brain-dependent mind, or self, the reverse is usually true of brain damage; indeed, in extreme cases there may be no apparent "person" in a body still physiologically intact except for its damaged brain. Brain damage may be likened to the "demoralization" or depersonalization we experience when we are tired or sick: at such times we also say that we are "not ourselves," and our behavior and feelings, like those of the brain-damaged person, usually change for the worse. But whereas such states are temporary, the depersonalization accom-

32. Jones, *Our Fragile Brains*, pp. 106-7.

panying certain types of brain damage is largely irreversible. Yet, writes Jones, because we are promised a full resurrection as embodied persons, such a cessation of the earthly self, although indeed tragic, should be no more metaphysically problematic to the Christian than the partial or complete death of the body.

Yet, cautions Jones, we must also wonder if such a complete "personal death" is always inevitable in the wake of brain damage. We know that through encouragement and appropriate therapy, un-committed parts of the brain can often take over the functions of damaged parts, particularly in younger people. Moreover, since we can judge only the external *behavior* of brain-damaged persons, we do not know what it is that has "died"—their basic, personal moti-vations or only their capacities to *execute* them. There have been cases of previously intelligent persons who, after suffering profound brain injury, have made heroic efforts to retain and exercise what vestiges of intellectual skills remained to them, and to communicate both their memories of normal existence and the frustrations accom-panying their ruptured state.[33] Thus, says Jones,

> It is unwise to discard an individual as a person, even in the face of major brain damage. True, the personality of the brain-damaged individual may be only a dim reflection of what it once was, and the choices open to such an individual may be tragically limited. Nevertheless, as long as some power to choose remains, that individual has not ceased to be a responsible personal agent. The framework of choice may have shifted to something quite unlike the framework employed when dealing with a brain-intact person, but in most instances it still exists. . . . If so, brain-damaged persons retain their status as persons, even though the range of alternatives open to them may be greatly narrowed.[34]

Finally, not content merely to settle ontological issues regarding the status of brain-damaged persons, Jones echoes the note of compas-sion that motivates so many perspectivalists toward a full understand-ing of the physical aspects of personhood. "Since personhood remains a crucial issue," he reminds us, "a Christian would wish to develop what personhood remains, rather than dismiss it as of little value. The

---

33. For a striking account of one such effort at self-recovery, see Alex-ander R. Luria, *The Man with a Shattered World* (Harmondsworth, U.K.: Penguin, 1975).
34. Jones, *Our Fragile Brains*, p. 108.

task becomes one of maintaining and perhaps enlarging whatever individual consciousness remains, as well as defending it from external onslaughts."[35] Such a careful and practically relevant application of the perspectivalist approach is of great help in advancing the Christian's understanding of embodied personhood.

Not surprisingly, Jones is also interested in the significance of the brain-mind relationship in "normal" persons whose brains are intact. Much of modern neuroscience has treated this as a one-way relationship, looking only at the effect of the brain on thinking or behavior. But Jones, as a Christian, shows a cautious interest in research that seems to show how, through biofeedback, thought processes may affect the brain more than we ever imagined. Biofeedback refers to a variety of techniques aimed at teaching people how to acquire control over certain physiological processes—most notably heart rate, blood pressure, muscle tension, and brain-wave activity. With the help of sensitive electronic instruments that portray and magnify these processes, persons use the resultant "feedback" to acquire a degree of voluntary control over their own physiological states.

As a perspectivalist who respects both the "I-story" and the "O-story" as well as their unity and mutual dependence, Jones gives biofeedback research qualified approval. "[It is] at least a highly provocative concept for understanding the interplay between the individual and the environment, and between the brain and its world."[36] He cites its modest success in teaching some persons how to reduce insomnia and chronic pain, and in helping others to reacquire the use of muscles and limbs that have been functionally impaired by strokes. Although biofeedback presently hovers around the fringes of scientific orthodoxy, Jones writes, it may "contribute to a new role of the patient in self-healing." Moreover, despite his loyalty to science as an institution, Jones shows an awareness of the negative role it has played in depersonalizing modern life. Thus he also says of biofeedback that "increased control of one's own body through one's own resources is surely a welcome development in an impersonal, technological culture."[37]

By contrast, Jones is distinctly uneasy about other types of so-called "new consciousness" movements such as Transcendental Med-

35. Jones, *Our Fragile Brains*, pp. 108–9.
36. Jones, *Our Fragile Brains*, p. 216.
37. Jones, *Our Fragile Brains*, pp. 218–19.

itation and drug-induced, extraordinary mental states. His reasons for this uneasiness stem both from his Christian anthropology and from his confidence, as a perspectivalist, in the objectivity and reliability of the scientific method. Advocates of Transcendental Meditation (TM) claim to teach bodily control and stress reduction, as biofeedback does, but without the mediation of technical apparatus. Moreover, they regularly cite (somewhat ambiguous) scientific evidence to show that their meditation techniques do attain such ends.

But the claims of TM also go much further. Its followers are said to experience a pure, cosmic consciousness that improves not only the minds and bodies of meditating individuals but also, by a kind of benign inoculative effect, the quality of life of entire areas that contain a minimum number of meditators. And while it claims to be a scientific rather than a religious movement, its assumptions are clearly those of Eastern mysticism. As Jones puts it, "TM seeks to change the state of consciousness rather than the condition of the external world. If enough people's consciousnesses are changed, the quality of life of their society will be changed. A Westerner finds it difficult to accept the rationale of that view until it is seen as the logical outworking of the Hindu notion that we project the material universe into existence by our collective consciousness of it."[38] (See also Chapter Two.)

Here we can see why Jones regards perspectivalism as the best safeguard of a Christian world view for the scientist. Being attracted to TM's stress on the power of pure consciousness, he concedes, is perhaps an understandable reaction to our overly mechanized Western life-style. But TM does not advocate the substitution of a mentalist monism for a materialist monism merely as a corrective. It goes on to identify each individual consciousness as a potential universe, which unifies all reality and transcends not only metaphysical distinctions but moral ones as well, so that right and wrong, compassion and indifference become equally meaningless categories. To guard against such seductions, Jones suggests, Christians need a view of persons and bodies that, as well as conceding creativity and moral agency to persons, also gives equal due to our God-ordained physical limitations and the dignity that God has bestowed on the physical world in general.

Moreover, he asserts, we need a view of the embodied person that guards against elevating individual, subjective experience to the

38. Jones, *Our Fragile Brains*, pp. 227–28.

status of ultimate metaphysical truth, something that happens not only in movements such as TM but also in those that advocate using drugs to heighten mental awareness and power. "In these movements," writes another Christian critic, "the external universe exists, not to be manipulated from the outside by a transcendent God, but to be manipulated from the inside by the self."[39] Jones thinks that a high view of science as conventionally practiced helps to guard against such heresies, inasmuch as it decries any investigation "in which the experimenter becomes the center of the experiment, in which the subjective displaces almost completely any hint of the objective. . . . [If science becomes] a natural history of [one's] own mind while in an altered state of consciousness, there can be no doubt that it is vastly different from conventional science. How can it warrant the name *science* at all . . . [if] it is based on the belief that one view of reality is as good as another, and one symbol system is as valid as any other?"[40] Thus Jones believes that the physical brain must be respected as the irreducible embodiment of the person, to preserve not only a high view of material creation but also a high view of objective science.

DUALISM VERSUS PERSPECTIVALISM: ONE DEBATE OR TWO?

By now the reader may have sensed that the debate between Christian dualists and perspectivalists is not merely a debate concerning the unity versus the duality of human existence. It is also—and I think just as profoundly—a debate concerning the status of empirical science in the lives of Christians. In other words, it is a debate about the extent to which Christians can rightly and zealously apply the scientific method to all facets of human life. For convenience I will label these two debates "the human-nature question" and "the place-of-science question." (We could, as in earlier chapters, also call them the anthropological question and the epistemological question.) Let me try to summarize the strengths and weaknesses of both dualism and perspectivalism with respect to each of these questions before articulating, in conclusion, my own position on this debate.

Concerning the human-nature question, we have seen that the features of dualism attractive to the Christian include its high view of

39. James W. Sire, *The Universe Next Door* (Downers Grove, Ill.: Inter-Varsity Press, 1976), p. 161.
40. Jones, *Our Fragile Brains*, pp. 233-34.

God's humanly inconceivable "otherness" and its respect for the mystery of his image in each of us. We have also seen that dualism is able to make sense of the Christian teaching that physical death is not the end of personhood, even prior to the resurrection of the body. By contrast, if persons are identified with their bodies or made as completely dependent on them as the perspectivalist insists they be, then, as philosopher C. Stephen Evans notes, "it is hard to explain why the cessation of the body's function is not the end of that person."[41] For many Christians in psychology this is not merely an academic question but a practical question as well. For nowadays not only pastors but also Christian psychologists counsel bereaved persons, and many of these psychologists share the confusion of pastors about what should be said to their counselees regarding the status of deceased friends and relatives.

Evans is correct when he says that the *Zeitgeist*, or spirit of our times, has definitely been against dualism. It has been denied as a live option by so many philosophers and scientists that pastors and psychologists often feel intimidated into following suit. Philosopher John Cooper has described the confusion of voices that has beset the Christian community as a result—a confusion that a strongly dualist view of human nature certainly avoids:

> Some anti-dualists openly affirm that at death we cease to exist until the resurrection. They are self-consistent in holding that questionable doctrine. . . . Most anti-dualists, however, are unintentionally inconsistent. They denounce anthropological dualism in their preaching and teaching and yet—often in the very same sermons and lectures—affirm doctrines such as the intermediate state which require it. The confusion thus created is not merely academic. I have encountered college students, catechumens, and relatively uneducated believers who are genuinely puzzled and even troubled by it.[42]

With regard to the place-of-science question, it has been noted that Christian dualists such as Stanley Jaki seem to have an unusual sensitivity to the anti-Christian motives that have permeated much of modern science. Far from turning either science or scientists into

---

41. Evans, *Preserving the Person: A Look at the Human Sciences* (Downers Grove, Ill.: InterVarsity Press, 1977), p. 103.
42. Cooper, "Dualism and the Biblical View of Human Beings," part 1, p. 13.

sacred cows exempt from the prejudices and historical limitations that affect the rest of us, these Christian dualists are keenly postmodern in their understanding of the metaphysical and cultural foundations of modern neuroscience. This is a corrective to unreflective scientism of which many Christians are still in need. At the same time, it is difficult to conclude that such dualists are obscurantist or anti-scientific when they include among their numbers internationally recognized neuroscientists like Eccles and Penfield.

Yet the dualist still has some unresolved problems regarding both the human-nature question and the place-of-science question. With regard to the first, there is still the problem of explaining just *how* the immaterial mind and the material body relate to each other. From the time of Descartes on, dualists have been content to affirm that mind affects body and that body equally affects mind. But this theory of causal interaction, in Evans' perceptive words, "does not seem adequate to account for the peculiarly intimate relationship which I have to my body. A threat to my body is a threat to *me*. The multitude of intimate relationships between physiological and mental happenings discovered by modern brain research, while perhaps compatible with dualism, do not seem congenial to it."[43]

With regard to the place-of-science question, a consistent dualist would seem to have no place whatsoever for a natural-science analysis of mind and behavior. Rather, he or she would regard the scientific method as illegitimately trespassing on a nonmaterial terrain, for the analysis of which its methods are quite inadequate. Yet in fact such militancy rarely comes to practical fruition among dualists, who seem no more likely to discourage young people from pursuing social science in its current form than they are to warn them away from physics or chemistry. In this respect it would seem that dualists themselves are not totally convinced of all of the implications of their viewpoint.

When we come to evaluate perspectivalism, we find a similar mixture of strengths and weaknesses concerning both questions. With regard to the human-nature question, we have learned that perspectivalists, with their high view of human unity within a material embodiment, are in no danger of denigrating the human body or falling short in their concern to understand and heal it. Nor are they likely to hesitate at the frontier where physiological brain functions

43. Evans, *Preserving the Person*, p. 104.

seem to powerfully affect the very foundations of personhood, provided that understanding and controlling the former seems to enhance—rather than limit—the latter. Despite their constant appeal to mechanical models in exploring human functions, they claim not to be materialist monists, since they recognize not only both the "I-story" and the "O-story" but, indeed, a great many different perspectives within each of these. Perspectivalists see human beings as unitary creatures encompassing many different aspects. Thus perspectivalists do not fear exploring this unity as exhaustively as possible in its material aspect, since they hold that such an analysis still accounts for only one perspective on the whole person.

On the place-of-science question, perspectivalists have the advantage of being supported by a very strong status quo. Science and its related technological achievements have so permeated our lives that, in the view of perspectivalists, it is unrealistic and even ungrateful to God to refuse its tools and its potential blessings. Perspectivalists stress that scientific and biblical accounts of human beings have different but complementary functions and purposes. To them the Bible is not a scientific text but an account of humankind's moral relationship to God and to each other. Conversely, they say, science tells us the "what" and the "how" of the material universe, but science cannot say who brought it about or for what purpose or with what moral ground-rules. Thus scientific accounts of people as part of the natural order are not seen as competing with the biblical account of persons as moral agents made in God's image. Moreover, the perspectivalist account confirms the legitimacy of Anglo-American social science as most of us know it. Although social scientists persist in studying person-oriented phenomena (such as values, choices, and beliefs) using an empirical and often causal approach, perspectivalists firmly defend the legitimacy of such an attempt. So long as the resulting analysis does not claim to be an ultimate and exhaustive understanding of human nature, they say, the scientist has the freedom to try out his or her tools on any topic that can be imagined.

But perspectivalism is not without its problems either. With regard to the human-nature question, one such problem seems to be not much different from the age-old "interaction problem" of classical dualism. "Of course," writes John Cooper, "the dualist must leave room in his theory for the interaction of different substances or entities—a baffling problem. But it is no more baffling than [the perspectivalist's] problem of how the diversity in human life can be conceived as a holistic unity."[44] In other words, it is one thing to *affirm* that a person is a unity made up of differing aspects; it is quite another to *show how* the multiple "O-story" and "I-story" perspectives fit together to form the personal unity to which perspectivalists pay such regular lip-service.

Yet this is a task for which perspectivalists are generally ill-equipped. For despite their repeated caveats about the need for multiple approaches, virtually all of them have been trained and are professionally practicing according to only *one* perspective—the natural-science approach, whose dominant metaphor for persons is causal and mechanistic. It sometimes seems to me that the perspectivalist resolution amounts to little more than academic eclecticism: every department in the university calendar is credited with representing a different yet essential aspect of humanity—and presumably if new disciplines emerge, new perspectives will be granted. But again, how do such diverse aspects come together in the holistic unity that perspectivalists repeatedly affirm? Moreover, why should Christians necessarily pattern their analysis of human aspects after contemporary academic vogues which themselves come and go?

With regard to the place-of-science question, it is difficult not to see perspectivalists as having mixed motives in giving traditional science such a high place. I pointed out in Chapter Five that perspectivalists are generally strong supporters of the unity-of-science thesis. That is, they hold that there is only one method that characterizes all genuine sciences, and that this consists of giving deterministic, causal explanations that are empirically testable. Since this has been both the ideal and the dominant reality in psychology since its formalization a century ago, it would certainly be convenient for those trained in this tradition to have it continue unchanged. In theory, as I have noted, perspectivalists affirm the need for multiple approaches to the study of human nature; in practice, however, they relegate to humanities scholars all the work of exploring the nonquantifiable, noncausal aspects of personhood. While the strict dualist seems to be saying that classical science is wrong to trespass on the territory of the mind, the perspectivalist almost seems to be saying the opposite: that the social

44. Cooper, "Dualism and the Biblical View of Human Beings," part 2 *Reformed Journal* 32 (Oct. 1982): 17.

and behavioral sciences, having begun by mimicking the natural sciences, must maintain an exclusively natural-science approach to human beings for the sake of a particular view of scientific unity.

A THIRD WAY?

How are the student and the concerned lay follower of psychology to react to these pros and cons of the dualist-perspectivalist debate? On the human-nature question, it may seem as if there is not much to choose between these two positions when all is said and done. We have already pointed out that dualists like Jaki have perspectivalist leanings, and that it is sometimes difficult to see the "O-story" and "I-story" analyses of the perspectivalist as much more than a subtle recasting of the old mind-body problem. In addition, thoughtful perspectivalists such as D. Gareth Jones frankly admit that their unity-in-diversity analysis of human nature cannot account for the intermediate state of individuals after death but prior to the bodily resurrection.

Motivated in part by his perception of this overlap, C. Stephen Evans has suggested a third way of approaching the human-nature question, a way that I believe is worth considering. He calls this position "minimal dualism," or the doctrine of "separable souls."[45] Evans begins by clarifying the distinction between substance (what something *is*) and function (what something *does*), and also the distinction between "separate" and "separable":

> "Separable" is a possibility word: hence this distinction involves the difference between what is the case, and what could be the case. Two things which are separate in some manner or other exist independently, though of course they may be interdependent in any number of ways. Two things which are separable do not necessarily exist independently. However, they are still "different" in the sense that they *could* exist separately in some sense of the word "could." . . . Minimal dualism is the claim that human souls (understood as selves or persons rather than as parts of persons or selves) and human bodies are related in the following way: *the soul is functionally separate from the body, but as a substance, it is only separable.*[46]

45. Evans, "Separable Souls: A Defense of 'Minimal Dualism,'" *Southern Journal of Philosophy* 19 (1981): 313–31.
46. Evans, "Separable Souls," p. 314.

Much of Evans' discussion recapitulates the historical debate between various kinds of dualists and various kinds of materialist monists, and tries to show why minimal dualism is philosophically defensible. For our purposes, however, it is only necessary to understand that Evans is saying this: the soul is the self, and the self of a human being is, in this life at least, thoroughly embodied. This embodiment is neither unnatural nor undesirable in the Christian view—but neither is it the only *logically necessary* way that the accountable, free, and creative self can function.[47] In the intermediate state, persons continue to function as selves without their earthly bodies; at the resurrection, Scripture implies, they will be *more* than their earthly bodies—"glorified bodies," in fact.

By contrast, the thorough (and limiting) embodiment of personal selves here on earth means that, for practical purposes, mental events are always identifiable with bodily events. As we have already seen, just *how* this embodiment takes place continues to be an empirical and theoretical challenge for neuroscientists. In light of current neurophysiology, however, it is more likely that mental events are identifiable with *global* (rather than strictly local) states of the brain, and even that there is considerable flexibility as to the pattern of some of these states, as we have already seen in the case of brain-damaged functions that are "taken over" by uncommitted parts of the cortex.

Nevertheless, even in earthbound persons mental events cannot be *reduced* to physiological language. Thus, with respect to the place-of-science question, minimal dualism does seem to preclude a thoroughly unified, deterministic approach to the science of the person. If persons have freedom, accountability, and dignity *despite* their physical embodiment, then, says Evans,

> it would seem that a [truly] scientific account of persons would *have to* take into account the unique features of human actions. . . . For example, explanations of actions might need to be non-deterministic and normative, or value-laden in character. . . .[This does not mean] that obscurantist roadblocks are placed in the path of any [existing] science. Scientists are free to explore the human body and bodily movements in any fashion they recognize as profitable, so long as they recognize that such bodily movements are not identical with thoughts and actions.[48]

47. See also Ronald L. Hall, "Dualism and Christianity: A Reconsideration," *Center Journal* 1 (Fall 1982): 43–55.
48. Evans, "Separable Souls," p. 329 (italics mine).

Regarding the place-of-science question, then, Evans seems to share my own inclination to look for a third way between dualism and perspectivalism. When various reformers speak of "humanizing" psychology, they are referring to two related emphases that are lacking in the perspectivalist resolution. The first is an emphasis on the need to humanize the *people* who are subjects of psychological research. The second is an emphasis on the need to humanize our understanding of the *psychologists* who are doing this research on others. The humanizing of psychology's research subjects basically means developing and using methods that can better do justice to the "I-story"—that is, to accounts of human behavior as seen by persons or groups themselves, in keeping with the rules and norms to which they adhere in a voluntary and accountable way. Participant observation, closer subject-researcher collaboration, and an approach that is more qualitative and descriptive (as opposed to quantitative and causally oriented) are the hallmarks of such reforms. (See especially Chapter Nine for examples.)

The humanizing of psychologists (and other natural and social scientists) refers to the need among members of such disciplines for critical self-reflection on the historical, cultural, and metaphysical assumptions that interact with the scholarly enterprise. We have seen that Jones, as a perspectivalist, decries the subjectivity of Transcendental Meditation and other, drug-induced states of personal consciousness. But perspectivalists, with their very high view of science, seem reluctant to admit that a kind of *corporate* subjectivity—analogous to Kuhn's paradigms—may affect entire cohorts of natural or social scientists, and that something is needed beyond the traditional safeguards of science itself to account for such effects.

Yet I suspect that few Christians in psychology would want to place a complete moratorium on the natural-science approach that currently dominates their discipline. Certainly I would not want to see it go. But many would, I think, like to see those methods "move over," as it were, and make equal room for others borrowed from the emerging traditions of the human sciences. In the chapters that follow, we will continue to confront both the need and the possibility for such reforms, including (toward the end of this section) specific examples of their implementation.

CHAPTER 7

BEHAVIORAL PSYCHOLOGY AT SEVENTY

If psychology is a science of the behavior of organisms, human or otherwise, then it is part of biology, a natural science for which tested and highly successful methods are available. . . . In the fifty years since a behavioristic psychology was first stated, facts and principles bearing on the basic issues have steadily accumulated.

—B. F. Skinner (1963)[1]

[There has been] a generalized deterioration of the romance with the neo-behaviorist paradigm in psychology. . . . With increasing boldness social psychologists have come to rely on an explanatory language granting the individual autonomous powers of self-direction. The stimulus world thus loses its powers of inexorable determination, and the individual becomes a creature of reasons as opposed to causes.

—Kenneth Gergen (1983)[2]

In the last chapter we discovered just how challenging it is for any psychologist—Christian or non-Christian; dualist, monist, or perspectivalist—to sort out the relationship between mind and brain, between the person and his or her inescapable earthly embodiment. Consequently, it should not surprise us that at various times scientists

1. Skinner, "Behaviorism at Fifty," in *Behaviorism and Phenomenology: Contrasting Bases for Modern Psychology*, ed. T. W. Wann (Chicago: University of Chicago Press, 1964), pp. 79, 84.
2. Gergen, "Theory of Self: Impasses and Evolution," in *Advances in Experimental Social Psychology*, ed. Leonard Berkowitz (New York: Academic Press, 1983), 17:85.

and social scientists have simply tried to avoid such a challenge either by ignoring mental phenomena completely or by reducing them to some other, more scientifically accessible level of discourse. To *reduce* the mind to the brain is one way of doing this; to *avoid* the mind and concentrate only on outwardly observable behavior is another. Although much-qualified in recent years, it is this latter legacy that underlies behavioral psychology. In this chapter we will explore the current state of this particular movement and examine some of its implications for Christians and others who hold to a high view of the person.

The reader will recall from Chapter One that the birth of behavioral psychology is usually dated in 1913, the year that J. B. Watson's paper, "Psychology as the Behaviorist Views It,"[3] was published. A half-century after the appearance of Watson's paper, B. F. Skinner assessed the state of "behaviorism at fifty" and concluded, as our opening quotation affirms, that the behavioral movement had more than justified Watson's initial hopes for it in terms of theoretical and applied successes. He implied, moreover, that these successes would probably continue to accumulate in the years to come. But twenty years after Skinner's mid-century assessment, social psychologist Kenneth Gergen has suggested that psychology's "romance with the neo-behaviorist paradigm" is waning, even though he is not so optimistic as to pronounce it totally dead.

It is probably fairer to say that the state of behavioral psychology at age seventy lies somewhere between these two contrasting views of its fate. In addition, as with the mind-brain controversy, Christians continue to differ—just as others do—in their responses to the various aspects of this movement. Few if any Christians profess agreement with behaviorism as a philosophical view of persons and their relationship to the world at large—what I have elsewhere called "ontological behaviorism."[4] At the same time, I know of none who align themselves with the most strident secular critics of applied behav-

3. Watson, "Psychology as the Behaviorist Views It," *Psychological Review* 20 (Mar. 1913): 158–77.
4. Mary Stewart Van Leeuwen, "The Behaviorist Bandwagon and the Body of Christ" in *Journal of the American Scientific Affiliation* 31: Part 1: "What Is Behaviorism?" (Mar. 1979): 3–8; Part 2: "A Critique of Ontological Behaviorism from a Christian Perspective" (June 1979): 88–91; Part 3: "A Critique of Applied Behaviorism from a Christian Perspective" (Sept. 1979): 129–38.

iorism—for example, with those who argue that behavioral control of any person by anyone else is to be rejected on principle.[5]

In what follows I will begin by reminding the reader of the basic theoretical, methodological, and applied contours of behavioral psychology. This will be a very cursory summary, based on the assumption that most readers will have had exposure to such material elsewhere. I will then go on to examine the current state of behavioral psychology's aims and achievements, and finally review how Christians in psychology, including myself, have responded to this important—and, until recently, dominant—movement in psychology.

THE SEVERAL FACES OF BEHAVIORAL PSYCHOLOGY

Psychologist Rodger Bufford, writing about behavioral psychology from a Christian point of view, aptly comments that, especially in its applied aspects, behavioral psychology is a mushrooming enterprise. "Even professionals in the forefront of the developing behavioral technology find it difficult to keep abreast of new developments," he cautions, adding that "critics tend to focus on features of behavior modification that do not reflect current thinking in the field."[6] Thus the reader must avoid regarding this area of psychology as something static; although its basic methodological and theoretical contours remain stable, both its technical vocabulary and its applications continue to diversify in the light of accumulating research. That research in turn is slowly having a moderating effect on the details if not the substance of basic behavioral theory.

There exist a great number of aids to understanding the technical aspects of behavioral psychology; in addition to the substantial treatment of it included in every introductory psychology text, entire books directed at a variety of audiences are devoted to explaining its principles and applications.[7] Moreover, B. F. Skinner's much-pub-

5. See, for example, Harvey Wheeler, ed., *Beyond the Punitive Society* (San Francisco: W. H. Freeman, 1973).
6. Bufford, *The Human Reflex: Behavioral Psychology in Biblical Perspective* (New York: Harper and Row, 1981), p. 114.
7. In addition to Bufford, *The Human Reflex*, see Howard Rachlin, *Introduction to Modern Behaviorism*, 2nd ed. (San Francisco: W. H. Freeman, 1976); and Alan E. Kazdin, *Behavior Modification in Applied Settings*, rev. ed. (Homewood, Ill.: Dorsey Press, 1980).

licized books on behaviorism—including his utopian novel *Walden Two*[8]—have made his name a household word, a rarity for social scientists in our culture.[9]

Respondent and Operant Conditioning: Emergence and Applications. The psychology student's introduction to behavioral psychology usually follows its historical development, beginning with Pavlov's turn-of-the-century work in Russia on classical—now called respondent—conditioning. In this type of learning a person or animal learns, in what appears to be an automatic fashion, to connect an already available response to a new stimulus. Thus Pavlov's dogs learned to associate salivation (a built-in response to food) with the ringing of a bell (a new stimulus that, through repeated pairings with the presentation of food, eventually came to elicit the salivation by itself). Respondent conditioning is so named because it is a relatively passive form of learning: autonomic bodily responses that are all "prewired" become connected by association to previously neutral events.

It was largely due to J. B. Watson that the idea of Pavlovian conditioning not only was brought to America but was also generalized to include human beings and, in fact, advocated as the paradigm for all of psychology. Although he himself had only a brief and truncated research career, Watson was convinced (and preached widely) that respondent conditioning was the basis of all human behavior. Children, he theorized, came into the world with only three innate—or unconditioned—responses: fear (i.e., the response to loud noise or lack of support), rage (i.e., the response to excessive bodily restriction), and love (which Watson reduced to enjoyment of physical stimulation). His conclusion that all other emotions and motivations were acquired simply by association with these three innate expressions is apparent in his oft-quoted claim of the 1920s:

> Give me a dozen healthy infants, well-formed, and my own specified world to bring them up in, and I'll guarantee to take any one at random and train him to become any type of specialist I might select—doctor, lawyer, artist, merchant-chief, and yes,

8. Skinner, *Walden Two* (New York: Macmillan, 1948); *Beyond Freedom and Dignity* (New York: Knopf, 1971); *About Behaviorism* (New York: Knopf, 1974); and *Particulars of My Life* (New York: Knopf, 1976).
9. A 1975 survey indicated that Skinner was the best-known scientist in America. See N. Guttman, "On Skinner and Hull: A Reminiscence and Projection," *American Psychologist* 32 (May 1977): 321-28.

even beggarman and thief, regardless of his talents, penchants, tendencies, abilities, vocations, and race of his ancestors.[10]

Needless to say, such a radical environmentalist stance toward the person was hardly calculated to endear Watson to the Christian subculture that he himself had actively rebelled against; it implied that neither the image of God, original sin, nor God's continuing sovereignty had anything to do with human behavior.[11] "It is no longer Satan who makes sin, but bad glands and unwise conditioning," announced Bertrand Russell on Watson's behalf in 1930,[12] thus helping to prolong the Christian community's already skeptical if not downright hostile assessment of this new discipline. There were exceptions, however. One theologian of the 1930s observed that Jonathan Edwards' theology of a "necessary world" could easily be rendered compatible with the general contours of Watsonian behaviorism. "A stimulus," he wrote, "is Edwards' 'motive,' and response is 'volitional behavior.' . . . A stimulus-response bond may be physical or it may be moral, but in both cases it is a certain connection. . . . Edwards' metaphysical principle of necessity is the modern methodological principle that all action is reaction."[13] Edwards, a Puritan writing in the eighteenth century, had been the champion of a thoroughgoing and consistent theological determinism, certainly based on his high view of God's sovereignty but also resulting from his respect for "that early modern philosophical and scientific knowledge which [later] made possible Skinner's work."[14]

Moreover, decades after Watson's death the potential for compassionate, therapeutic use of respondent-conditioning principles began to attract some Christians to behavioral psychology in the same way that brain science, for all its potential hazards and abuses, had begun to motivate others. The most typical procedure based on re-

10. Watson, *Behaviorism* (New York: Norton, 1970), p. 94.

11. See "John Broadus Watson—Autobiography," in *A History of Psychology in Autobiography*, ed. Carl Murchison (Worchester, Mass.: Clark University Press, 1936), 3:271–81; and also Paul Creelan, "Religion, Language, and Sexuality in J. B. Watson," *Journal of Humanistic Psychology* 15 (June 1975): 55–77.

12. Russell, "The New Generation," reprinted in his *Why I Am Not a Christian* (London: Unwin, 1967), p. 113.

13. Joseph Haroutunian, *Piety Versus Moralism* (New York: Harper and Row, 1932), p. 225.

14. James W. Woelfel, "Listening to B. F. Skinner," *The Christian Century*, 30 Nov. 1977, p. 1114.

spondent-conditioning principles has come to be known as *systematic desensitization*, and is frequently used to help people overcome debilitating phobias. Fearful reactions to a particular stimulus situation are considered to be conditioned acquisitions. By replacing these fearful responses with more relaxed ones in a gradual and systematic fashion, the behavioral psychologist can often effect a relatively permanent reversal of the phobic reaction.[15]

Nevertheless, techniques such as systematic desensitization are few compared to the vastly greater repertoire of applications based on a second kind of learning known as *operant conditioning*. If respondent conditioning involves learning to connect an autonomic response to a new stimulus presented *prior* to that response, operant conditioning may be seen as the opposite: the learning of a new—and in this case active—response to an already familiar stimulus (or, in operant-learning vocabulary, a "reinforcer") that now *follows* that response and is conditional upon it.

Operant conditioning is so named because it involves not behaviors that are autonomic but rather those that an animal or person actively uses to "operate" in the environment—chewing, moving around, manipulating objects, vocalizing, and grooming to name but a few. The efficacy of operant conditioning lies in discovering what things in the environment are reinforcing to the organism—that is, things for which the person or animal will work—and then making the receipt of that reinforcement contingent upon the performance of a certain action. B. F. (Burrhus Frederick) Skinner (1904–   ) is the name most closely associated with the basic animal research (although not most of the human applications) involving operant conditioning. As a young undergraduate he was intrigued by translations of Pavlov's laboratory reports and by Watson's writings on respondent conditioning with children. By his own report he began identifying himself as a behaviorist as early as 1927, by which time he had decided to pursue graduate studies in psychology.[16]

Skinner and his students at Harvard continued to refine their knowledge of operant-learning principles, as Pavlov had done with respondent-conditioning principles. They showed how a desired response could be "shaped" by first reinforcing clumsy, random approximations of it, then gradually requiring closer approximations for the

15. See Cyril M. Franks, ed., *Assessment and Status of the Behavioral Therapies* (New York: McGraw-Hill, 1968).
16. Skinner, *Particulars of My Life*, p. 229.

same reward. Strictly speaking, such procedures were not new: animal trainers had been using them in one way or another for centuries. But for the first time these procedures were being studied in a controlled and systematic fashion. Skinner also showed how various extended patterns, or "schedules," of reinforcement yielded different patterns of response, and how "secondary" reinforcers could be linked to primary, drive-reducing ones such that an animal would respond to the one in order to be able to work for the other.

As a strong believer in the continuity of animals and human beings, Skinner has been convinced that these operant-conditioning principles would remain basically unchanged when applied to people. Yet in his own research career he has rarely departed from the use of animal subjects—the major exception being his research on programmed learning and teaching machines, where individualized, step-by-step presentation of material is reinforced by immediate feedback about the correctness of the response.[17] Nevertheless, Skinner has consistently maintained not just that operant conditioning is *one* type of human learning but in effect that it is the *only* significant kind. He insists that both positive and negative behaviors are learned by their consequences, so much so that one could, in principle, construct a behaviorist utopia so carefully and scientifically planned that only good behavior would be reinforced and bad behavior, as a result, would gradually be totally extinguished.[18]

A convinced evolutionist, Skinner argues that the entire history of human and animal species can be understood as the interplay of learned and genetically predisposed behaviors. Individual members of species learn by trial and error those behaviors that result in essential, biologically based reinforcers, such as food, shelter, and access to sexual objects. But if, through random genetic mutation, certain members of the species become better equipped to pursue such goals (e.g., birds develop beaks that help them pick up grain, or males develop keen senses of smell that help them to detect when females are in heat), then it is these individuals and their offspring who are most likely to survive. Either way, Skinner suggests, it is the survival demands of the *environment* that dictate both immediate and genet-

---

17. See, for example, Richard C. Atkinson, "Teaching Children to Read Using a Computer," *American Psychologist* 29 (Mar. 1974): 169–78.
18. See Skinner's *Walden Two* for such a utopian vision, and for a critical Christian analysis, see Van Leeuwen, "The Behaviorist Bandwagon," part 2.

ically shaped behaviors. It is true, he concedes, that in human cultures many "secondary" reinforcers such as intellectual and political prestige have become attached to these primary, biological reinforcers—but this in no way obliterates the fact that all human values and accomplishments are really to be credited to the controlling pressures of the environment, and consequently that all notions of human freedom and inherent dignity—indeed, perhaps even the mind itself—are merely illusions.

Such assumptions—which, as Skinner admits, go beyond the actual accomplishments of behavioral psychology—constitute behaviorism as a world view. Nevertheless, Skinner insists, such a world view is increasingly supported by the accomplishments of those who use operant techniques in applied, human situations. Representative examples include the use of basic reinforcers such as food to aid in the resocialization of severely regressed mental patients, and the eventual conversion of entire institutions into "token economies" in which plastic chips serve as secondary reinforcers to inmates who must earn them, then exchange them for individually desired rewards. More individualized schemes have often been used in classrooms to extinguish undesirable behavior and systematically reinforce more acceptable responses, or to teach autistic children how to talk and interact in meaningful ways.[19]

I have briefly summarized the origins, principles, and applications of the two major streams of behavioral psychology, those of respondent and operant conditioning. This brings me to the heart of my consideration of this movement, in which I will focus on several enduring issues that the movement raises in light of a Christian understanding of personhood. I preface this, however, with a consideration of some essential distinctions among types of behavioral psychologists, including those who call themselves Christians.

Three Types of Behavioral Psychologists. So far we have taken a cursory look at both the origins and some common applications of respondent and operant conditioning. I have also pointed out that B. F. Skinner, the acknowledged living patriarch of the behavioral movement, goes well beyond the findings of laboratory and field research to proclaim behaviorism to be a metaphysical theory about the organization of all species' behavior throughout time. It is possi-

19. For a more detailed review, see Franks, *Assessment and Status of the Behavioral Therapies,* or Kazdin, *Behavior Modification in Applied Settings.*

ble, however, to call oneself a behavioral psychologist—as many Christians, and others, do—without espousing Skinner's full-blown world view, which credits the physical world—and, in the long run, the forces of evolution—as the source of all human behavior. To be a "methodological" behaviorist, as opposed to an ontological or "metaphysical" behaviorist, one must merely adopt the behaviorist analysis as a working assumption, saying in effect, "Let us suppose, as a scientific hypothesis, that human behavior *is* totally explicable in terms of its environmental consequences. What kinds of *methods* should we then use to test this hypothesis and its related implications?"

The answer to this question, from J. B. Watson's time on, has emphasized sticking as closely as possible to publicly observable behaviors (as opposed to inferences about unobservable mental activities). It has also appealed to controlled experimentation using objectively operationalized variables and independent replication of findings—in short, a strictly natural-science-oriented approach.[20] But within this broad, unifying definition of methodological behaviorism there is a broad spectrum of behaviorists, from conservative to liberal. The former are more strictly Skinnerian in their refusal to infer mental events between observable behaviors and their reinforcers, preferring to search for effects that are powerful enough to yield predictability and control at the individual level as opposed to the merely statistical level. More liberal methodological behaviorists feel freer to infer the existence of mental processes and are generally more flexible and pragmatic with regard to methodology. Their guiding criterion seems to be the acceptance of whatever empirical methods will facilitate an understanding of both simple *and* complex human behavior.[21] It is probably accurate to say that most Christians in behaviorist circles (indeed, Christian perspectivalists generally) adhere to this more liberal version of methodological behaviorism.

Besides metaphysical and methodological behaviorists (who theorize and/or do basic research), there is a growing cadre of applied behavior modifiers who are much less exercised by questions about human nature or the nature of proper scientific inquiry than by the

---

20. See Michael J. Mahoney, *Cognition and Behavior Modification* (Cambridge: Ballinger, 1974), chap. 1; and Mary Stewart Van Leeuwen, *The Sorcerer's Apprentice: A Christian Looks at the Changing Face of Psychology* (Downers Grove, Ill.: InterVarsity Press, 1982), chap. 1.

21. Mahoney, *Cognition and Behavior Modification*, pp. 18–19.

business of testing and refining behavioral techniques in real-life settings. It is primarily this area of behavioral psychology that accounts for the movement's continuous growth, with its steady proliferation of professional organizations and journals. [22] The concerns of applied behavioral psychologists are increasingly wide-ranging, and include (besides examples previously noted) the reduction of test anxiety and hallucinations, the control of substance abuse and overeating, the reorienting of sexual preferences, the elimination of compulsive habits, the cognitive modification of depressive and other negative states, the reconditioning of negative interaction patterns between spouses, and the self-modification of bodily states through biofeedback. Techniques derived from respondent-conditioning principles are generally subsumed under the rubric of *behavior therapy*, while those derived from operant-conditioning principles are lumped under the label of *applied behavior analysis*. [23]

ENDURING ISSUES FOR CHRISTIANS

In assessing the current status of behavioral psychology in light of a biblical anthropology, at least three issues are of enduring importance—especially given the widespread publicity that has attended both Skinner's writings and those of his critics, secular and Christian. [24] The first of these issues hearkens back to an issue raised several times in the first part of this book—namely, the question about whether behavioral scientists are practicing a *single* or a *double* standard of humanness with regard to themselves and the people they study. I will argue that most of the concern about both metaphysical and applied behaviorism arises when the impression is given that behavioral psychologists are a different and somehow more privileged

22. Examples are *Behavior Research and Therapy* (published since 1962); *Behavior Therapy* (published since 1970); *Journal of Applied Behavior Analysis* (published since 1968); *Journal of Behavior Therapy and Experimental Psychiatry* (published since 1979); and *Journal of the Experimental Analysis of Behavior* (published since 1957).

23. See, for example, the bibliographies of Bufford, *The Human Reflex;* Kazdin, *Behavior Modification in Applied Settings;* Mahoney, *Cognition and Behavior Modification;* and Richard B. Stuart, ed., *Behavioral Self-Management* (New York: Brunner/Mazel, 1977).

24. See especially Wheeler, *Beyond the Punitive Society;* Van Leeuwen, "The Behaviorist Bandwagon"; Arthur Koestler, *The Ghost in the Machine* (Chicago: Gateway Editions, 1967); and Francis A. Schaeffer, *Back to Freedom and Dignity* (Downers Grove, Ill.: InterVarsity Press, 1972).

group of people than those whom they study, and when it is implied that they therefore have both the ability and the right to become a species of managerial elite within society. When the limitations of such assumptions are conceded, the specter of totalitarian behavioral control is greatly diminished.

The second issue is connected to the first: if behavioral psychologists are of "one blood" with the rest of humankind—no more and no less unique, as a group, than other normal adults—then it would seem to follow that they have no more inherent ability to control others than others have to control them. In more technical terms, we need to examine the existence and power of *countercontrol*, a phenomenon that Skinner and others have acknowledged to exist[25] but that, according to one reviewer of the behavioral literature, is "a seldom cited consideration in our discipline."[26]

The final issue concerns the place of the *human mind* in a behavioral analysis. Elsewhere I have noted that Skinner and other conservative behaviorists have so reduced the mind to mere behavior that they have virtually espoused a position of "mental processlessness." That is, they have accorded the environment such total control over behavior that any accompanying mental activity is seen as merely an epiphenomenon—a species of "noise" accompanying and resulting from our behavior but having no controlling or self-transcending status of its own.[27] This position, although still held by some doctrinaire Skinnerians, is being increasingly eclipsed by a more cognitive behavioral psychology in which the mutual influences of mind, body, and external environment (and the resulting difficulty in predicting and controlling individual behavior) are freely acknowledged. Related to this is an increasing emphasis on people's ability to become (and the desirability of having them become) *their own* behavior modifiers—an emphasis, in other words, on the phenomenon of *self-control*. Let us examine each of these three issues in turn.

A Double Standard of Humanness? I will begin my consideration of this question by reminding the reader of two essential aspects of the history of behavioral research. First of all, recall that behavioral psychologists have invoked, as either a metaphysical or a working assumption, a close evolutionary continuity between animals and

25. See in particular Skinner, *About Behaviorism*, chap. 12.
26. Mahoney, *Cognition and Behavior Modification*, p. 224.
27. VanLeeuwen, "The Behaviorist Bandwagon," part 2.

people—so close that the basic behavioral principles established using animal subjects are assumed to apply without much qualification to people. Second, recall that, in their desire to be strictly scientific, the pioneers of behavioral psychology (such as Pavlov and Skinner and their students) studied the behavior of their animal subjects in very closely controlled environments. That the Skinner box, in which a rat or a pigeon is at least mobile, is relatively less constraining than the harness and headgear that Pavlov used with his dogs in no way lessens the fact that the researcher literally has absolute control over the animal, deciding where it will live, when and what it will eat, whether it will breed, and how and when it will be used as a research subject. Indeed, once the animal has been "contaminated" by participation in one study, it will not normally be used in another but instead will be "sacrificed" (a common euphemism for the killing of laboratory animals), thus confirming the absolute character of the researcher's control. We can fairly say, then, that basic behavioral research has been done with organisms of "limited powers in limiting environments."

The first human applications of behavior therapy and applied behavior analysis were done under similarly artificial conditions. For example, a technique known as *aversion therapy*, which employs respondent-conditioning principles, has been used to reorient alcoholics, drug addicts, and sexual deviates. But most of the subjects of such research have also suffered from other mental disturbances, and none of them have had any choice about their incarceration and treatment, since public authorities had referred them because of antisocial or criminal behaviors.[28] The essence of this technique is the pairing of the deviance-related stimulus (such as a glass of liquor) with an extremely unpleasant stimulus such as a painful electric shock or a drug that produces temporary nausea. The result is often the successful conversion of the originally attractive stimulus into one that the patient now wants to avoid. For the moment I am not concerned with the ethics of imposing such treatment without the informed consent of the patient (an issue to which I will return later). I simply want to point out that the behavioral reversals obtained by this

28. See Joseph Wolpe, "The Experimental Foundations of Some New Psychotherapeutic Techniques," in *Experimental Foundations of Clinical Psychology*, ed. R. J. Bachrach (New York: Basic Books, 1962); and Joseph Wolpe and Arnold K. Lazarus, *Behavior Therapy Techniques* (New York: Pergamon Press, 1966).

method tend to occur in coercively limiting environments using persons whose mental capacities are often impaired by the very problem (drug dependency, alcoholism) for which they have been referred in the first place.

The same is true of the first heady successes of applied behavior analysis, which is based on operant-conditioning principles. In 1949 an institutionalized "vegetative idiot" was taught to earn food by lifting his right arm to a vertical position—almost the first sign in his eighteen years of life that he was capable of learning anything. Later applications of operant conditioning, as I have previously noted, included teaching autistic children how to talk, training mental patients to engage in socially acceptable behaviors, and teaching retarded children simple school skills.[29] Again, the success of these methods was associated with a double limitation: all of the persons involved had limited or impaired reasoning abilities, and all were constrained to stay in their respective settings on the authority of someone else. It is with these conditions—enforced institutionalization combined with a degree of cognitive impairment on the part of the subject—that the behavioral psychologist can most closely approximate the situation of the Skinner box—that is, a high degree of control over an organism who, by virtue of a variety of limitations, is not the intellectual peer of the investigator.

It is difficult, for me at least, to understand how behavioral psychologists could ever have assumed that such a one-way relationship of control would generalize beyond the animal in the laboratory or the impaired human being in an institution to adults of normal intelligence in more ordinary settings. Yet it seems that many of them did just that. By virtue of their scientific knowledge (and the assumption that it would always be used benignly), social scientists were envisaged as a special elite who both could and should be the managers of a behaviorally planned society. Skinner's behaviorist utopia, which he invented in 1947 in *Walden Two*, assumes the possibility and praises the virtues of just such a society. And in his introduction to the reissue of the book in 1976 he indicates that his faith in such a vision has grown, not dwindled, in light of the intervening accomplishments of behavioral technology:

---

29. For an account of these early studies in applied behavior analysis, see W. K. Honig, ed., *Operant Behavior: Areas of Research and Application* (New York: Appleton-Century-Crofts, 1966).

What is needed is not a new political leader or a new kind of government, but further knowledge about human behavior and new ways of applying that knowledge to the design of cultural practices. . . . The choice is clear: either we do nothing and allow a miserable and probably catastrophic future to overtake us, or we use our knowledge about human behavior to create a social environment in which we shall live productive and creative lives and do so without jeopardizing the chances that those who follow us will be able to do the same. Something like Walden Two would not be a bad start.[30]

In such an analysis it is human beings—and, in particular, a more highly evolved, scientific elite among them—who both understand and know how to correct the human condition. They are, it seems, a group of people who have so transcended the limits of their own genetic endowment and past conditioning that they are "ideal observers" of the human scene. Indeed, in *Walden Two* Skinner transfers the theological language of an omniscient, morally perfect God (a remnant from his own Presbyterian youth?) to the figure of Frazier, the designer of this perfectly planned, behaviorally controlled society.[31]

Such hubris in the guise of benevolence is not displayed by Skinner alone. C. R. Jeffery, for example, is a metaphysical behaviorist whose particular target is the American judicial system. He criticizes it because it adheres to an outdated doctrine of moral responsibility rather than a totally deterministic view of criminal behavior. In his view it is this frustrating relic of the Judeo-Christian tradition that prevents truly effective behavior modification of criminals from taking place. "The standard for criminal responsibility is now [individual] mental responsibility," he writes. "The standard we are suggesting is harm to others, social protection, and the prevention of crime. . . . Treatment can be a function of criminal law if it is designed within a physical, rather than a mentalistic, model of man."[32]

Jeffery thinks that sociologists, behavioral psychologists, genet-

30. Skinner, "Walden Two Revisited," introd. to *Walden Two*, rev. ed. (New York: Macmillan, 1976), p. xvi.
31. For a more detailed analysis of Skinner's use of biblical imagery in *Walden Two*, see Van Leeuwen, "The Behaviorist Bandwagon," part 2.
32. C. R. Jeffery and Ina Jeffery, "Psychosurgery and Behavior Modification: Legal Control Techniques Versus Behavioral Control Techniques," *American Behavioral Scientist* 18 (May–June 1975): 706.

icists, and psychobiologists should be the only expert witnesses on criminal behavior and its treatment—not, as is now the case, psychiatrists and others committed to a prescientific distinction between full versus diminished responsibility in criminals.[33] From a biblical perspective on persons, the problem with such a position is not just its attribution of too *little* responsibility to ordinary people but its implicit attribution of too *much* responsibility to the social scientist. It is a view that refuses to see the scientist as a human being who is as finite and fallen as the persons he or she studies. "Who do we find when we get inside the man with the white lab coat?" asks Christian cultural critic Francis Schaeffer. "We find a faulty, lost man, don't we? Where are these great, benevolent manipulators going to come from? Talk about utopia! This is the most utopian concept of all."[34]

Among less doctrinaire behaviorists, however, there are signs that this double standard is beginning to change. Thus Michael Mahoney, a cognitively oriented behaviorist, warns his readers that only if we regard the scientist as a "fallible information processor" will we begin to understand human thought in all its complexity.[35] Far from being the direct product of external reinforcers and internal biology (as in extreme behaviorism), human behavior in Mahoney's analysis is strongly mediated by active and far-from-disinterested thought processes—processes, moreover, from which scientists are in no way exempt:

> [As human beings] we selectively filter environmental input and actively construct experiential regularities. We anticipate future events, and often distort our perception of them to enhance conformity with our expectations. All of this suggests that the human being is a frequently deluded organism whose beliefs and behaviors are stubbornly molded by perceptual bigotry. The implications of this view of man, however, strike a little closer to home when we are reminded that scientists are human and that scientific research is itself comprised of belief-behavior patterns. The scientist is not exempt from the mediational influences which dramatically affect human action. While awareness of those influences may reduce their distorting impact, it is unlikely that they can ever be totally eliminated. Moreover, the average

33. Jeffery, *Criminal Responsibility and Mental Disease* (Springfield, Ill.: Charles C. Thomas, 1967).
34. Schaeffer, *Back to Freedom and Dignity*, p. 29.
35. Mahoney, *Cognition and Behavior Modification*, p. 294.

scientist seldom applies his technical knowledge to himself. Ostensibly, his is the only "immaculate perception."[36]

Such an analysis represents a dramatic shift from traditional behaviorism—both metaphysical and methodological.[37] Moreover, it reinforces two persistent themes of this volume, being both postmodern in its understanding of science and (as a consequence) very supportive of the explicit integration of value considerations into both scientific theory and scientific research. That Mahoney's own value system is a liberal-humanist one not entirely compatible with Christianity[38] should not blind us to the fact that he is at least explicit about its existence and content, and also about its influence on his own work:

> The realization of the personal fallibility of the scientist suggests two major conclusions. First, our pursuit of knowledge is far from objective in any technical sense of that term. The data is *always* filtered. Second, the growth of knowledge is not a self-directing process. Our successive approximations toward "truth" might be more accurately described as successive embellishments of assumptive worlds. That is, the growth of knowledge is dramatically influenced by our expectancies and selective questioning of nature.[39]

Thus, by refusing to exempt themselves or their scientific work from the conditioning influences they ascribe to others, neobehaviorists such as Mahoney are helping to eradicate the double standard that has plagued their ranks for too long.

The Reality of Countercontrol. I have already noted that neobehaviorists of a cognitive orientation now tend to reject the notion that a person's environment (whether external or internal) determines his or her behavior in a nonreciprocal fashion. In a review documenting the progress of this theoretical shift, Frederick Kanfer comments,

36. Mahoney, *Cognition and Behavior Modification,* pp. 289–90.
37. Mahoney, however, tries to demonstrate the *fallibility* of empirical science using the *methods* of empirical science—a common paradox that can also be seen, for example, in Irwin Silverman, *The Human Subject in the Psychological Laboratory* (New York: Pergamon Press, 1977); and in Robert Rosenthal and Robert L. Rosnow, *Artifact in Behavioral Research* (New York: Academic Press, 1969).
38. See Mahoney, *Cognition and Behavior Modification,* chaps. 15 and 16, for an elaboration of his own value system.
39. Mahoney, *Cognition and Behavior Modification,* p. 290.

The emphasis on the reciprocal interaction between a person and his environment implies the need for a thorough investigation of the "pull value" of a client's behavior on his social environment, and a careful assessment of the attitudes and actions [he] elicits from the people with whom he interacts. . . . A person is the product of his environment. His behavior, in turn, shapes the environment and, thus, the individual is able to modify the conditions under which he lives. A philosophy that credits a person with potential for active alteration of his environment is the antithesis of a mechanistic, passive, environmentally-determined picture of Man—a concept of man-as-machine which has its modern roots in Watsonian classical behaviorism.[40]

However, I have also noted that this human capacity for countercontrol has been a largely underexamined topic in behavioral psychology. One reason for this neglect has been the assumption that the one-way, behavioral management techniques developed in the laboratory should simply be transferred to those human situations where they are most likely to work. This explains the enormous concentration of field research and applied work in settings such as schools, correctional institutions, and mental-health facilities—places where subjects, many of whom are either immature or cognitively impaired, are kept in environments with a greater or lesser degree of isolation (approximating gigantic Skinner boxes). Yet it is to this massive, often impressive, but highly *unrepresentative* body of literature that doctrinaire Skinnerians appeal when, in Michael Novak's words, "[they see] the whole field of human behavior reduced to a science and, more than a science, to a technology." He adds, "Unavoidably, such a vision is an act of faith, a project rather than an accomplishment."[41]

Skinner himself speaks ambivalently about the human capacity for countercontrol. While conceding its existence and even invoking it as a potential defense against despotic control by others, the bulk of his writings openly stress or covertly assume that what subjects *think* about conditioning procedures imposed on them is causally irrelevant to the outcome.[42] Philosopher Max Black summarizes and comments on it this way:

40. Kanfer, "The Many Faces of Self-Control, or Behavior Modification Changes Its Focus," in *Behavioral Self-Management*, pp. 4–5.
41. Novak, "Is He Really a Grand Inquisitor?" in *Beyond the Punitive Society*, p. 238.
42. See Skinner, *Beyond Freedom and Dignity* and *About Behaviorism*.

Skinner regards serious reference to such allegedly "mentalistic" factors as motive, intention, and the like as being, at best, Aesopian and, strictly speaking, inadmissible in a truly scientific account. . . . The pigeon, we may presume, cannot reflect upon his conditioning, and if a man under conditioning knows what is being done to him, that makes no difference to the administered reinforcements. . . .

Skinner will retort that men are controlled anyway, whether by propaganda, the threat of force, education, indoctrination, or love. Well, all these things affect us, to be sure, but that hardly amounts to control, in the sense of manipulation. Common sense would hold that men are sometimes manipulated and sometimes not. The differences, turning as they do upon the knowledge and consent of those involved, are crucial.[43]

In addition to such philosophical considerations, comprehensive reviews of the literature on applied behavior modification now tend to concede that, even in closed settings using cognitively impaired or immature subjects, the success rate of various behavioral techniques is modest.[44] Desensitization procedures are fairly reliable when the fears involved are very specific, but not when anxiety is ill-defined or diffuse. Token economies work well for short-term problems (although even in these cases the *persistence* of the effects of treatment is difficult to maintain), but they usually cannot reorient a total lifestyle based on a pervasive character disorder such as alcoholism or sexual perversion. Classroom programs are often successful, but only if primitive rewards such as candy and toys are replaced as soon as possible by less tangible and more intermittent reinforcers such as free activity time or teacher's praise and attention. "In general," writes one reviewer of the applied literature, "behavior therapy and behavior modification methods have been shown to be somewhat superior

43. Black, "Some Aversive Responses to a Would-Be Reinforcer," in *Beyond the Punitive Society*, p. 128.

44. See, for example, the following: John M. Atthowe, Jr., "Behavior Modification, Behavior Therapy and Environmental Design," *American Behavioral Scientist* 18 (May–June 1975): 637–55; Leonard Krasner, "Behavior Therapy," in *Annual Review of Psychology*, ed. Paul H. Mussen and Milton R. Rosenberg (Palo Alto, Calif.: Annual Reviews, 1971), 22: 483–532; A. E. Bergin, "The Evaluation of Therapeutic Outcomes," in *Handbook of Psychotherapy and Behavior Change*, ed. S. L. Garfield and A. E. Bergin (New York: John Wiley, 1978), pp. 217–70; and M. R. Goldfried and M. M. Linehan, "Basic Issues in Behavioral Assessment," in *Handbook of Behavioral Assessment*, ed. A. R. Ciminero, K. S. Colhoun, and H. E. Adams (New York: John Wiley, 1977), pp. 15–46.

to other forms of therapy. However, difficult disorders do not produce very positive results, and it still has to be demonstrated that the effects of therapy are persistent. What success there is suggests that treatment must involve many techniques, be comprehensive, and involve aftercare."[45]

Moreover, when we move from impaired or immature persons to those of normal, adult intelligence, Black's "common sense" appeal to the power of human reflexivity as having counterconditioning potential has even more support. Albert Bandura, a learning theorist at Stanford University, has pointed to the failure of the North Koreans to produce (under conditions very much like those of a Skinner box) more than a handful of permanently brainwashed converts among their G.I. prisoners of war, and concludes that human control on the scale envisaged by Skinner is simply not possible.[46] Bandura's colleague Ernest Hilgard believes that mass control of human behavior is theoretically possible but realistically improbable "because there are too many bright people who would never go along."[47] Michael Mahoney now admits that facing up to the existence of human counter-control was "one of the most humbling experiences of my early career." All too often, he adds, even young children will deliberately *avoid* their preferred reinforcers just *because* they have discerned that these are being used to shape their behavior.[48] "In general," concludes another reviewer of the literature (himself an experienced researcher of token economies), "*behavior modification does not work if the client is not motivated to accept the intervention.*"[49]

It is somewhat ironic that the behavioral community has taken this long to acknowledge the reality and power of countercontrol, because it has always advertised, as one of the benefits of operant conditioning, the simplicity of its principles and the ease with which its applied techniques can be used even by nonprofessional ward attendants, parents, and other caretakers. But if these principles and techniques are so easily learned, why should we be surprised when even impaired persons (let alone normally intelligent adults and chil-

---

45. Atthowe, "Behavior Modification," p. 646.
46. Bandura, as quoted in *Annual Editions: Readings in Psychology* (Guilford, Conn.: Dushkin Publishing Group, 1972), pp. 7–13.
47. Hilgard, as quoted in *Annual Editions*, p. 11.
48. Mahoney, *Cognition and Behavior Modification*, chap. 13.
49. Atthowe, "Behavior Modification," p. 649 (italics mine).

dren) discern the patterns of manipulation being used on them and decide to do some manipulating of their own?

Attempts to change behavior permanently (as opposed to temporarily and opportunistically) simply do not work when the target of manipulation is a human being who knows or has guessed the nature of those manipulations and refuses to accept the process or its goals or both. He may, as C. S. Lewis observed over a quarter of a century ago, decide to "cheat [his captors] with apparent success,"[50] cooperating with the program only long enough to be released from it, then reverting to type once more. But he may decide not even to do that. One perceptive prison inmate, writing about a behavior-modification program in a Michigan correctional facility, demonstrated both a clear understanding of the techniques being applied to him and a stubborn unwillingness to cooperate with them:

> [Tokens] are distributed by the guards and psychiatric staff on their own arbitrary discretion. . . . Inmates are awarded tokens for proper responses, such as "Good morning sir, How are you sir? Yes sir," etc. . . . During group therapy, the prisoner's therapist will point out what problems an inmate has, and whether they're real or not, that inmate is required to solve his problem in the group. If the inmate doesn't try to solve this problem forced on him, then he's not co-operating with the behavior modification program, which results in a hard way to go on all fronts. . . .
>
> The guards put on a front of politeness, concern, and friendship. I had had enough of cells, guards, and phoniness those few hours between the 6th and 7th of April, and refused to eat or talk to anyone.[51]

Countercontrol, then, is a very real phenomenon, one that testifies to the existence of human freedom even as we are *relatively* constrained by our biological heritage and our social and natural environments. It is to be hoped that behavioral psychologists, as they come to understand this more and more, will be less inclined to make exaggerated claims for their techniques or (in the case of metaphysical behaviorists) for their world view. But as we have noted before and will see again in this chapter, world views are rarely abandoned as the

---

50. Lewis, "The Humanitarian Theory of Punishment," Reprinted in *God in the Dock,* ed. Walter Hooper (Grand Rapids: Eerdmans, 1970), p. 290.
51. W. A. Nicholson, "Michigan Intensive Program Center," *R. T.: A Journal of Radical Therapy* 6 (Spring 1975): 5.

result of mere empirical evidence, regardless of stated professional standards to the contrary.

The Return of the Person. We might summarize the foregoing discussion by asserting, as I have before, that human beings are irreducibly reflexive. That is, they are capable of analyzing the part they are playing in a given situation and, on the basis of that self-examination, capable of initiating changes such that they are not the same as they were before that reflexive examination began. When members of liberation movements speak of the importance of "consciousness-raising" with their recruits, they are acknowledging that once persons begin to question, or "reflect upon," their previously taken-for-granted position, they are on their way to reorganizing their circumstances in potentially significant ways. Indeed, such reflexivity, as we know from the example of biofeedback, extends even to aspects of physiological functioning previously assumed to be beyond conscious control. When persons are able to monitor their own bodily functions with the aid of instruments, they are often able to change them within certain limits. Thus we can see why Cambridge sociologist Anthony Giddens defines reflexivity as "the rational basis of freedom."[52]

None of this is to gainsay the *relative* efficacy of conditioning or to attribute to human beings a greater degree, or consistency, of rational self-examination than they actually possess as finite, sinful, and emotion-laden creatures. But even Donald MacKay—who, as we have seen, invokes a thoroughly mechanical picture of persons within his perspectivalist position—appeals to the concept of "logical indeterminacy" to account for this reflexive capacity. He suggests that even if our actions were completely predictable to a "super-scientist," our knowledge of the content of those predictions (or even merely the fact that someone was making them) would render them immediately out-of-date and therefore no longer true for us in particular.[53]

Earlier in this chapter I spoke of the efforts of some theologians to reconcile the biblical and the behaviorist views of personhood by

52. Giddens, *Studies in Social and Political Theory* (New York: Basic Books, 1977), p. 28. See also Mary Stewart Van Leeuwen, "Reflexivity in North American Psychology: Historical Reflections on One Aspect of a Changing Paradigm," *Journal of the American Scientific Affiliation* 35 (Sept. 1983): 162–67.

53. See MacKay, *The Clockwork Image: A Christian Perspective on Science* (London: Inter-Varsity Press, 1974); and *Human Science and Human Dignity* (London: Hodder and Stoughton, 1979).

appealing to the sovereignty of God over all of creation—a species of theological determinism. Yet neither Scripture nor the accumulating corpus of behavioral research can be interpreted this simply. We have seen that countercontrol, which depends on the existence of human reflexivity, emerges as an important feature of the conditioning process. Moreover, the bondage of the will and the sovereignty of God are not the only themes in biblical anthropology. Unless we are to assume that the *imago Dei* was totally eradicated at the Fall, we must see human beings as capable, at least in part and at times, of self-transcending insight and real choice. In Francis Schaeffer's words,

> To a Christian, though man may undergo a good deal of conditioning, he is not only the product of conditioning. Man has a mind; he exists as an ego, an entity standing over against the machine-like part of his being. [To hold otherwise is to say] that not only morals, but every vestige of everything that makes human life valuable from the standpoint of what God meant us to be as men in His image is eradicated.[54]

The Growing Emphasis on Self-Control. Behavioral psychologists' accumulating knowledge about countercontrol is related to another significant shift in their theoretical and applied activities: the idea that persons, both in principle and in practice, can sometimes be their own behavior modifiers. On the practical level the cost of individualized therapy coupled with the perennial shortage of trained therapists has also prompted a growing interest in teaching self-control techniques. Such methods include self-relaxation techniques; systematic desensitization of phobias by putting oneself through a graduated stimulus hierarchy (suggested, but not administered, by a therapist); exaggerated role-playing, which involves overt rehearsal of the more adaptive behaviors to which one aspires; and self-study, or the rational examination of one's problems and the circumstances that evoke them. All these, and more, are now standard considerations in textbooks of behavioral psychology.[55]

Again, no claims are made regarding the uniqueness of these methods per se. As Skinner has noted in one of his earlier books,

---

54. Schaeffer, *Back to Freedom and Dignity*, p. 36.
55. See, for example, Stuart, *Behavioral Self-Management*; Kazdin, *Behavior Modification in Applied Settings*; Robert Sherman, *Behavior Modification: Theory and Practice* (Monterey, Calif.: Brooks-Cole, 1973); and Michael Mahoney and Carl E. Thoresen, *Self-Control: Power to the Person* (Monterey, Calif.: Brooks-Cole, 1974).

people have always found ways to control their own behavior for the sake of avoiding temptation or building up weak but desirable habits.[56] What is new is the ongoing program of systematically analyzing and testing such methods, then teaching them to a lay population. And while it is true that the basic research literature on self-control is still rather scanty, practical applications representing a range of successes continue to proliferate.

Behavioral psychologists address the idea of self-managed therapy with varying degrees of optimism. On the one hand, Robert Sherman asserts,

> The basic principles of learning are presumably the same whether the therapist or the individual himself arranges the treatment contingencies. Therefore the individual may be taught to be his own therapist in administering certain behavior modification methods. . . . He may desensitize himself from a phobic reaction, or use aversive conditioning to rid himself of a bad smoking habit. On the preventive side, skills such as self-relaxation and interpersonal expressiveness may enable one to become more behaviorally effective. . . . In either case, we attempt to teach the individual self-controlling responses which he may use to control the probability of other responses, either adaptive or maladaptive.[57]

On the other hand, Alan Kazdin is more cautious in his assessment of the self-control phenomenon. These methods, he points out, vary merely in the *degree* to which clients are in charge of their own treatment. It is true that in any therapeutic encounter that is self-chosen, clients are "in control" inasmuch as they can quit the program whenever they wish. But within this basic parameter of informed consent, the involvement of the therapist ranges from frequent contact and elaborate contractual obligations to the client's independent purchasing and use of self-help books in the absence of any personal contact with a therapist. While he concedes that involving clients in their own treatment is "probably advisable wherever possible," Kazdin points out that persons left on their own tend to drop out of self-modification programs at an alarming rate, and he suggests that for most people external social support is essential for

---

56. Skinner, *Science and Human Behavior* (New York: Macmillan, 1953).
57. Sherman, *Behavior Modification*, p. 133.

therapeutic success.[58] If coerced treatment breeds reaction, counter-manipulation, or attempts at "conning" the therapist, unregulated self-help programs have opposite problems: they allow persons to rationalize their lapses, alter their standards capriciously, and become careless about essential record-keeping.[59]

Nevertheless, for several clearly laudable reasons the study and use of self-modification programs continues to grow. On the ethical level their use helps behaviorists to avoid anxieties and accusations about being coercive. On the practical level they extend the knowledge and benefits of certain techniques to laypersons who might otherwise not be able to afford treatment. Their use also helps to reduce the putative gap between professionals and laypersons, thereby demystifying behavioral psychology and making the quest for human understanding and treatment a collegial rather than a strictly professionalized undertaking. For all these reasons Christians can welcome the growing emphasis on self-control in behavioral literature.

AMBIVALENCE ABOUT MIND AND MORALS

Neobehaviorists, we have seen, are facing up to the existence of human reflexivity and its implications for self-control and counter-control. But, strangely enough, many do so while continuing to affirm a view of persons that precludes any real freedom—that is, the kind of freedom necessary to hold persons morally accountable for their actions. In other words, many neobehaviorists concede that countercontrol exists in the sense that events occurring in a person's head have a potentially controlling influence over other events. But they then go on to say that those "events inside the head" are themselves wholly determined by the forces of nature and nurture and are in no way indicative of any measure of personal transcendence. In B. F. Skinner's words,

> A scientific analysis of behavior must, I believe, assume that a person's behavior is controlled by his genetic and environmental histories rather than by the person himself as an initiating, creative agent. . . . We cannot prove, of course, that human behavior as a whole is fully determined, but the proposition becomes

58. Kazdin, *Behavior Modification in Applied Settings*, p. 275.
59. Bufford, *The Human Reflex*, chap. 4.

more plausible as facts accumulate. We must surely begin with the fact that human behavior is always controlled.[60]

That the "accumulating facts" of applied behavioral psychology have in reality yielded a very ambiguous picture of control in no way diminishes the faith of metaphysical behaviorists. "Behavior is always modified whether or not a particular behavioral program is specifically designed for this purpose," writes Alan Kazdin. "Because there are conflicting sources of control, the net effect varies across individuals. [But] control is no less control just because there are variations in the final success."[61] And Michael Mahoney, despite his acquired respect for the realities of countercontrol, hastens to add that "deviation from prediction, however, should not be mistaken for a capriciousness in nature. . . . The [countercontrolling] subjects are being 'deviant' only in the sense that they are responding in a manner which contradicts the experimenter's contingencies. This is a far cry from being indeterminate. They are still exhibiting performance regularities, albeit frustrating ones for their would-be controllers."[62]

Statements of this sort are of interest not only because they confirm that metaphysical behaviorism (at least on the level of lip service) is still alive and well, but also because they fly in the face of the Popperian philosophy of science to which psychology as a whole claims to adhere. As we have previously seen, Popper's "falsificationist" criterion requires that scientists be able to specify the kinds of disconfirming evidence that would lead them to abandon the theory to which they adhere. Yet, as with other scientists, psychologists are in fact very slow to accept any empirical evidence as disconfirming their cherished theories.[63] Those who are metaphysically committed to a deterministic world view will, like Kazdin and Mahoney, simply explain away any contradictory evidence, and continue to state—ex cathedra, as it were—that "control is no less control just because there are variations in the final success." This is further reason to affirm, as I did in Chapter One, that science and religion are not such separate activities as we have been led to believe. Both involve adherence to metaphysical faith-commitments that cannot, in the final analysis,

60. Skinner, *About Behaviorism*, pp. 208, 221.
61. Kazdin, *Behavior Modification in Applied Settings*, pp. 309–10.
62. Mahoney, *Cognition and Behavior Modification*, p. 245.
63. See especially Imre Lakatos, "Falsification and the Methodology of Scientific Research Programs," in *Criticism and the Growth of Knowledge*, ed. I. Lakatos and A. Musgrave (New York: Cambridge University Press, 1970).

be controverted simply by appealing to empirical evidence, however important this may be.

The ambivalence of even liberal behaviorists about the status of the mind leads in turn to ambiguities regarding the ethics of behavioral control. On the one hand, as both Christian and humanist critics of behaviorism have pointed out, a totally mechanized universe leaves no place for moral pronouncements of any sort, holding as it does that moral preferences, like every other kind of attitude, are solely the product of material and social forces, whose differing combinations totally relativize the status of any resulting beliefs. On the other hand, it is rare to find textbooks on behavioral psychology whose authors do not include a section on ethical considerations.

Figure 7.1 presents the ethical "checklist" drawn up by the Association for the Advancement of Behavior Therapy. It is a set of guidelines that have been phrased in such a manner as to apply to all types of intervention (for example, psychosurgery and drug-related treatments) and not just those that emerge from behavioral psychology. A perusal of this list shows that concern for the client's trust, privacy, informed consent, and long-term (not just immediate) interests are recurring themes. There is also an insistence that therapists know their own limitations as well as those of the techniques being considered, and that they carefully monitor both professional and public relations in every kind of treatment program.

Certainly all of this is both admirable and reassuring to Christian and non-Christian consumers alike. But when we recall that many behavior modifiers still express a philosophical commitment to a view of human beings as passively determined and therefore morally neutral, then we must ask, what is the *source* of such laudable concern? Is it the moral goodness of behavioral psychologists—are they, as persons, better than their theories? (One would hope so; for if one must choose between acting morally and being logically consistent with one's theories, then surely it is better to be known for the former.) Or is it, on the other hand, merely enlightened self-interest—a reluctant recognition that since total control over clients' lives would raise too much public outcry, it is better to settle for limited control than be forced out of business entirely. If so, then the negative, behaviorist utopia imagined by C. S. Lewis in *That Hideous Strength* is far from impossible, for one would expect behavior modifiers who acted opportunistically in an era concerned with human rights to act just as

Figure 7.1. Example of an Ethical Checklist for Behavior Modifiers (from "Ethical Issues for Human Services," *Behavior Therapy* **8 [Jan. 1977]: v–vi).**

A. Have the goals of treatment been adequately considered?
   1. To insure that the goals are explicit, are they written?
   2. Has the client's understanding of the goals been assured by having the client restate them orally or in writing?
   3. Have the therapist and client agreed on the goals of therapy?
   4. Will serving the client's interests be contrary to the interests of other persons?
   5. Will serving the client's immediate interests be contrary to the client's long-term interest?

B. Has the choice of treatment methods been adequately considered?
   1. Does the published literature show the procedure to be the best one available for that problem?
   2. If no literature exists regarding the treatment method, is the method consistent with generally accepted practice?
   3. Has the client been told of alternative procedures that might be preferred by the client on the basis of significant differences in discomfort, treatment time, cost, or degree of demonstrated effectiveness?
   4. If a treatment procedure is publicly, legally, or professionally controversial, has formal professional consultation been obtained, has the reaction of the affected segment of the public been adequately considered, and have the alternative treatment methods been more closely reexamined and reconsidered?

C. Is the client's participation voluntary?
   1. Have possible sources of coercion on the client's participation been considered?
   2. If treatment is legally mandated, has the available range of treatments and therapists been offered?
   3. Can the client withdraw from treatment without a penalty or financial loss that exceeds actual clinical costs?

D. When another person or an agency is empowered to arrange for therapy, have the interests of the subordinated client been sufficiently considered?
   1. Has the subordinated client been informed of the treatment objectives and participated in the choice of treatment procedures?
   2. Where the subordinated client's competence to decide is limited, have the client as well as the guardian participated in the treatment discussions to the extent that the client's abilities permit?
   3. If the interests of the subordinated person and the superordinate

Figure 7.1. *Continued*

persons or agency conflict, have attempts been made to reduce the conflict by dealing with both interests?

E. Has the adequacy of treatment been evaluated?
1. Have quantitative measures of the problem and its progress been obtained?
2. Have the measures of the problem and its progress been made available to the client during treatment?

F. Has the confidentiality of the treatment relationship been protected?
1. Has the client been told who has access to the records?
2. Are records available only to authorized persons?

G. Does the therapist refer the clients to other therapists when necessary?
1. If treatment is unsuccessful, is the client referred to other therapists?
2. Has the client been told that if dissatisfied with the treatment, referral will be made?

H. Is the therapist qualified to provide treatment?
1. Has the therapist had training or experience in treating problems like the client's?
2. If deficits exist in the therapist's qualifications, has the client been informed?
3. If the therapist is not adequately qualified, is the client referred to other therapists, or has supervision by a qualified therapist been provided? Is the client informed of the supervisory relation?
4. If the treatment is administered by mediators, have the mediators been adequately supervised by a qualified therapist?

---

opportunistically during a more totalitarian era in which those rights were substantially eroded.[64]

It is, of course, impossible to know which of these two attitudes is most characteristic of the behavioral community as a whole. But there is evidence that some behavior modifiers have regulated their activities only in response to strong external pressure. This is particularly true of token-economy schemes based on operant-conditioning principles. Because operant conditioners have placed so much emphasis on rewarding desirable behavior rather than punishing undesirable behavior, it has been deceptively easy to assume that no legal

---

64. Lewis, *That Hideous Strength* (London: John Lane-the Bodley Head, 1945).

objections would possibly be raised about such benign principles. But as court and legal experts have learned more about these schemes, they have discovered that the effectiveness of positive reinforcers usually requires that a state of deprivation precede them—a state often severe enough to be classed as inhumanly punitive.

Many token economies in prisons, hospitals, and training schools have accorded inmates certain amenities (such as meals, beds, personal clothing, and access to recreational facilities) only after they have acquired enough "tokens" or "points" for acceptable behaviors. But precedents set in recent legal cases have established that certain things previously used as earned reinforcers must now be accorded inmates as a matter of basic rights.[65] In *Wyatt v. Stickney* (1972), such rights include a comfortable bed, screens or curtains to secure privacy, a locker for personal belongings, nutritionally adequate meals, reasonable clothing, and the right to receive visitors, attend religious services, get physical exercise, and have access to a television set.[66]

The reaction of the behavioral community to such controls has been mixed. Many have complained that the recent court decisions have ruled out the use of therapy programs before there is even a chance to assess their efficacy. They have also insisted that inmates' rights must be balanced by a concern for the wider society whose norms they have violated. C. R. Jeffery, for example, argues that if we may incarcerate people without their consent in the first place, then surely we may provide therapy for them without their consent also.[67] By contrast, others have counseled cooperation with the law, not only to avoid lawsuits that may be directed at them but also in the interest of finding more creative and humane programs that are in keeping with civil libertarian concerns.[68]

Among Christians, too, there are mixed reactions to recent trends in behavioral psychology, and it is with a consideration of these that we will end this chapter.

65. See, for example, Reed Martin, *Legal Challenges to Behavior Modification* (Champaign, Ill.: Research Press, 1975); and David B. Wexler, "Behavior Modification and Legal Developments," *American Behavioral Scientist* 18 (May–June 1975): 679–84.
66. For an elaboration, see Wexler, "Behavior Modification and Legal Developments."
67. See Jeffery and Jeffery, "Psychosurgery and Behavior Modification."
68. See, for example, Martin, *Legal Challenges to Behavior Modification.*

CHRISTIAN RESPONSES TO BEHAVIORAL PSYCHOLOGY

As indicated at the beginning of this chapter, Christians in general have rejected metaphysical behaviorism, which elevates chance but adaptive genetic mutations and the environment to the status of prime movers over all animal and human behavior. At the same time, most Christian analysts, for a variety of reasons and to varying degrees, have accepted the notion of conditioning as one form of learning. Moreover, Christian perspectivalists applaud methodological behaviorism as an epistemological tool without explicitly embracing behaviorism as a metaphysical system.

Catholic theologian Michael Novak suggests that Skinner's stress on the controlling power of the social environment is in many ways more compatible with Catholic notions of community than is the "Protestant principle" that "each man is his own priest and pope, each conscience inviolable, each person a source of autonomy and dissent."[69] We not only are buttressed but need to be buttressed by environmental and social supports as weak creatures trying to serve God, says Novak. He reminds readers that both the teachings of Scripture and the practices of early Christianity confirm the folly—if not the impossibility—of any person's trying to be captain of his or her own ship, isolated from external influence.

Protestant scholar James Woelfel agrees that exposure to Skinner's extreme doctrines may be a salutary corrective for contemporary Christians:

> Neither classical nor modern Christian thought has faced with utter seriousness the heavy "weight" of biology and environment as they shape human actions. . . . Skinner's work is an invaluable, if clearly limited, reminder to Christians of some of the implications of our earthly creatureliness and interdependence within the web of nature and society.[70]

Such views are supported theologically by concepts such as grace and providence, according to which it is God, not individuals (nor the impersonal forces of environment and evolution), who upholds the universe at all times and is to be credited with any positive actions we take. Indeed, even the notion of sin has the suggestion of inevitability

---

69. Novak, "Is He Really a Grand Inquisitor?" p. 232.
70. Woelfel, "Listening to B. F. Skinner," p. 1116.

about it. "Our sin is not merely personal," Novak reminds us. "The entire social order is flawed and damaging to all. At no historical time was the cultural tissue of human life supportive of humane, creative acts; the reinforcers often bring out the worst in us. The 'sin' is original; the sickness, the plague, is inescapable."[71]

No Christian analyst goes so far as to invoke Skinnerian thought in order to abolish all notions of human responsibility. Many, however, point out that the themes of freedom and inevitability coexist in a puzzling tension in Scripture, and that this poses not only theological dilemmas but practical moral dilemmas as well. In Woelfel's words, "How can I respond compassionately to the *bondage* in your and my character and actions while at the same time nurturing the elusive, *unbound* dimension of our selfhood, [for] it is just such a balanced response to persons that the data of human behavior demand of us."[72]

Along similar lines, David Myers, appealing to the literature of social psychology on attribution, points out that we all too easily blame the environment for *our* misdeeds ("I couldn't help it") while crediting our own creativity and autonomy for all of our positive accomplishments. Conversely, we tend to "blame" other people for *their* misdeeds ("He brought it on himself") while underrating their personal responsibility for their achievements. Against this self-elevating, other-denigrating tendency, Myers suggests, the Bible calls us to be severe with ourselves but compassionate toward others, invoking more personal responsibility for our own failures but considering how the weight of nature and nurture has conditioned the lapses of others.[73]

On yet another practical level, Christians vary in the enthusiasm with which they embrace behavior-modification techniques, although most, including me, accord them a legitimate place in human interaction while also recognizing their mixed character.[74] Being weak and finite, we need both immediate and long-range incentives (although not always of a strictly material nature) to keep us working toward acceptable goals. Moreover, Scripture not only speaks of God

71. Novak, "Is He Really a Grand Inquisitor?" p. 233.
72. Woelfel, "Listening to B. F. Skinner," p. 1116 (italics mine).
73. Myers, *The Human Puzzle: Psychological Research and Christian Belief* (San Francisco: Harper and Row, 1978), chap. 10.
74. See, for example, Bufford, *The Human Reflex*; Van Leeuwen, "The Behaviorist Bandwagon"; and Edward P. Bolin and Glenn M. Goldberg, "Behavioral Psychology and the Bible," *Journal of Psychology and Theology* 7 (Fall 1979): 167–75.

as both the rewarder and the punisher of human behavior but makes clear that this authority, within limits, is transferred to certain human relationships.

Rodger Bufford, writing in *The Human Reflex*, is probably the most enthusiastic and explicit advocate of a behavioral analysis of child-rearing, Christian education, and pastoral and evangelistic activity. Taking for granted the scriptural legitimacy of the authority of parents, pastors, and teachers, Bufford gives detailed suggestions about how each of these "shaping" roles can be made more efficient and attractive by an appeal to behavioral principles and techniques. My own preference would be for a somewhat less hierarchical analysis of the Christian community, with more stress placed on the reality of *mutual* accountability and authority, and more consideration given to the process by which children must progress from a position of dependent obedience to one of responsible coequality within the Body of Christ. But these are differences of emphasis rather than of basic principle, since all Christian analysts seem to agree that behavioral control is legitimate and necessary but only within carefully defined spheres of authority.

More serious is the charge of social scientist Bruce McKeown that Christians *cannot* claim to be merely methodological (as opposed to metaphysical) behaviorists because of the impossibility of separating one's anthropology from one's epistemology. "In spite of its contributions to social analysis and behavioral therapy," writes McKeown, "behaviorist psychology substitutes another set of myths and fictions for those it rejects. By denying traditional myths and symbols, behaviorism becomes totalitarian and thus symbolic of a secular age."[75]

McKeown is concerned with the way in which some Christians "overtranslate" the Bible into behaviorist language as a means of integrating the two, and thereby distort the unique complexity of Scripture's various genres:

> [In such an analysis], eschatological doctrine is equated with positive reinforcement, the conscience functions as a negative reinforcer, and the beatitudes are analogous to a system of token rewards. Indeed, it is asserted that Hebrews 11:6 establishes God as a positive reinforcer. At issue in this translation, more than its being trite and superficial (comparable to declaring God as my

75. McKeown, "Myth and Its Denial in a Secular Age: The Case of Behaviorist Psychology," *Journal of Psychology and Theology* 9 (Spring 1981): 12.

"co-pilot" or "cosmic pal") is that *it legitimizes the fiction of behaviorist metapsychology*, and in doing that it debases religious language and symbolism and sterilizes, if not destroys, traditional religious images, meanings, and significance. The translation is dangerous because it substitutes a new set of symbols for those essential to historic Christian faith.[76]

Replies to such criticisms usually invoke some version of the perspectivalist resolution. Calling God a "positive reinforcer" is not the same as saying he is *nothing but* a positive reinforcer, protests Bufford. Furthermore, he notes, if we are forbidden to translate biblical themes into the language of contemporary culture, then the writing of any creedal statement or catechism is equally suspect.[77]

As we saw in Chapter Six, both these positions have their problems. On the one hand, it is difficult to see how "territorialists" such as McKeown can both limit the application of behaviorist concepts and at the same time grant them the necessary freedom to make the "contributions to social analysis and behavioral therapy" that he concedes they have made. On the other hand, as we have also seen, integrators of a perspectivalist bent are, by both training and inclination, overly focused on only a single perspective—namely, the natural-science perspective. It is good behavioral theory to hold that people tend to become and believe in what they habitually *do*. Consequently, it is at best inconsistent and at worst naive for Christian behavioral psychologists to assume that they can adopt a mechanistic perspective on persons as a mere working hypothesis, to be used day after day in their professional lives, and never be affected by its associated metaphysic. We are constantly in danger of being seduced by our own metaphors—which is just another way of saying that anthropology and epistemology are intimately intertwined in any study of the person.[78]

Although I am still not inclined to pronounce simple resolutions to this in-house debate, I continue to suggest that, at this point in

76. McKeown, "Myth and Its Denial in a Secular Age," p. 19 (italics his).
77. Bufford, "On the Possibility of Integration: Response to McKeown's Characterization of Behavioral Psychology as Myth," *Journal of Psychology and Theology* 9 (Spring 1981): 21–25.
78. Van Leeuwen, *The Sorcerer's Apprentice*, chap. 2. This represents a shift from my earlier analysis in "The Behaviorist Bandwagon." At that time I was readier than I am now to concede the possibility of a neat separation between metaphysical and methodological behaviorism.

time, the greater burden of proof rests with the perspectivalist. Literacy in natural science is the major—and in some places the only—training requirement for would-be psychologists. Consequently, there is a greater—not a lesser—need to balance this with true literacy in other areas as well. In this respect McKeown's point is well-taken: biblical language has its own special nuances and ways of seeing the world that need detailed hermeneutical attention on their own level. Yet there is a persistent tendency among Christian behaviorists to assume that merely *being* a Christian is sufficient to turn oneself into a biblical scholar who can accurately integrate both perspectives. It is high time that we conceded otherwise.

CHAPTER 8
THE COGNITIVE REVIVAL

This traditional belief, this conviction that we are really different, and that all that is wondrous and awesome (and fearful) about us is due to our intellect, is being made credible and respectable again by the new empirical discipline called cognitive science.

—Morton Hunt[1]

The aim [of biblical wisdom literature] is to put a stop to the erroneous concept that a guarantee of success [is] to be found simply in practising human wisdom and in making preparations. Man must always keep himself open to the activity of God, an activity which completely escapes all calculation; for between the putting into practise of the most reliable wisdom and that which actually takes place, there always lies a great unknown. . . . [Thus] only he is really wise who does not consider himself wise. To consider oneself wise is a sure sign of folly.

—Gerhard Von Rad[2]

In Chapter Six we explored the current contours of the brain-mind debate among Christians. In Chapter Seven, by contrast, we surveyed the current landscape of behavioral psychology, a movement that originally sought to evade the brain-mind problem entirely, either by simply ignoring the mind or by reducing it to an illusory by-product of biological or environmental processes. In this chapter we

1. Hunt, *The Universe Within: A New Science Explores the Human Mind* (New York: Simon and Schuster, 1982), p. 14.
2. Von Rad, *Wisdom in Israel* (Nashville: Abingdon Press, 1972), p. 101.

return to psychology's study of the mind as we consider the relatively new area broadly known as "cognitive science." This corpus of theory and research on the human mind represents an interdisciplinary as well as a psychological endeavor, an endeavor that some people— like Morton Hunt, author of the first opening quotation—believe to be the obvious successor to behaviorism. Hunt's book is entitled *The Universe Within*, a phrase that expresses his confidence in the mind's present powers and future possibilities. Indeed, at one point he turns amateur theologian and suggests that the attitude of the writer of Genesis 1:27 ("So God created man in his own image . . .") can rightly be described as "*hubris* justified" in portraying human beings as "little replicas of the almighty."[3]

Even a layperson of modest biblical literacy can recognize that this is very crude exegesis. Nevertheless, Hunt's enthusiasm for the cognitive revival in psychology raises an important point. In previous chapters, particularly in the last one, I have taken pains to argue that unless we assume that the *imago Dei* was permanently eradicated by the Fall, we must regard human beings as capable—at least in part and at times—of the kind of insight, choice, and creativity essential to their calling as accountable stewards over the creation. For this reason alone, many Christians in psychology have welcomed the gradual eclipse of behaviorism by the growing renaissance of cognitive studies.

On the other hand, Scripture also gives us, in Genesis 11, an account of the attempt to build the Tower of Babel—a story to which Hunt makes no reference at all but that C. S. Lewis used as the basis of his apocalyptic novel, *That Hideous Strength*.[4] In the original story we find that while God concedes humankind's *ability* to realize its project ("This is only the beginning of what they will do; and nothing that they propose to do will now be impossible for them"—v. 6), he concludes that their *motivation* is distorted in wanting to "make a name" for themselves by building "a tower with its top in the heavens" (v. 4). Consequently, the project cannot continue; God sows linguistic confusion among the builders and scatters far and wide the resulting groups that can no longer communicate with each other.

Here we have the use of human intellectual and technical skills—abilities originally endowed by God himself—being cut short by God when their guiding motives are self-glorifying and conse-

3. Hunt, *The Universe Within*, p. 157.
4. Lewis, *That Hideous Strength* (London: John Lane-the Bodley Head, 1945).

quently blasphemous. Nor is this theme unique to the Tower of Babel account, for as Von Rad (author of the second opening quotation) makes clear, knowing one's limits and discerning what is possible and prudent within God-ordained norms is the essence of the biblical concept of wisdom. If the danger inherent in behavioral psychology is reductionism, the opposite danger lurks within the cognitive revival—that of elevating human rationality to the point where it claims to replace God. Thus the problem that confronts us as Christians is this: How do we give adequate acknowledgment to the power and complexity of human thinking while at the same time trying to discern the limits of what it can and should do? How, in other words, do we walk the fine line "between reductionism and self-deification"?[5]

Because the renaissance of cognitive studies is a relatively recent phenomenon, it may be difficult to give a definitive answer to such a question. Among Christians, participation in the cognitive revival is still rather limited. What work exists is overwhelmingly concentrated on the relationship between cognitive and moral development, a topic popularized by Harvard's Lawrence Kohlberg and one of considerable interest to Christians inasmuch as it has practical relevance for the ethical and even religious socialization of children.[6] But this work, flowing from Jean Piaget's theories of cognitive development, represents only one stream of the current cognitive revival. What is needed now is a summary of each of the streams of influence and their current status, in light of which I will return to the above question and attempt at least a tentative answer.

THE INTELLECTUAL ROOTS OF CURRENT COGNITIVE SCIENCE

From previous chapters of this book, the reader knows that efforts to understand human thinking predate the Greeks and continue through to the work of contemporary neuroscientists. Twentieth-

5. I owe this trenchant phrase to C. Stephen Evans, "The Concept of the Self as the Key to Integration," keynote address given at the meeting of the Christian Association for Psychological Studies, Chicago, April 1983.
6. Kohlberg, "Stage and Sequence: The Cognitive-Developmental Approach to Socialization," in Handbook of Socialization Theory and Research, ed. D. Goslin (New York: Rand McNally, 1969). See also Craig Dykstra, Vision and Character: A Christian Educator's Alternative to Kohlberg (New York: Paulist Press, 1981); and Thomas C. Hennesy, ed., Values and Moral Development (New York: Paulist Press, 1976).

century psychology, however, has been dominated by a behaviorist paradigm that has discouraged if not totally proscribed the exploration of the mental processes that mediate environmental input and behavioral response. How, then, has the revival of cognitive studies come to pass? In roughly chronological order of their appearance, the three influential factors are (1) Piaget's work on cognitive development; (2) the linguistic theorizing of Noam Chomsky; and (3) the possibilities opened up by computer technology in the field known as artificial intelligence. Let us examine each of these in turn.

Piaget's Work on Cognitive Development. The extent of American psychology's commitment to a behaviorist paradigm can be seen in the fact that not until 1969 did the American Psychological Association present its Distinguished Scientific Contribution Award to someone who represented an entirely different tradition. He was a European whose continental reputation had been established as far back as the 1920s with his first five books on children's cognitive development. That person was Jean Piaget (1896–1980), whose ideas continue even after his death to stimulate a tradition of research and theory that is a challenge to conservative behaviorism. For Piaget rejected the behaviorist contention that the laws of learning (by which is meant respondent and operant conditioning only) are the same for all ages, taking pains to demonstrate how modes of thinking *change* from one developmental stage to the next, particularly in children and adolescents.

Piaget's view of cognition was influenced by both neo-Kantian and neo-Darwinian ideas, yielding what one writer has called a kind of "evolutionary rationalism."[7] Beginning his intellectual career as a biologist studying the structural adaptations of mollusks, Piaget was at the same time much drawn to Henri Bergson's theory of "creative evolution," according to which species changes occur not just by random, quantum-jump mutations (as Darwin had maintained) but also through active processes initiated by individual organisms in the process of coping with the environment.[8] According to Bergson, the source of this active capacity for self-change was a divine *élan original,* and as the young Piaget struggled to reconcile his Reformed Protestant upbringing with the materialist assumptions of current biology,

7. Joseph F. Rychlak, *Introduction to Personality and Psychotherapy,* 2nd ed. (Boston: Houghton Mifflin, 1981), chap. 11.
8. Bergson, *Creative Evolution,* trans. Arthur Mitchell (London: Macmillan, 1911).

Bergson seemed the ideal compromise. As Piaget later wrote of this period in his youth,

> I recall one evening of profound revelation. The identification of God with life itself was an idea that stirred me almost to ecstasy because it now enabled me to see in biology the explanation of all things and of the mind itself. . . . The problem of knowing (properly called the epistemological problem) suddenly appeared to me in an entirely new perspective and as an absorbing topic of study. It made me decide to consecrate my life to the biological explanation of knowledge.[9]

However heterodox it might seem compared with biblical theism, Piaget's metaphysical vision was in many ways to sustain him through more than six decades of productive work, thus reinforcing Thomas Kuhn's insistence on the importance of a scientist's "ideas about the order of nature" to his or her research.

In Piaget's case, however, this biological orientation was augmented by a second interest in cognitive theory that was sparked while he pursued his doctoral research on mollusks. One of his professors, the logician A. Reymond, was interested in both psychology and the philosophy of science, and taught that "logic stems from a sort of spontaneous organization of acts."[10] That same phrase might be used to summarize Piaget's theory on cognitive development: our increasingly sophisticated and abstract knowledge of the world begins in—but gradually and increasingly transcends—the biologically innate, reflex actions with which we begin postnatal life. Moreover, just as the mollusk's structural adaptations to the stream are conditioned by the physical environment yet grapple with it in an active and not totally predetermined way, so human thought processes are a never-ending "equilibration" between deference to environmental givens ("accommodation" in Piaget's terms) and the creative imposition of our *own* progressively changing thought processes upon that reality—what Piaget called "assimilation."

While such a reading of cognitive development clearly allows for the possibility of individual differences in ways of conceptualizing reality, Piaget maintained that human beings' shared biological heritage, coupled with their common subjection to a set of universal

---

9. Piaget, "Autobiography," in Richard I. Evans, *Jean Piaget: The Man and His Ideas*, trans. Eleanor Duckworth (New York: Dutton, 1973), p. 11.
10. Piaget, "Autobiography," p. 113.

physical laws, results in stages of cognitive development demonstrably similar in all persons. Cognitive growth begins with the "sensorimotor" period of infancy, during which children gradually learn both the capacities and the limitations of their sense organs and motor equipment, then proceeds to what Piaget called the "preoperational" period—a stage remarkable for its linguistic achievements but, to Piaget, just as remarkable for its evidence of undeveloped logic in the child. Unable to distinguish between superficially changed appearances and deep-seated consistencies, the preoperational child thinks that a tall, skinny glass holds more juice than a squat mug, even though both contain exactly eight ounces. He or she also finds it difficult to maintain consistent classification rules in a sorting task, or to understand that "All dogs are animals" does not imply that "All animals are dogs." While these logical confusions disappear in the following stage, even then children still find it difficult to use their newfound logical skills in abstract or symbolic form. They can, however, do quite well if the logical task is embodied in concrete examples and materials (such as actual containers of juice or pictures of animals)—hence Piaget's application of the term "concrete operational" to describe this stage of cognitive development. But it is only during adolescence or later in industrialized nations (and sometimes not at all among preliterate peoples) that full-blown "formal operational" thinking appears, and with it the capacity to reason abstractly, test hypotheses systematically, and argue according to a consistent set of logical rules in the manner required by scientific thought.[11]

To summarize Piaget in a slightly different way, we might say that neurological development interacting with common environmental experiences results in adult persons who possess common notions of inclusion, space, time, causality, and other cognitive "operations." Although such a theory bears some resemblance to Kant's doctrine of a priori organizations of thought, to Piaget these operations were not strictly a priori, since they depend for their emergence on the properly paced interaction of persons with their physical and social environment from birth through adulthood. It was Piaget's painstaking dem-

11. For a good introduction to Piagetian theory and research, see John L. Phillips, Jr., *The Origins of Intellect: Piaget's Theory*, 2nd ed. (San Francisco: W. H. Freeman, 1975); or Herbert Ginsburg and Sylvia Opper, *Piaget's Theory of Intellectual Development: An Introduction* (Englewood Cliffs, N.J.: Prentice-Hall, 1969).

onstration of this developmental process with hundreds of children (including his own) that eventually won him great acclaim from empiricist-oriented American psychologists, even though his observational methods did not include the particular blend of control, quantification, and laboratory experimentation so long regarded as normative in American psychology. To this day a host of neo-Piagetians on both sides of the Atlantic keep alive his tradition of research and theorizing, and many have become key figures in the current revival of cognitive studies. [12]

The Emergence of Psycholinguistics. Piaget, we have noted, was a rationalist to the extent that he saw the human mind as "preprogrammed" to interact with the environment according to a universal set of developmental stages leading to a uniform type of adult rationality. Such an analysis is quite at odds with classical behaviorist learning theory, which tries to explain all types of learning by appealing to simple association, reinforcement, or imitation. According to behavioral principles, persons of whatever age learn to emit socially approved responses (such as "7 + 2 = 9") because they have experienced the pairing of these elements so often, and/or because they have been selectively rewarded for the approved response, and/or because they have observed valued role-models doing likewise. Besides reducing all cognitive accomplishments to unreflective associative processes, such an analysis also tends to relativize them: it sees no necessary human universals in thought or language but only the results of shifting patterns of reinforcement, themselves merely the product of the survival contingencies of a given environment.

Piaget's insistence on the developmental character of human logic represents one rebellion against behaviorist reductionism. The psycholinguistic work inspired by Noam Chomsky, to which we now turn, represents yet another. Chomsky (born in 1928 in Philadelphia) was the child of a Hebrew language scholar whose work in the area of historical linguistics led his son to consider linguistics as a professional career. At the time of Chomsky's formal training, however, linguists seemed more concerned to catalogue the ways in which

---

12. See, for example, Jerome S. Bruner, Robert Oliver, and Patricia Greenfield, *Studies in Cognitive Growth* (New York: John Wiley, 1966); David Elkind and John H. Flavell, eds., *Studies in Cognitive Development* (New York: Oxford University Press, 1969); Jerome S. Bruner, *Beyond the Information Given* (New York: Norton, 1973); and John W. Berry and Pierre R. Dasen, *Culture and Cognition* (London: Methuen, 1974).

languages *differ* than to discover what they have in common. Moreover, the favored model of language acquisition was a behavioral one, according to which children learn to emit words for which they have been arbitrarily reinforced or which they have consistently heard from their elders. A similarly behavioral analysis was invoked to explain the grammatical character of sentences. According to the left-to-right probabilistic model, called the Markov model, the occurrence of each word in a sentence is determined by the immediately preceding word or series of words, each unit serving as the stimulus for the next in a way determined by past serial associations.

As far back as 1951, however, certain prominent psychologists were becoming uneasy with this simple "chain model" of language. In particular, the neuropsychologist Karl Lashley, whom we discussed in Chapter Six, argued that both language production and language comprehension depend on knowledge of "a generalized pattern" that the person holds in his or her head throughout the entire sentence and that is "imposed on the specific acts as they occur."[13] But it was the publication of Chomsky's *Syntactic Structures* in 1957 that both revolutionized linguistics and gave birth to the subarea of psychology now known as psycholinguistics.[14]

In *Syntactic Structures* Chomsky develops a number of cogent arguments against the behavioral model of language acquisition and production. To begin with, if we learn only those responses for which we are consistently reinforced, how are we to explain the enormous number of unique sentences, never heard before, that even a five-year-old child can generate? Second, if sentence production and comprehension depend on word-to-word serial associations, how is it that we can embed "sentences within sentences" (such as "The book that Mary Van Leeuwen is writing is to be published by Eerdmans"), keeping the connection between subject and main verb in our heads even though one or more subordinate clauses intervene? Third, the perceived grammaticality of a sentence in no way depends on the frequency with which its component words have previously been experienced together. When we read the first couplet of Lewis Car-

---

13. Lashley, "The Problem of Serial Order in Behavior," in *Cerebral Mechanisms in the Brain*, ed. L. A. Jeffress (New York: John Wiley, 1951).
    14. Chomsky, *Syntactic Structures* (The Hague: Mouton, 1957). For a readable introduction to psycholinguistics, see Dan I. Slobin, *Psycholinguistics* (Glenview, Ill.: Scott, Foresman, 1971); and for a more technical treatment, W. Weskel and T. G. Bever, eds., *The Structure and Psychology of Language* (New York: Holt, Rinehart and Winston, 1972).

roll's *Jabberwocky* (" 'Twas brillig, and the slithy toves / Did gyre and gimble in the wabe"), we recognize it as a sentence even though it contains nonsense words that we've never heard before—in fact, we can memorize it more easily because of that. On the other hand, a string of words (e.g., "Goes down here is not large feet are the happy days") can be generated such that adjacent pairs of words all have a high probability of previous occurrence—yet this does not suffice to make it a sentence.[15] Finally, Chomsky appeals to our ability to unravel the meaning of ambiguous sentences as further evidence against the behavioral model. A sentence such as "They are visiting professors" is clearly ambiguous (is it "they" who are visiting the professors, or the professors who are visiting somewhere away from home?). Yet at some preconscious level the reader will automatically appeal to the context of the sentence to decide whether to treat "visiting" either as an adjective (describing the professors) or as part of a verb (describing the action of "they"). This is something that the Markov chain model cannot account for.

All of this has led Chomsky and his followers to conclude that children must be *born* with the neural equipment to infer the principles that underlie the grammatical structure of all languages. It is this innate potential, they contend, that explains the success and speed of language acquisition, the similarities of syntax shared by the world's four-thousand-odd languages, and the fact that we can translate one language into another, even managing to decipher the written records of long-dead languages such as ancient Babylonian. It also helps to explain our apparent possession of what Chomsky called "transformational grammar," a set of implicit but highly consistent rules for rearranging sentence elements—for example, going from present to past tense, from active to passive voice, and from statements to questions. This too is something we seem to learn without formal coaching or item-by-item reinforcement. By middle childhood, for example, we simply "know" that "The cat was chased by the dog" is equivalent to "The dog chased the cat," and we can quickly change from active to passive (or vice versa) sentences we have never heard before.

What sorts of things do self-styled psycholinguists do with this recent explosion of rationalist linguistic theorizing? In brief, they look for ways to test empirically the various Chomskyan hypotheses

15. This example is taken from Slobin, *Psycholinguistics*, p. 9.

about language acquisition, comprehension, and production. One particularly fertile field has been that of developmental psycholinguistics, for although Piaget provided a paradigm for the growth of logical-scientific thinking in children, he was notably uninterested in the nature of the language development that must precede and embed such thinking. Through the recording and analyzing of the utterances of many children from birth on, a set of stages has been identified through which children of all language communities seem to pass en route to fully grammatical speech. One such stage, around the age of two years, is that of the "two-word utterance." This stage (characterized by phrases such as "Stove hot!" and "Allgone milk!") seems to have its own unique rules and predictable regularities. A later and also much-investigated stage is one that is characterized by the "overregularization" of simple past-tense verbs ("I comed," "It breaked," "He goed," and so on). Here too we have utterances that parents never reinforce or role-model, and that seem to indicate that children are acquiring (in this case, temporarily *over*acquiring!) the deep, syntactical rules that govern their language. That such overregularization has been identified in children of many language groups again suggests that both the innate structure and the maturational rate of the human brain may have predisposed the development of a universal grammar that emerges in identifiable stages.[16]

Adult verbal behavior has also been a target of psycholinguistic research. For example, it seems that it is not so much the *length* as the grammatical *complexity* of sentences that places limits on their memorizability: research has shown that adults can easily remember sentences with one or two relative clauses, but that sentences with three or four self-embedded clauses prove much more difficult for them to recall.[17] Transformational grammar theory also predicts that simple, declarative sentences (e.g., "The cat ate the fish") will be more easily retained than the same sentences "transformed" by the addition of more and more grammatical "tags"—such as negative constructions, negative passive constructions, and negative, passive, interrogative constructions (e.g., "Has the fish not been eaten by the cat?"). This has been tentatively confirmed by empirical investigations.[18] A third

---

16. See Slobin, *Psycholinguistics*, chap. 3.
17. See George A. Miller and Stephen Isard, "Free Recall of Self-Embedded English Sentences," *Information and Control* 7 (1964): 292–303.
18. See H. B. Savin and E. Perchonock, "Grammatical Structure and the Immediate Recall of English Sentences," *Journal of Verbal Learning and Verbal Behavior* 4 (Oct. 1965): 348–53.

prediction of Chomskyan linguistics is that we cognitively store sentences according to their "deep," or intended, meanings rather than by their superficial syntactical structure. This too has been empirically tested: persons who listen to a passage of prose and who are later exposed to modified, single sentences from the same passage can easily spot subtle changes of *meaning* that have been introduced, but they have a harder time detecting changes of mere syntax (e.g., from active to passive) that leave the original meaning intact.[19]

These are a few of the many types of cognitive research inspired by Chomsky's linguistic theories. More strongly nativist in his rationalism than Piaget, Chomsky has made what seems to be a strong case for certain innate linguistic capacities in human beings. Does the cybernetic revolution that has led to studies of "artificial intelligence" in computers support or debunk this conclusion regarding the uniqueness of human cognition? Let us turn to this final contribution to cognitive science to find out.

Human Cognition and Artificial Intelligence. Ulrich Neisser, a contemporary cognitive psychologist at Cornell, has remarked that the advent of the computer more than anything else has been responsible for the reemergence of cognitive studies. It is largely due to the computer revolution, he suggests, that "technical journals once top-heavy with articles on animal behavior are now filled with reports [on] perception, memory, attention, pattern recognition, problem-solving, the psychology of language, cognitive development, and a host of other problems that had lain dormant for half a century."[20] There seem to be two reasons behind the influence of which Neisser is speaking. First of all, as even the layperson with a home computer appreciates, computers enable researchers to conduct experiments more easily and to analyze large and complex bodies of data quickly and more exhaustively. They are therefore ideal helpmates for dealing with the multifaceted theories and sets of data that are more characteristic of cognitive research than of behavioral research. But more importantly to some cognitive scientists, it has been suggested that the activities of the computer *itself* are similar to human cognitive processes. It is this hypothesized similarity that has led to the develop-

19. Jacqueline S. Sachs, "Recognition Memory for Syntactic and Semantic Aspects of Connected Discourse," *Perception and Psychophysics* 2 (Feb. 1967): 437–42.

20. Neisser, *Cognition and Reality: Principles and Implications of Cognitive Psychology* (San Francisco: W. H. Freeman, 1976), p. 5.

ment of the field known as artificial intelligence, often abbreviated simply as AI.

Computers receive information, manipulate symbols, store things in a so-called "memory," retrieve them as needed, classify inputs, recognize patterns, and perform a host of other functions that people do, accomplishing many of them with much greater speed and reliability. To some cognitive scientists the question about whether computers do these things in the same *manner* as people is less important than the fact that they do them at all. The existence of computers has simply served to reassure these scientists, in a discipline so strongly wedded to behavioral models, that cognitive activities are real. But to others, computer processes either *are like* mental processes or *are themselves* mental processes, depending on whether one has espoused a "weak AI" or a "strong AI" position. It will be instructive to look at each of these positions briefly.[21]

According to the weak AI position, the computer is at the very least an extremely useful tool for the study of the mind. Weak AI theorists do not go so far as to insist that the appropriately programmed computer literally *has* a mind, but they do maintain that if one can simulate one's theoretical *understanding* of certain cognitive processes on a computer, then this helps to confirm the correctness of such a theory. Indeed, some go as far as to suggest that in the future all psychological theories will be written in the form of computer programs.

An example will best show how this is carried out. At Yale University Roger Schank, a computer scientist, and Robert Abelson, a social psychologist, have been exploring how it is that people understand narrated events.[22] In particular, they note, it is characteristic of human beings that they can often answer questions about such events even though the pertinent information was not explicitly included in the story itself. Suppose that I were to tell you the following story about a recent restaurant experience: "I went to the Hungry Lion last Friday and ordered some stuffed sole. When it arrived, I was very pleased with it, and as I left, I gave the waitress a large tip before

21. "Strong AI" and "weak AI" positions are the terms used by John Searle. See his "Myth of the Computer," *New York Review of Books*, 29 Apr. 1982, pp. 3–6; and also his "Minds, Brains, and Programs," in *The Mind's I: Fantasies and Reflections on Self and Soul*, ed. Douglas R. Hofstadter and Daniel C. Dennett (New York: Basic Books, 1981), pp. 353–73.

22. See Schank and Abelson, *Scripts, Plans, Goals and Understanding: An Inquiry into Human Knowledge Structures* (Hillsdale, N.J.: Lawrence Erlbaum, 1977).

paying my bill at the cashier's desk." If I then asked you the question "Did I eat the sole?" you would undoubtedly answer "yes," even though nothing has actually been said about my eating the fish. The reason for this is that, as members of a culture in which eating out is commonplace, we have gradually acquired a set of "understandings" about restaurant behavior and norms that allow us to infer certain events from certain others.

Schank and Abelson have programmed their computer to be able to answer similar questions based on implicitly held information; They have focused on what they call "restaurant scripts." This requires very complex programming indeed, much more so than an earlier (and also much-discussed) question-answering program known as DOCTOR. That earlier program, created by Joseph Weizenbaum of M.I.T., was designed to simulate the responses of a nondirective, Rogerian psychotherapist talking to a client.[23] But it did so by being programmed to react in stereotypical fashion to key aspects of sentences typed into its memory bank. Thus, for example, any submitted sentence that ended in a question mark automatically produced the typed reply "Why do you ask?" Any submitted sentence containing the phrase "I might" (as in "I might be suffering from depression") automatically triggered the reply "Why aren't you sure?" But Schank and Abelson's SAM program (short for "Script Applier Mechanism") must do much more than react to key phrases, word pairs, and punctuation marks. It must have built into its memory information about typical restaurant scenarios upon which it draws according to specified rules.

Schank and Abelson's "conceptual dependency theory" leads them to view restaurant (and other) scripts as gigantic causal chains: each action within the script must be completed satisfactorily before the next can be carried out. It is these causal chains and their preconditions for a variety of different restaurant settings that are built into the SAM program in such a way that ordinary English-language questions can be entered, their implicit as well as their surface content recorded and compared to the memory bank's holdings, and a retranslated English answer correctly given back. Figure 8.1 is a "sketch" of one type of restaurant script that Schank and Abelson have drawn up using their shorthand terms to represent various aspects of their theory. This is not the computer program per se but a kind of conceptual

23. See Weizenbaum, *Computer Power and Human Reason: From Judgment to Calculation* (San Francisco: W. H. Freeman, 1976).

Figure 8.1. An Example of a Schank & Abelson "Restaurant Script" (from Schank and Abelson, *Scripts, Plans, Goals and Understanding* [Hillsdale, N.J.: Lawrence Erlbaum, 1977], pp. 43–44).

Script: RESTAURANT
Track: Coffee Shop
Props: Tables
     Menu
     F-Food
     Check
     Money

Roles: S-Customer
     W-Waiter
     C-Cook
     M-Cashier
     O-Owner

Entry conditions: S is hungry
     S has money

Results: S has less money
     O has more money
     S is not hungry
     S is pleased (optional)

Scene 1: Entering

S **PTRANS** S into restaurant
S **ATTEND** eyes to tables
S **MBUILD** where to sit
S **PTRANS** S to table
S **MOVE** S to sitting position

Scene 2: Ordering

(menu on table)   (W brings menu)   (S asks for menu)
S **PTRANS** menu to S

                                    S **MTRANS** signal to W
                                    W **PTRANS** W to table
                                    S **MTRANS** 'need menu' to W
                                    W **PTRANS** W to menu

                 W **PTRANS** W to table
                 W **ATRANS** menu to S

            S **MTRANS** food list to CP(S)
          ·S **MBUILD** choice of F
            S **MTRANS** signal to W
            W **PTRANS** W to table
            S **MTRANS** 'I want F' to W

                 W **PTRANS** W to C
                 W **MTRANS** (ATRANS F) to C

C **MTRANS** 'no F' to W
W **PTRANS** W to S

                         C **DO** (prepare F script)
                         to Scene 3

W **MTRANS** 'no F' to S
(go back to *) or
(go to Scene 4 at no pay path)

Scene 3: Eating

C **ATRANS** F to W
W **ATRANS** F to S
S **INGEST** F
(Optionally return to Scene 2 to order more;
otherwise go to Scene 4)

Scene 4: Exiting

      S **MTRANS** to W
        (W **ATRANS** check to S)
    W **MOVE** (write check)
    W **PTRANS** W to S
    W **ATRANS** check to S
    S **ATRANS** tip to W
    S **PTRANS** S to M
    S **ATRANS** money to M
(no pay path): S **PTRANS** S to out of restaurant

---

precursor to it in the form of a flow diagram; nevertheless, it will suffice to give the reader an idea about how SAM eventually carries out its task of analyzing stories.[24]

What does such an exercise, if successful, tell us about human cognition? According to what we have labeled the weak AI position, it is this: because the computer cannot do anything it is not programmed to do, it cannot "model" human processes unless they are broken down and reconceptualized in exhaustive detail. Thus, by having to think out in painstaking detail the cognitive process they are trying to simulate, AI researchers hope to learn more about them. As Schank and Abelson explain it,

> Whenever an AI researcher feels he understands the process he is theorizing about in enough detail, he then begins to program it to find out where he was incomplete or wrong. It is the rare researcher who can detail a theory, program it, and have the program work right away. The time between the completion of the theory and the

24. An actual example of a computer run of SAM is included in Schank and Abelson, *Scripts*, pp. 190–204.

completion of the program that embodies the theory is usually extremely long. In modelling such complex processes as comprehension of language, there are more things to keep track of than a human trying to be conscious of each variable can manage. Understanding at such a level of complexity is a relatively subconscious process in everyday life.

What AI has to contribute to psychology is exactly this experience with modelling processes. An AI researcher asks what the input is and what the output is for every subprocess he deals with. In asking these questions he recognizes, at the very least, the nature and number of the subprocesses that must make up the entire process he wishes to model.[25]

Computer modeling of cognitive processes, then, forces the AI researcher to make explicit much that the mind normally carries out with only partial awareness. (There is an old adage to the effect that you don't understand something until you have successfully taught it to someone else; now it is held that you don't understand it until you've been able to program it into a computer!) Whether this exercise in explicitness and its subsequent computer simulation really mirror the processes of our minds in attending to, say, restaurant stories is quite another question. But weak AI theorists believe that at the very least such computer simulations can help to enrich as well as to test theories of cognitive processes.

How does the strong AI position differ from the position we have just described? One of its most provocative expressions can be found in *The Mind's I,* a book of readings and reflections assembled by computer scientist Douglas Hofstadter and philosopher Daniel Dennett.[26] In its most extreme form (to which these two scholars adhere), strong AI theory is characterized by three propositions. First, it holds that the human mind is simply a very complex digital-computer program. In other words, strong AI adherents see mental states simply as computer states and all mental processes as computational in nature. Note that it is the program and not its embodiment in the computer per se that is crucial: according to strong AI theory, *any* system able to work with an appropriate program would be capable of

25. Schank and Abelson, *Scripts,* p. 20.
26. See note 21. In cognitive psychology the most forceful expression of the strong AI position comes from Allen Newell and Herbert Simon. See their *Human Problem Solving* (Englewood Cliffs, N.J.: Prentice-Hall, 1972); and also Simon's *The Sciences of the Artificial,* 2nd ed. (Cambridge, Mass.: M.I.T. Press, 1981).

mental states in the same way that we are. Second, the strong AI position sees neurophysiology as largely irrelevant to an understanding of the mind. In this view the mind is an abstraction, and human brains are only one of its many possible embodiments; any other "computer" with the right program, or "software," would have a mind too. Thus Hofstadter and Dennett speak of "the emerging view of the mind as software or program—as an abstract sort of thing whose identity is independent of any particular physical embodiment."[27]

Third, strong AI proponents appeal to what is known as the "Turing test" as the most adequate criterion for labeling a system truly "intelligent" in the human sense of that word. In the 1950s computer scientist Alan Turing proposed that if a human being could interact with another entity in such a way as to be unable to distinguish it from another human being, then that entity should be labeled intelligent.[28] Weizenbaum's DOCTOR program is often cited as the most dramatic example of an artificial entity that has "passed" the Turing test: after people type their questions into the computer so programmed and get its nondirective replies, some actually begin to take its responses seriously, become emotionally attached to it, and insist that it really did "understand" them. Several psychologists even added DOCTOR to their counseling resources. What had been intended partly as a parody and partly as an early attempt at text-analysis programming had begun to take on a life of its own. For the Turing test proposes in essence that "if a system can convince a competent expert that it has mental states, then it really has those mental states."[29]

But DOCTOR notwithstanding, it needs to be understood that most of the material cited by strong AI adherents runs far ahead of actual AI accomplishments. Despite their own academic comments, Hofstadter and Dennett's volume is top-heavy with "thought experiments," extracts from science-fiction writings, and appeals to a kind of technology-based mysticism. We are asked, for example, to imagine having our bodies dismantled in space and their complete blueprints electronically transmitted to earth, "where a receiver, its reservoirs well-stocked with the requisite atoms, will almost instantly produce, from the beamed instructions—you!" Or we are asked to

27. Hofstadter and Dennett, The Mind's I, p. 15.
28. Turing, "Computer Machinery and Intelligence," excerpted in Hofstadter and Dennett, The Mind's I, pp. 53–68.
29. Searle, "The Myth of the Computer," p. 5.

envisage a time when we will annually have "tapes" made of our minds, preparing us for the possibility that brain damage might require their implantation to restore us to our former selves.[30] The use of such visionary scenarios does not in itself invalidate the strong AI position. Indeed, I have already stressed more than once how important the role of imagination is in facilitating eventual scientific breakthroughs. It does mean, however, that any evaluation of strong AI claims cannot be made on the assumption that computer simulation accomplishments are anywhere near what is described in such imaginative exercises.

SOME CRUCIAL QUESTIONS

What is the common denominator behind the current interest in cognitive development, psycholinguistics, and artificial intelligence? Obviously it is the age-old question regarding the nature and uniqueness of human thought processes. Most Christian readers will sense that each of the above areas of study has potentially great significance for the task of elaborating our biblical understanding of the person. Knowing that we have been created to have accountable dominion over the earth, Christians have traditionally assumed that thinking must be a crucial feature of the *imago Dei*. Affirming with Paul that God has created a unified human race from a common ancestral strain, (Acts 17:26), we feel instinctively drawn to Chomsky's conclusion that the basic neural equipment for language production and comprehension seems to be innately similar in all people. The confusion of Babel was not absolute: that we can and do learn each other's languages according to a common "deep grammar" seems an affirmation not only of human unity but also of God's grace—here is yet another sphere of life where he did not leave us totally isolated in our sin. Moreover, understanding that adults have special responsibilities for children (e.g., Eph. 6:1–4), who in turn are understood to grow only slowly into their own adult responsibilities, many Christians have been attracted to Piaget's analysis of the cognitive stages by which children slowly progress toward fully adult rationality.

On the other hand, with the formalization of artificial intelligence as a field of inquiry, some Christians have begun to feel uneasy. They are alternately impressed and alarmed by the futuristic

30. Hofstadter and Dennett, *The Mind's I*, pp. 3, 243.

scenarios offered by the "artificial intelligentsia" (as the AI community is often called) on the basis of their actual or projected research. In the words of Allen Emerson, a Christian mathematician, and Cheryl Forbes, a Christian journalist,

> The union between man—the old Adam—and an artificial intelligence creates a new Adam, a whole whose sum is greater than its parts. What we have is a creature not made by God in his image, but made by us in our image. We will stand to this creation as God stands to us. At the same time, the machine mind will in certain ways far surpass our own—even surpass those minds that originally created it. It would be like having the ability to surpass God, which, of course, is what we have been trying to acquire since the Garden of Eden.[31]

These writers seem to be troubled by two possibilities they see implied in the AI phenomenon. First, they wonder whether the emergence of "intelligent machines" might in some way threaten our own unique status as God's agents, however finite and sinful we may be. Second, they wonder whether the mere *attempt* to create such machines "in our own image" may be trespassing the creative limits God has imposed on us as mere human beings. AI, it seems, may either reduce us or tempt us to self-deification.

These are understandable questions that I have found myself wondering about also. However, on reflection, it seems to me that both of them are somewhat premature. In my estimation it is more important for Christians to understand just how *little* agreement there is among psychologists concerning the nature of *human* intelligence and, this being the case, how presumptuous it is to talk about an "artificial" approximation to something the "real" nature of which is so disputed. So let us consider just what various psychologists mean when they do talk about human intelligence, and compare this to what Scripture means when it speaks about something both related and different—namely, *wisdom* (and Scripture has much more to say about wisdom than about intelligence). Then we may be prepared to return to the question that Emerson and Forbes have posed about artificial intelligence and that I asked earlier concerning cognitive science generally: How, in this fast-growing area of psychology, do

---

31. Emerson and Forbes, "Living in a World with Thinking Machines," *Christianity Today*, 3 Feb. 1984, p. 14.

Christians walk the fine line between reductionism and self-deification?

HUMAN INTELLIGENCE: A DISPUTED PHENOMENON

"The short answer to the question, 'What is intelligence?' is that we are just not sure!"[32] So begins one introductory text on the topic of human intelligence. A second, more technical review of the topic is no more confident, admitting at the outset that "the concept of intelligence has never had a recognized position among the systematic constructs in any comprehensive psychological theory."[33] None of this theoretical uncertainty, however, has prevented the growth of a huge intelligence-testing industry or the attempt to explain intelligence by continuous, post hoc analyses of myriads of such test results. How can this be? How is it that psychologists claim to be able to "measure" something with an essential nature on which they are either unclear or profoundly divided?

Part of the answer lies in the history of the intelligence-testing movement itself, and part in the philosophy of science that has surrounded it from its early years. A century ago in Great Britain, Francis Galton based the first tests of "intellectual strength" on purely sensory measures such as visual acuity, color discrimination, breathing power, and force of handgrip. His assumption was that since all we know comes to us via the senses, good senses must mean good intellect. But whatever we *don't* know about intelligence a century later, we at least do know that Galton was wrong on this score: colloquially expressed, brains and brawn do not reliably go together!

In contrast to Galton, Alfred Binet, working in turn-of-the-century France, adopted a largely atheoretical, pragmatic approach to the problem of intelligence. His mandate from the government was to find a way to spot that minority of children unable to profit from regular schooling. To do this he did not need to have a developed theory of intelligence; he needed only to find out what, in fact, the majority of children *could* do at a variety of age levels and then devise

---

32. David W. Pyle, *Intelligence: An Introduction* (London: Routledge and Kegan Paul, 1979), p. 1.
33. J. P. Guilford, "Theories of Intelligence," in *Handbook of General Psychology*, ed. Benjamin B. Wolman (Englewood Cliffs, N.J.: Prentice-Hall, 1973), p. 630.

a way of sampling it efficiently and accurately. Thus he devised, by guess and intuition, a series of "stunts" (as he called them) to present to a large sample of Paris schoolchildren. Whenever he found a stunt, or question, that about seventy-five percent of a given age group could pass, he retained it as an item that could determine "normal ability" for that age, provided that performance on that item also correlated well with the children's actual progress in school. In none of this did Binet claim to be answering the question "What is intelligence?" His test items were merely a set of age-graded, trial-and-error derived tasks, performance on which correlated well with children's progress through the Paris school system.[34]

Binet's evasion of the problem fit in well with the *operationist* philosophy of science that dominated psychology in the first half of the twentieth century. Operationism holds that a phenomenon can be defined merely in terms of the scientific operations used to investigate it, with little or no recourse to its theoretical underpinnings. Thus Lewis Terman, an early American psychologist, defended the thesis that one could measure intelligence before knowing what it was, just as physicists had measured electricity before knowing about its fundamental nature. Edwin G. Boring concurred: intelligence, he asserted, "must be defined simply as the capacity to do well in an intelligence test."[35]

What, then, do we know about intelligence tests after close to a century of their routine use in the Western world? We know that their scores seem to break down into "clusters" of items that "hang together" in the sense that a score on one item tends to be predictive of a score on other items in the cluster. Thus a person doing well on verbal comprehension items also tends to score well on word fluency, analogues, and sentence memory: all of these items, and others, contribute to what is labeled a "verbal intelligence" score. Persons who do well at jigsaw-puzzle items also tend to do well at block-design tasks, or recognizing figures in various orientations—a so-called "performance" or "spatial-mathematical" cluster. We also know that I.Q. scores are good predictors of school and college success (or lack of it), but that they are not particularly good predictors of final success or prominence in the adult work world.

34. See also Mary Stewart Van Leeuwen, "I.Q.ism and the Just Society," *Journal of the American Scientific Affiliation* 34 (Dec. 1982): 193–200.
35. Boring, "Intelligence as the Tests Measure It," *New Republic*, 6 June 1923, p. 35.

Nor are they, at any developmental stage, good for spotting creativity of either an artistic or intellectual sort, since the test items are designed to elicit a single, correct answer ("convergent thinking") as opposed to encouraging the unrestricted range of associations ("divergent thinking") that seems to be a feature of creative intelligence.[36] Finally, the tests themselves are, quite bluntly, ethnocentric. Because the tests were standardized using samples of only white, native-born Americans or Europeans, when they are administered to a non-native or nonwhite person, the resulting score represents only how well that person has performed relative to a norm that, when originally set, never took his or her cultural group into account.[37]

What, then, do intelligence-test scores really tell us? I believe that Jerome Kagan expressed it best when he said that "they tell us the extent to which a person has become familiar with the vocabulary, the preferred thinking styles, and the current intellectual problems of western, middle-class society."[38] Now this is not unimportant information; indeed, it can be highly useful information even in a non-Western society, provided it is that society's wish to become industrialized after the Western pattern as quickly and as efficiently as possible. But just what *are* these "preferred thinking styles," and how normative are they, both in the statistical and the biblical sense?

To answer this question, let us return briefly to Piaget's work on cognitive development. For as you may recall, Piaget maintained that human beings' shared biological heritage, combined with their exposure to a common physical world, leads to a common pattern of cognitive development everywhere—a pattern culminating in a type of adult thinking that includes the ability to reason abstractly, to test hypotheses systematically, and to argue according to a consistent set of logical rules. Unlike I.Q. tests, the Piagetian "clinical-experimental" approach does not rely on tightly timed, single-answer items. It is, on the contrary, relaxed and open-ended, more akin to playing a

36. For a comprehensive technical introduction, see R. L. Thorndike and E. Hagen, *Measurement and Evaluation in Psychology and Education*, 4th ed. (New York: John Wiley, 1977).
37. See, for example, N. J. Block and Gerald Dworkin, *The I.Q. Controversy* (New York: Random House, 1976); Pyle, *Intelligence*; and Michael Cole and Sylvia Scribner, *Culture and Thought* (New York: John Wiley, 1974).
38. Kagan, as quoted in *The I.Q. Myth*, narr. Dan Rather, CBS Documentary Films, 1975.

game and having an accompanying conversation than to taking a test. Nevertheless, what Piagetians are trying to assess (although they would not assign a numerical score to it) overlaps considerably with the kind of "thinking style" that the designers of I.Q. tests are also taking pains to assess.

Perhaps the best way to understand what is meant by adult, formal operational thought—the typically valued Western thinking style—is to consider a couple of the Piagetian "games" by which this is assessed.[39] In one "game" an older child may be presented with five small beakers, each containing a clear, colorless liquid, and told that some unspecified combination of them will result in a yellow solution. The child is then asked if he or she will try to discover what that combination is by mixing the various solutions together in a sixth, empty beaker. The child who is not fully capable of formal-operational thinking will not approach this problem systematically but merely try combinations of various liquids at random, with no way of accounting for which ones have been tried and eliminated as solutions. The child who is a formal-operational thinker, by contrast, will proceed according to an overall strategy. If the liquids can be called A, B, C, D, and E, he or she will try A + B, then A + C, then A + D, then A + E, and so on until all pairs are exhausted. If none of these double combinations work, the child will experiment with triple combinations just as systematically—A + B + C, A + B + D, A + B + E, B + C + D, B + D + E, and so on—then with all possible combinations of four, and finally (if no yellow solution has yet developed), with all five together.

Here is another example. A child is shown a simple "house" made of 60 one-inch wooden cubes. This roofless house, the dimensions of which are, say $3'' \times 4'' \times 5''$, sits on a $3'' \times 4''$ base called an "island." The child is asked to imagine that the house and island are swept away in a storm, and that a new house, with exactly the same number of "rooms" (i.e., one-inch cubes), must be built on a neighboring island, the dimensions of which (also unlabeled) are $2'' \times 10''$. The child's challenge is to understand that the house made of 60 "rooms," or cubes, can be rebuilt on a $2'' \times 10''$ base and only have to be three stories high. They must, in other words, understand that in

---

39. See, for example, John H. Flavell, *The Developmental Psychology of Jean Piaget* (New York: Van Nostrand, 1963).

terms of volume a 2″ × 10″ × 3″ structure is the same as a 3″ × 4″ × 5″ one.

Here is a final example. A child is asked to sort some randomly ordered pictures of animals into two piles that are "in some way alike." In point of fact, the pictures include various types of dogs plus various other mammals, and the child who is not quite formal-operational can usually sort these two piles easily. But then he or she is asked to consider two abstract questions about the piles, or categories: "If all the dogs in the world were to die, would there be any mammals left?" and "If all the mammals in the world were to die, would there be any dogs left?" In most cases only the child fully capable of formal operational thinking can answer both questions correctly and, more important, know *why* the answers are correct. In effect, the child must apply a kind of self-made symbolic logic and say, in so many words, "Because not all mammals are dogs, there would be some other mammals left if all the dogs died," and conversely, "Because dogs are also mammals, if all the mammals died, then no dogs would be left."

Formal Operational Thought: An Addiction of the Western World. From these examples the reader will have a better sense of what is meant by "intelligence" as it is understood, valued, promoted, and studied in the Western world. Such a concept of intelligence assumes facility of verbal comprehension and production not only in ordinary language modes but also in abstract, symbolic-logic modes. It favors very strongly the capacity to ignore concrete particulars in order to focus on abstract features of a problem situation. It also gives high marks for the capacity to manipulate variables in a controlled and orderly fashion, and for the capacity to mentally reassemble existing structures in new ways that conserve essential features of the original. In terms of I.Q. tests, the faster and more accurately a person does the tasks designed to assess these skills, the higher his or her score will be.

It is largely our recognition and promotion of these formal operational skills (particularly since the scientific and industrial revolutions) that have made our technological society the mixed blessing that it is today. Moreover, it is these capacities—or aspects of them—that are most easily mimicked by today's AI computer programs. Given certain "algorithms," or fixed working procedures, a computer can solve in very short order not only Piaget's five-beaker problem but, indeed, a similar problem involving dozens or hundreds of such beakers. By systematically testing all possible, permissible combinations (and without falling prey to either the mental exhaustion or the memory lapses that plague human beings), appropriately programmed computers win chess games, evaluate logical syllogisms, and even help to calculate the molecular structure of new chemical compounds. Other programs known as "expert systems" circumvent the time and memory space demanded by algorithmic programs by simulating human "heuristic" thinking—that is, by applying broader principles of exploration and rules of thumb such as those developed by highly experienced doctors diagnosing diseases.[40]

Does all this make such machines or their programs "intelligent," even in our limited, Western sense of the word? Nowadays that depends on who is answering the question. According to scholars like Hofstadter and Dennett, the mere application of the highly behavioral Turing test is sufficient to reach a conclusion: if, in interacting with a computer program, human beings can be fooled into thinking that there really *is* another human being "at the other end of the line" (as many people did with Weizenbaum's DOCTOR program), then that program *is* an intelligent entity like ourselves. Others quite rightly insist that such a criterion is a simplistic evasion of the need to explore what is involved in all the complexities of human thought.

Philosopher John Searle compares the use of the Turing test to the following imaginary scenario. Suppose a person who doesn't know Chinese memorizes a rule book for the manipulation of Chinese characters: he or she learns how to focus on certain parts of a presented sequence of characters, how to rearrange them, and how to send back another sequence of characters. These rules say nothing about the meaning of the characters but merely explain how to "compute" them, but because the person applies the rules correctly and sends back what turn out to be intelligible Chinese sentences, the person giving and receiving the sentences can't tell the invisible rule-follower from a native-speaking Chinese. But, says Searle, we who understand the real situation would never say that the person who only applies Chinese character rules mechanistically "understands" Chinese. Neither then, he concludes, are we justified in attributing understanding to computer programs, the Turing test notwithstanding.[41]

40. See Hunt, *The Universe Within;* and also the entire Dec. 1983 issue of *Psychology Today.*
41. Searle, "Minds, Brains, and Programs."

But such disputes about human intelligence and its artificial approximations beg the even larger question to which I have already referred—namely, how justified are we in the excessive honor that we *do* give to formal operational thinking humanly *or* artificially carried out? Is such a thinking style even as universal as we assume it is? And if it is not, is it really the fundamental feature of the *imago Dei* that Christians in the Western world tend unreflectively to assume it is?

To answer the first two questions, we need only look at the cross-cultural evidence that has been assembled in response to Piaget's claims regarding the universal course of cognitive development toward a formal operational endpoint. Piaget's own original research was conducted entirely with European children, and with these subjects the nature of cognitive stages as well as their order and rate of progression accorded obligingly with his theory. This was also the case when later replications of his studies were done with American children. Embarrassments to the theory appeared only when younger Piagetian researchers began to test his theory in non-Western societies. Even with appropriate modifications in test materials and instructions, it gradually became clear that in many cultures almost no adults reach the stage of formal operations, and, indeed, many do not even perform consistently at the concrete operational level usually attained by Western children by about age seven.[42]

Some neo-Piagetians continue to try to salvage a general theory of cognitive development in the midst of these anomalies. One of their motives in doing so is clearly a laudable one: they realize that demonstrating a universal course for cognitive development would be a decisive refutation of any ideology of Western, white, racial superiority. But for Christians there is still another level of discourse to consider: it seems to me that this failure to confirm the universality of our own preferred brand of thinking reopens the entire question regarding the nature of real intelligence as an aspect of the *imago Dei*. Nor are Christians the only persons exercised by questions of this sort. Indeed, to date much *more* reflection on such issues has been done by scholars in another world view tradition—namely, classical Marxists and neo-Marxists associated with the Frankfurt school of critical

42. A good review of cross-cultural Piagetian studies is Pierre R. Dasen, "Cross-Cultural Piagetian Research," *International Journal of Psychology* 3 (Spring 1972): 23–29. Also reprinted in John W. Berry and Pierre R. Dasen, *Culture and Cognition* (London: Methuen, 1974).

theory.[43] Some of their questions are very thought-provoking, even if their preferred solutions are not.

Two critics from this tradition, Susan Buck-Morss and Allan Buss, have suggested that the criterion for cognitive maturity established by Piaget (and, by extension, the intelligence test) is laden with both class and cultural bias.[44] For thinkers in the broadly Marxist tradition, cognitive development is *not* as ahistoric as Piaget claimed it was. Rather, the world and nature come to be understood via cognitive categories that evolve socially, as human needs dialectically interact with changing social and economic realities. Thus particular thinking styles arise from and change through differing, communally human responses to the challenges of survival and production.[45] Such an analysis has the advantage of being able to account for the existence of different styles, whereas Piaget's theory can only chart the course of a cognitive style typical of highly industrialized nations that rely on scientific thinking and its offshoots in technology as a way of understanding and controlling the environment.

Buss further argues that the roots of our attachment to formal operational thinking go back to the progressively increasing desire of human beings to dominate nature. To some extent, he concedes, such an orientation *is* universal and transhistorical in that, at all times and in all places, human beings must struggle to gain a degree of mastery over their physical environment. But, he points out, this human tendency took a quantum leap in the Western world at the time of the Enlightenment and has since reached its pinnacle in the instrumental rationality that characterizes all industrialized nations, be they capitalist *or* communist in ideology. Consequently, it should come as no surprise that Piaget, himself a product of Western, industrialized society, was in many ways afflicted with scientistic tunnelvision. He is on record as stating that the only absolute, knowable

43. See, for example, Jürgen Habermas, *Knowledge and Human Interest* (Boston: Beacon Press, 1971); and Max Horkheimer, *Critical Theory* (New York: Seabury Press, 1972).
44. See Buck-Morss, "Socio-Economic Bias in Piaget's Theory and Its Implications for Cross-Culture Studies," *Human Development* 18 (1975): 35–49; and Buss, "Piaget, Marx, and Buck-Morss on Cognitive Development: A Critique and Reinterpretation," *Human Development* 20 (1977): 118–28.
45. See, for example, A. R. Luria, *Human Brain and Psychological Processes* (New York: Harper and Row, 1966); and L. S. Vygotsky, *Thought and Language* (Cambridge, Mass.: M.I.T. Press, 1962).

truths are those discoverable through the scientific method. Any other kind of thinking—metaphysical, critical, or the like—was to him merely a species of "wisdom . . . the taking up of a vital position . . . which man as a rational being finds essential for co-ordinating his different activities, even if it is not knowledge, properly so-called. For although there can be several wisdoms, there exists only one [scientific] truth."[46] Piagetian and other Western-based theories of intelligence do not adequately describe universal thinking styles; they merely describe the nature and development of a particular style of scientific reasoning dear to the heart of Western man.

Wisdom in Israel—and Elsewhere. What lessons have Christians to learn—or perhaps I should say relearn—from the concerns of the critical theorists that I have just summarized? To begin with, Christians of the Western world must always be on guard against baptizing what may be largely cultural preferences with the seal of orthodox approval. As sojourners, not natives, of the present time-period, we are called to be critical watchers of our society and its institutions, not merely unreflective participants in it. Fortunately, we do have some recent Christian role-models to look to for a biblically based critique of our technological society and the narrowly based concept of intelligence that keeps it running. Jacques Ellul's *Technological Society* is a classic in this regard, as are the writings of the late E. F. Schumacher.[47]

In his best-known work, *Small Is Beautiful*, Schumacher combines his roles as a Christian economist, businessman, and government advisor to launch a series of warnings about the directions in which our nature-mastering priorities are taking us as a culture. He points out (as Ellul does) that although science and technology are the products of human intelligence, they also tend to develop according to their own inherent laws and principles, which are very different from those of humankind and the creation in general. Technology is not inherently self-regulating: it recognizes no self-limiting principles regarding size, speed, or violence. Thus, in its wake human beings become dehumanized adjuncts to machines; the ecosystem groans in

46. Piaget, *Insights and Illusions of Philosophy*, trans. Wolfe Mays (New York: New American Library, 1971), p. xiii.
47. Ellul, *The Technological Society* (New York: Random House, 1964); and Schumacher, *Small Is Beautiful: A Study of Economics As If People Mattered* (London: Abacus Books, 1974), and *A Guide for the Perplexed* (New York: Harper and Row, 1977).

protest as its fragile balance is continually violated; and in our greed for "more, farther, quicker, and richer" our nonrenewable resources face imminent exhaustion.

In terms of power and numbers, those prepared to halt this insane overapplication of Western intelligence are few indeed. For the most part, says Schumacher,

> I see people who think they can cope with our crisis by the methods current, only more so. I call them the people of the forward stampede. . . . Let us admit that [they] have all the best tunes, or at least the most popular and familiar tunes. You cannot stand still, they say; standing still means going down; you must go forward; there is nothing wrong with modern technology except that it is as yet incomplete. . . . There are no insoluble problems. The slogans of the forward stampede burst into the newspaper headlines every day with the message "a breakthrough a day keeps the crisis at bay."[48]

Those few who do plead for a new life-style in the West, who ask to return to the norms within which human beings and the creation were intended to function, Schumacher calls "the home-comers":

> The term "home-comer" has, of course, a religious connotation. For it takes a good deal of courage to say "no" to the fashions and fascinations of the age and to question the presuppositions of a civilization which appears destined to conquer the world; the requisite strength can be derived only from deep convictions. If it were derived from nothing more than fear of the future, it would be likely to disappear at the decisive moment. The genuine "home-comer" does not have the best tunes, but he has the most exalted text, nothing less than the gospels. For him, there could not be a more concise statement of his situation, of *our* situation, than the parable of the prodigal son.[49]

To Schumacher, the beatitudes from the Sermon on the Mount are also suggestive in terms of a redefinition of intelligence and its goals in the West. What the beatitudes mean for us today, he writes, is a realization of the truth that we are *not* demigods but spiritually bankrupt people; that we are *not* emerging into a technological golden age but have much to repent of in sorrow; and that we need to rediscover a gentle touch in our dealings with the human and non-

---

48. Schumacher, *Small Is Beautiful*, pp. 129–30.
49. Schumacher, *Small Is Beautiful*, p. 130.

human creation, to be willing to return to life-styles of a smaller and more humane scale. This means not a wholesale rejection of technology but a refusal to let it develop as if human beings and the creation did not matter or were of only secondary importance to the so-called march of progress.

The New Testament is continuous with the Old in voicing such warnings about the limits of human intelligence. In his book *Wisdom in Israel* Gerhard Von Rad makes much of the fact that proverbial wisdom in the Bible does draw freely on the fruits of common human experience, including even that of Israel's pagan neighbors. Yet, he points out, there is a difference: for again and again these lists of wisdom sayings are interrupted with the reminder that, without the knowledge and fear of God, human intelligence is bound to go awry.[50] Moreover (and this is perhaps the crowning indictment of our worship of formal-operational thought), biblical wisdom constantly stresses that while human beings must be prudent, intelligent, and diligent in observing their world and making use of its resources, their best and most sincerely laid plans are still subject to the sovereign will of God. The sayings of Proverbs are telling in this regard:

The plans of the mind belong to man, but the answer of the tongue is from the Lord. (16:1)

A man's mind plans his way, but the Lord directs his steps. (16:9)

Many are the plans in the mind of a man, but it is the purpose of the Lord that will be established. (19:21)

No wisdom, no understanding, no counsel, can avail against the Lord. The horse is made ready for the day of battle, but the victory belongs to the Lord. (21:30, 31)

We have now seen that cultural critics, both Christian and non-Christian, unite with biblical scholars in warning us about our confidence in and idealization of formal operational thinking styles. To these we can add the voices of that small minority of cross-cultural psychologists who have studied non-Western thinking from a sympathetic perspective. Among the most perceptive of these investigations has been Mallory Wober's work in Uganda. Wober explored not cognitive attainment per se but rather the projective responses of

---

50. See, for example, Prov. 1:7; 2:6; 9:10; 15:33; 16:7–12; also Job 28:28; Ps. 111:10. See also Von Rad, *Wisdom in Israel*, chaps. 4 and 6.

Africans to the very *idea* of intelligence, and compared these to the responses of Westerners.[51] The contrasts that emerged are fairly striking. For Americans "intelligence" conjures up associations of energy, speed, novelty, individuality, and competitive power. For Africans who lead traditional life-styles, almost the opposite picture emerges: intelligence is regarded as slow, careful, and steady; tradition-honoring, not tradition-breaking; and corporately possessed and shared, not individualistic. Even more striking is the finding in another study that as Africans are progressively exposed to Western education, their concept of intelligence becomes more Westernized and their respect for traditional religious beliefs dwindles.[52] But this is so only up to a point, for among the *most* highly educated Africans, there was a marked tendency to *return* to traditional values once more. It is as if, once they had become saturated with the ways of the West, they began to suspect that they were selling their birthright for what might turn out to be a dubious blessing.

These Africans may be more fortunate than most of us in the West, for they at least have a living recollection of life in a society that, while often not Christian, was certainly saturated with a respect for the supernatural. Thus, among such groups it is not only the lack of industrialization that retards formal operational thought, but also the fact that their view of nature as *religiously animated* has placed a brake on their impulses to master nature, and hence on the kind of instrumental rationality that results. And we Christians of the Western world may need to ask a question that many of our missionaries have found themselves posing—namely, just who needs to learn from whom in all of this? In the process of bringing the gospel to non-Western groups, may we not be learning that God in his grace has also spared such groups some of the ravages of our own culture's intensely secular rationalism?

SOME TENTATIVE CONCLUSIONS

We have now examined the character and some of the limitations of the Western world's concept of intelligence, an intellectual style

51. Wober, "Towards an Understanding of the Kiganda Concept of Intelligence," in *Culture and Cognition*, pp. 261–80.
52. See Gustav Jahoda, "Supernatural Beliefs and Changing Cognitive Structures Among Ghanaian University Students," *Journal of Cross-Cultural Psychology* 1 (June 1970): 115–30.

heavily prejudiced in favor of what Piaget called adult, formal operational thought. In passing we have also noted that some aspects of formal operational thought can be programmed into digital computers with relative ease, an accomplishment that makes many people wonder if human intelligence is really so special after all. In light of these explorations, we now return to the question with which we began the chapter: How can Christians in psychology welcome the cognitive revival and its rejection of behaviorist reductionism while avoiding two other mistakes just as serious as that reductionism: first, the mistake of attributing too *much* to human cognition as an aspect of the *imago Dei,* and second, the mistake of attributing too *little* to it in light of the accumulating feats of artificial intelligence?

Setting aside for the moment the question of the normativeness of formal operational thought, let us first evaluate the challenge of the AI "revolution." I have already noted that it is a matter of hot debate among philosophers and AI researchers as to whether the Turing test is an adequate test of the presence of a real mind, or real understanding, in a computer program. Like John Searle (of the "Chinese characters" scenario), I am convinced that it is not. Moreover, I agree with Searle that it may be largely due to the computer's relative rarity (up until now) that it has acquired its mystique and accrued such fantastic speculation about its potential powers. "As computers and robots become more common," writes Searle, "as common as telephones, washing machines, and forklift trucks, it seems likely that this aura will disappear and people will take computers for what they are—namely, useful machines."[53] He may well be right; it will be difficult to continue agonizing metaphysically about something that now promises to become as much a part of the household scene as a toaster or a typewriter.

In addition, members of the AI community have stressed that although they can program computers to perform prodigious formal operational feats, the more routine and "simple" cognitive operations that *precede* such adult thinking are extraordinarily elusive. Computerized robots can play chess, manipulate abstract logical symbols, and chase down tax evaders; but they are still notoriously poor at perceptual pattern-matching, processing natural language, and climbing stairs—things that even a three-year-old does with tremendous versatility.[54] "Why were we able to make AI programs do such grown-up

53. Searle, "The Myth of the Computer," p. 6.
54. See Hunt, *The Universe Within,* and the articles of the various contributors to the Dec. 1983 issue of *Psychology Today.*

things before we could make them do childish things?" ask AI specialist Marvin Minsky. "Perhaps it is because adult or expert thinking is often somehow simpler than a child's commonsense!"[55] As AI researchers are discovering, there is a great deal going on in terms of perception, comprehension, and execution when a toddler responds to the request to "Put away your building blocks!"—so much so that common sense now appears to be more complex and not so "common" (in the sense of "unimportant") after all.

On the other hand, it has become routine even among the AI laity to talk about computers in an anthropomorphic way, as if they *did* share our commonsense understanding. Most of us can recall an occasion when we had an unsatisfying interaction with the local automatic bank-teller and found ourselves saying things like "It doesn't want to give me the money because it doesn't understand that my paycheck has been deposited." True, the use of such language may be only a species of shorthand, a way of rendering the machine more "user-friendly," or (in colloquial language) understandable. But again, we must guard against being seduced by yet another of our own metaphors. Such talk may all too easily persuade us either to limit our norms for human intelligence to "whatever the machines can do" (recall that it used to be "whatever I.Q. tests measure") or, conversely, to fool ourselves into thinking that interaction with machines is a potentially adequate substitute for true human communication.

This, I think, leads us back to the heart of the matter. I submit that the computer revolution is not nearly so revolutionary as we are being told to believe it is. On the contrary, it is merely the most recent step in a process that the Western world committed itself to decades—even centuries—ago. Since the time of the Enlightenment the Western world has more than eagerly traveled the twin roads of technologization and secularization. Emerging from both of these, and now enshrined as the Western norm for "intelligence," is a species of thinking that is rationalistic, individualistic, materialistic (in both senses of the word), and power-oriented. Thus the fundamental question is *not* whether machines will take over our formal operational thinking but whether formal operational thinking as we have understood it and deified it is really the kind of thinking we should be aspiring to as exclusively as we do.

What the Old Testament praises as "wisdom" has two primary

55. Minsky, as quoted in Patrick Huyghe, "Of Two Minds," *Psychology Today* 17 (Dec. 1983): 34.

themes, we have discovered: the first is the fear of the Lord; the second is a recognition of our own limitations under his sovereignty. The "fool" of the Proverbs is not the person whom we would call mentally retarded (a frequent modern application of the term), but rather the person (or society) of *whatever* mental endowments who refuses to recognize creational norms and personal limits. By this criterion the mentally handicapped adult who lovingly and carefully tends a garden or sweeps a floor is wiser, and less of a fool, than the scientist who helps design an atomic bomb with no regard for its possible future use. Schumacher is right when he suggests that we cannot divorce our theories of human intelligence from our convictions about what is normal, in the moral sense, for all of life—for the creation, for individual persons, and for interpersonal relations of every sort.

Perhaps it is here that Christians can make a modest start on their own "cognitive revival." Rather than begging the question about the importance of formal operational thought, as we are prone to do with the rest of our society, perhaps we need to identify and help to facilitate life-styles and cognitive styles more in keeping with the home-comers' priorities of which Schumacher wrote. And we need to return to Scripture and try to understand better just what is involved in the kind of intelligence that is the *true* expression of the *imago Dei*. Until then, as Schumacher reminds us, we are identifying ourselves not with the biblically wise home-comers but with the people of the forward stampede, who may be the real "fools" in the biblical sense of the word.

In so rethinking the received view of intelligence, Christians will have the support of an articulate and growing minority within psychology itself. For example, Robert Zajonc (who shares with Piaget the distinction of having received the APA's Distinguished Scientific Contribution Award) has recently argued that emotional (including value) judgments are largely independent of and often prior to cognitive operations. Cognitive psychologists of an information-theory orientation have long worked on the assumption that, in Zajonc's words, "affect is post-cognitive."[56] They have assumed, in other words, that feelings of like or dislike, anger, shame, surprise, and guilt are produced in persons only *after* certain cognitive processes discrim-

56. Zajonc, "Feeling and Thinking: Preferences Need No Inferences," *American Psychologist* 35 (Feb. 1980): 151.

inate, identify, and weigh the features of a situation. Thus, if the error of behaviorism was the reduction of thought to motor activity, the error of information theory, says Zajonc, has been the reduction of emotions and value judgments to epiphenomena of cognition.

But there is accumulating evidence that it has been a mistake to regard feeling and valuing in this secondary way. For although our emotions affect our conscious thinking and vice versa, it now appears that each is mediated by a different hemisphere of the brain. Moreover, while less articulate and more global in its functioning than the left hemisphere, the right hemisphere (which processes affect much more than cognition) may be both more efficient *and* no less accurate than the left in perceiving relevant aspects of a stimulus situation.[57] Formal operational thought (which is largely left-brain) is in many ways very exhausting: we can note that champion chess-players often lose several pounds of body weight during a tournament despite being well-fed and almost totally sedentary throughout. In this respect at least, it may be a blessing that we can now turn over to computers many of the most wearying aspects of analytic thought. But if our *left* brains are thus to be less taxed and perhaps less valued than they have been in the past, we need to learn much more about the structure and advantages of *right*-hemispheric functioning.

It has been found, for example, that when persons are coached to encode memory items by means of emotional or value associations (which are thought to be mediated primarily by the right hemisphere), these are retrieved more accurately and quickly than when they are categorized according to formal operational "tags"—such as the length of the word or the part of speech it represents. It is also the case that persons are able to make highly accurate inferences about the emotional tone of recorded utterances even when these are in unknown languages, or if in one's own tongue, have had their purely cognitive content obliterated by means of electronic masking, filtering, or random splicing of the tape.[58] By such studies experimental psychologists are beginning to fathom how human beings use their minds in other than formal-operational, left-brain-mediated ways.

I suspect, however, that none of the foregoing will come as a surprise to most clinical and counseling psychologists. As Zajonc

57. For a brief but clear survey of brain-hemispheric theory and research, see Sally P. Springer and Georg Deutsch, *Left Brain, Right Brain* (San Francisco: W. H. Freeman, 1981).
58. See Zajonc, "Feeling and Thinking," for a pertinent bibliography.

himself admits, "The separation of affect and cognition, the dominance and primacy of affective reactions, and their ability to influence responses when ordinary perceptual recognition is at chance level are all very much in the spirit of Freud, the champion of the unconscious."[59] Thus, after close to half a century of neglect in the academic arena, the insights of clinicians into the primacy and complexity of our emotional selves are receiving a renewed hearing. What this portends, I hope, is a progressive closing of the gulf that separates psychology's "two cultures"—on the one hand, that of academic psychology (with its stress on operationalization, control, and probabilistic generalizations), and on the other hand, that of the clinic and the counseling office (with their stress on the individual case-study, the phenomenology of the whole person, and the primacy of affect and values).

Such closure, if it takes place, would bode well not only for a more complete psychology of the person but also, I believe, for a more complete psychology of religious faith. Elsewhere I have analyzed this same "two cultures" phenomenon within the church itself, showing how some Christians instinctively seem to gravitate toward church traditions that are rational, confessional, and homiletic, while others eschew these for churches that are more liturgical, aesthetic, and mystical in their emphases.[60] Yet it is hard for me to believe, either biblically or experientially, that human beings were created to choose either the analytic or the intuitive mode as primary. Both in their day-to-day life as well as in their more specifically faith-expressing activities, persons need to cultivate that wholeness that comes only when the linear, analytic processes of formal operational thought are balanced by the intuitiveness, globality, and vulnerability of feeling.[61] It is precisely in the fostering of such a balance that we may weather the cognitive revival without falling prey to either reductionism or self-deification.

---

59. Zajonc, "Feeling and Thinking," p. 172.

60. Mary Stewart Van Leeuwen, "Cognitive Style, North American Values, and the Body of Christ," *Journal of Psychology and Theology* 2 (Spring 1974): 77–88.

61. See also Robert C. Roberts, *Spirituality and Human Emotion* (Grand Rapids: Eerdmans, 1982).

CHAPTER 9

SOCIAL PSYCHOLOGY:
A Battleground
Between Two Paradigms

Social psychologists want to discover causal relationships so
that they can establish the basic principles that will explain
the phenomena of social psychology.
—Judson Mills[1]

The aim of social psychologists should be to give man more
choices, not to demonstrate how few he actually has.
—Ragnar Rommetveit[2]

By now the reader will be used to the fact that I have frequently
chosen opening quotations for chapters that reflect the existence of
tension or controversy about a given area of psychology. Today we
could say that in most of the areas of psychology this tension is
embodied in a debate about both the nature of human beings and, by
extension, the methods that psychologists should use to study them.
Are human beings largely to be viewed in their material aspects,
passively subject to the forces of their internal and external environments, and therefore best studied through methods and metaphors
borrowed from the natural sciences? Or, on the other hand, are
human minds, however physiologically dependent, so capable of cre-

1. Mills, "The Experimental Method," in *Experimental Social Psychology*, ed. Judson Mills (New York: Macmillan, 1969), p. 412.
2. Rommetveit, as quoted by Lloyd H. Strickland, Frances E. Aboud,
and Kenneth J. Gergen, *Social Psychology in Transition* (New York: Plenum
Press, 1976), p. 7.

ative analysis and reflexive self-scrutiny as to make us more masters than pawns of our environments, and therefore better studied through methods that depart from those of traditional natural science?

Nowhere in present-day psychology are these anthropological and methodological issues more hotly debated than they are among social psychologists. That is why in this chapter I have chosen to treat social psychology as a kind of bridge between the predominant, natural-science traditions of Anglo-American psychology and their lesser-known (but fast-growing) alternatives—what I will call the human-science approaches. I will begin with a brief look at the immediate history of mainstream, positivistic social psychology and its standard research concerns. Then I will show how social psychology—a subdiscipline hardly half a century old—is in a state of self-admitted crisis. It has separated into two conflicting subcultures, each of which almost totally rejects the approach and methods of the other. I will then summarize the assumptions and growing work of two human-science-oriented movements that are challenging the hegemony of the older tradition in social psychology. In light of all this I will try to show that the Christian psychologist's mandate to walk the fine line "between reductionism and self-deification" (as C. Stephen Evans phrases it) is nowhere more intriguingly challenged than it is in social psychology—which, for all its ferment, may well be the area of psychology most potentially open to explicitly Christian theorizing in the future.

A CRISIS WITH A HISTORY

Few social psychologists would quarrel with Gordon Allport's oft-quoted definition of their field: "Social psychologists regard their discipline as an attempt to understand and explain how thought, feeling, and behavior of individuals are influenced by the actual, imagined, or implied presence of human beings."[3] In other words, while sociologists tend to be more concerned with overall *group* characteristics as a function of historical, economic, religious, and other factors, social psychologists try to understand the dynamics and effects of various kinds of social interaction on the "thought, feeling,

3. Allport, "The Historical Background of Modern Social Psychology," in *Handbook of Social Psychology*, ed. Gardner Lindzey (Cambridge, Mass.: Addison-Wesley, 1954), 1:3.

and behavior of *individuals.*" (Despite these differences of focus, however, there is still some disciplinary overlap. Both sociologists and social psychologists study small-group dynamics, for instance, and some members of each discipline have an interest in how individuals acquire and execute social roles.)

There is also general agreement among social psychologists regarding the historical background of social psychology within the context of psychology as a whole, which itself became formalized as a discipline only a century ago.[4] At that time, when Wilhelm Wundt first attempted his laboratory analysis of mental structures, there was no apparent place for an explicitly social psychology. In Wundt's highly atomistic scheme, all incoming stimuli were reduced to patterns of sensation (of light, sound, smell, etc.), and all resulting behavior was seen as derivable from the basic psychological processes of sensation and association. It is of interest that Wundt himself eventually tired of this "bricks-and-mortar" approach (as one of his early critics termed it) to the mind, and turned his attention instead to social behavior, using a historical approach rather than an experimental and psychophysical approach. It is also significant that almost no standard texts in the history of psychology refer to Wundt's later work in any detail, preferring only to lionize him as the father of experimental psychology.

By the turn of the century, however, William James was arguing strongly for the identification of influences and behaviors that were irreducibly social rather than mere combinations of physical elements and motor movements. By the 1930s the exodus to America of the German *Gestalt* psychologists had further moved those in the discipline to think in terms of patterned perceptions and behaviors in which the whole was more than merely the sum of its parts. Almost all social psychologists date the actual formalization of their discipline from 1933, the year that German psychologist Kurt Lewin came to America. They are, however, quite divided over the significance of Lewin's work for social psychology today. This is not surprising, for

4. For historical treatments of social psychology more recent than Allport's, see, for example, Kenneth J. Gergen, *Toward Transformation in Social Knowledge* (New York: Springer-Verlag, 1982), on which this chapter's treatment draws considerably. For a more traditional interpretation from a positivistic viewpoint, see Leon Festinger, ed., *Retrospections on Social Psychology* (New York: Oxford University Press, 1980); and Clyde Hendrick, "Social Psychology as an Experimental Science," in *Perspectives on Social Psychology*, ed. C. Hendrick (Hillsdale, N.J.: Lawrence Erlbaum, 1977).

Lewin, like Wundt, manifested a fundamental ambivalence in his view of persons and consequently in his notions of how they should be studied by psychologists.

When Lewin arrived in America to take up a post at the University of Iowa, American psychology was dominated by a species of neobehaviorism that insisted that all human activity could be explained by reference to either internal physiological drives or external environmental reinforcers. The possibility that human beings might significantly *construe* (as opposed to passively *receive*) the events and influences of the social environment was rarely considered worthy of investigation. Consequently, when Lewin produced his classic equation, $B = f(P,E)$ [behavior is a function of both the person *and* the environment], it represented for its time a very un-American attempt to reconcile very different approaches to the person. On the one hand, "P," the person, was seen as being capable of a deliberate and selective perception of surrounding social events. On the other hand, Lewin's "E" (the actual social and physical environment) also had a strong ontological status and could not be dismissed as a mere figment of P's imagination. For Lewin the result was a deliberate union of what Kenneth Gergen has called *endogenic* and *exogenic* epistemologies: the latter "grant[s] priority to the external world in the generation of human knowledge [while the former] denote[s] those theories holding the processes of the mind as pre-eminent."[5]

This view of persons as at least partially active in construing their own social world led Lewin to favor a research method that has been characterized as "experimental phenomenology."[6] That is, in addition to exposing subjects to experimental manipulations of social influence and measuring their effects on behavior or perceptions, Lewin took pains to obtain a great mass of descriptive data on the meaning of the total situation *as seen by the subject*. This was indeed a radical departure from the Skinnerian notion of the subject's mind as an impenetrable "black box," and even from the ruling neobehaviorist concession that one could assign "hypothetical constructs" to the black box but must infer their existence through behaviorally anchored measures—operationalized by the experimenter but never by the subject.

In a somewhat twisted and inconsistent manner, Lewin's endo-

5. Gergen, *Toward Transformation in Social Knowledge*, p. 175.
6. J. DeRivera, *Field Theory as Human Science: The Contributions of Lewin's Berlin Group* (New York: Gardner Press, 1976).

genic orientation—admitting, respecting, and studying the active cognitions of the subject in a social situation—has persisted in social psychology to this day, and may even be said to predate the cognitive revival in psychology as a whole. For instance, as early as the late 1950s, a number of social psychologists turned their attention to a phenomenon known as "cognitive dissonance." In the classic experiment of this genre, naive subjects are persuaded, by the offer of varying sums of money, to make a public proclamation of an attitude that is really contrary to what they believe. The result under certain circumstances is that many of the subjects come to believe what they originally said only with reluctance and ambivalence. According to cognitive dissonance theory, these subjects cannot tolerate the inconsistency of having behaved contrary to their own attitudes (especially if they cannot justify the prevarication in terms of having received a lot of money for it). Consequently, they reduce the resulting cognitive dissonance by bringing their attitudes in line with their behavior.[7]

A great deal of research on cognitive dissonance has followed in the wake of these early studies.[8] But more significant for our purposes are the reasons behind the enthusiasm with which social psychologists have embraced such cognitive theories of social behavior. According to one prominent participant in the field, Elliot Aronson,

> The early dissonance experiments sounded a clarion call to cognitively-oriented social psychologists, proclaiming in the most striking manner that *human beings think;* they do not always behave in a mechanistic manner. When in situations which allow them to think, human beings engage in all kinds of cognitive gymnastics aimed at justifying their own behavior.[9]

Such a statement (which is typical of social psychology's pride in having resisted naive behaviorism) might make social psychology

7. See, for example, Arthur R. Cohen, "An Experiment on Small Rewards for Discrepant Compliance and Attitude Change," in *Explorations in Cognitive Dissonance*, ed. Jack W. Brehm and Arthur R. Cohen (New York: John Wiley, 1962), pp. 73–78. For a theoretical treatment, see Leon Festinger, *A Theory of Cognitive Dissonance* (Stanford, Calif.: Stanford University Press, 1957).

8. For a recent review of the dissonance literature, see R. A. Wicklund and Jack W. Brehm, *Perspectives on Cognitive Dissonance* (New York: John Wiley, 1976).

9. Aronson, "Persuasion Via Self-Justification: Large Commitments for Small Rewards," in *Retrospections on Social Psychology*, p. 10.

seem very attractive to the uninitiated Christian reader. On the one hand, by affirming people's susceptibility to environmental influence, it anchors them firmly to the natural order. On the other hand, by suggesting that persons creatively restructure their cognitions of self and others, it also suggests that freedom and responsibility—what in Chapter Four we called accountable dominion—are also irreducible human attributes. But upon closer examination we will see that this balanced view is not really the norm and that mainstream social psychologists, despite their disclaimers to the contrary, have in fact rejected Lewin's original paradigm in favor of an anthropology and epistemology that are still largely behaviorist.

POSITIVISM IN MAINSTREAM SOCIAL PSYCHOLOGY

In the fifty or so years since its inception, social psychology has gradually acquired a repertoire of topics around which most of its research and theory revolve. One much-researched topic is that of attitudes—how they are acquired, preserved, and changed. A definite bent toward democratic political activism among social psychologists can be seen in the fact that a good deal of attitude research focuses on the causes, consequences, and ways of changing the prejudiced opinions of various groups. Similar concerns are reflected in the many studies of conflict, aggression, and altruism so commonly found in social-psychology journals and textbooks. Other broad research topics include the processes by which people are attracted to and form impressions of other persons, the circumstances under which individuals resist or conform to social influence, and the processes by which children acquire and learn to abide by the social norms of their families and cultures.

There is no denying the importance of these topics or their attractiveness to students who sincerely want to contribute to the understanding and solution of enduring social problems. Nor do social psychologists claim to have a monopoly on the study of these phenomena; on the contrary, they are more than willing to cooperate with political scientists, sociologists, and social and political philosophers in the study of attitudes, group dynamics, socialization, conflict resolution, and the like. But at the same time, mainstream social psychologists seem to regard themselves as a special—and even somewhat superior—breed as compared with scholars in these other disciplines. Morton Deutsch, a productive social psychologist in the area of conflict research, gives us an example of this attitude in his introduction to a recent review of the conflict literature:

> I shall not review here the writings about conflict from the social philosophers, limiting myself to the era of modern social psychology. However, it is my impression that a careful reading of their work would leave most of us with a sense of humility and also a feeling of pride: humility at the recognition that few of our ideas are new; pride at the realization that, unlike the social philosophers, we are part of a scientific tradition which tests its ideas through experimental research in order to eliminate those that cannot survive rigorous, empirical examination. [10]

Mainstream social psychologists, then, seem to consider the results of their own social research to be more reliable and valid than those of other disciplines pursuing similar topics, because their results have been arrived at by empirical—and especially experimental—means. In this connection it is of interest that the anthology from which Deutsch's remarks are taken (and to which many of the acknowledged giants of American social psychology have contributed) contains not a single reference to the work of either Thomas Kuhn or Michael Polanyi, whose arguments against naive objectivism in science we considered in the first chapter of this book. [11] It is rare, in fact, for mainstream psychologists to make any reference to the philosophy of science underlying their work, self-conscious as they still are about being a cut above the philosophers from whom they separated a century ago. But an underlying philosophy of science still exists in social psychology, and on the rare occasions when it is specifically acknowledged, it is seen to share with the rest of psychology a distinctly Popperian prejudice. As summarized by social psychologist Kenneth Gergen,

> Perhaps the chief assumption underlying contemporary behavioral research is that general theoretical statements are subject to empirical evaluation. During the hegemony of logical positivism the empirical validity of a given hypothesis was primarily linked to the frequency of its empirical confirmation. [Now] many feel

10. Deutsch, "Fifty Years of Conflict," in *Retrospections on Social Psychology*, p. 46.
11. The same myopia characterizes two other recent state-of-the-discipline collections, Hendrick's *Perspectives on Social Psychology* and Mills' *Experimental Social Psychology*.

this view has been supplanted by Popper's falsification doctrine. On this account, a theory is scientific only to the degree that it can specify what range of observations would be incompatible with it, and a theory is proved superior as it withstands attempts at falsification.[12]

Moreover, Gergen argues, mainstream social psychology has almost completely abandoned Lewin's original concern to give both the human mind *and* the external environment equal status in the formation of beliefs, attitudes, and cognitions. Rather, it has become largely exogenic in its epistemology, "granting nature pre-eminent status in guiding or fashioning mental processes." In turn, this metatheoretical orientation has committed social psychology to an increasingly truncated range of theories and methods. In Gergen's words,

> [It has committed] the discipline to some form of stimulus-response theory [and] also carries with it strong implications for preferred forms of methodology. In particular, if the stimulus world is superordinate and antecedent to psychological process, and the latter is responsible for behavior, required is a methodology that precisely traces the connections among the stimulus-response elements. And, because elements within the psychological and behavioral sphere are fundamentally dependent on conditions within the pre-eminent sphere of the stimulus world, the most sensible course of research is to alter stimulus conditions systematically and to observe the resulting repercussions. The favored methodology can thus be none other than the controlled experiment. Metatheory, theory, and method are interlocking and mutually reinforcing. . . . In effect, by the late 1960's, social psychology had witnessed the apotheosis of neobehaviorism.[13]

How does this joint commitment to behaviorist theory and (wherever possible) an experimental methodology manifest itself in the actual research of the best-known social psychologists? We have already cited one example from the area of cognitive dissonance studies: by the judicious manipulation of social influences and monetary incentives in a controlled setting, subjects are induced to experience what is thought to be cognitive dissonance, and subsequent

---

12. Gergen, *Toward Transformation in Social Knowledge*, p. 69.
13. Gergen, *Toward Transformation in Social Knowledge*, pp. 126, 183.

attitude changes are then recorded. Similarly, in the study of conformity, naive subjects may be placed in a situation where their judgments (of a physical stimulus or of an issue assigned for discussion) are subjected to counterjudgments of actual or implied others (in reality confederates of the experimenter), and any resulting opinion shifts are noted. In the study of helping behavior, mock emergencies may be carefully staged (in either the laboratory or the field situation) under a variety of preselected conditions and their effectiveness in generating altruistic responses from naive subjects or bystanders recorded. In research on interpersonal attraction, subjects are often exposed to what they think are written descriptions of another person; in reality, the content of these descriptions is manipulated by the experimenter to be like or unlike the self-description of the subject in order to see to what degree persons are attracted to those they perceive as being similar to themselves.

Analogous experimental techniques could be cited in the areas of socialization, conflict, group decision-making, and other research topics of social psychology, but the above will suffice to exemplify what has indeed been a dominant preoccupation within the field. Nonexperimental studies (such as surveys, simulations, and naturalistic observations) do exist, but they do not command nearly as much status—or as much space—in the major journals of social psychology. For example, in the most influential of these, the *Journal of Personality and Social Psychology*, the percentage of purely experimental studies increased from about thirty percent in 1949 to eighty-seven percent by 1969. By contrast, a 1968 review of naturalistic observation in social psychology revealed that only fifteen percent of three hundred studies referenced had been published in the four major journals of social psychology. [14]

Such a pervasive theoretical and methodological behaviorism may seem strangely at odds with Elliot Aronson's statement, recorded earlier, that social psychologists are distinguished from behaviorists by the respect that they accord human thought processes. And it is certainly true that students of cognitive dissonance, attitude change, interpersonal attraction, and the like explicitly acknowledge that

14. These two reviews are K. L. Higbee and M. G. Wells, "Some Research Trends in Social Psychology During the 1960's," *American Psychologist* 27 (Oct. 1972): 963–66; and K. E. Weick's "Systematic Observation Methods," as quoted in Gergen, *Toward Transformation in Social Knowledge*, pp. 126–27.

these phenomena are essentially mental in character. But two inconsistencies should be noted with regard to this position. The first is that, for the most part, these cognitive processes are not assumed to have any autonomy. Rather, they are seen as largely "made" to happen by means of immediate social influences (real or experimentally contrived), just as a rock dropped from the hand is "made" to obey the law of gravity. Thus the cognitive orientation of social psychologists might better be described as a species of "mental behaviorism": it allows that cognitive processes exist, even in some complexity, but it makes them almost totally subservient to external environmental pressures.

By this accounting, human reflexivity either does not exist or is merely a minor feedback loop with the environment that can effectively be ignored or controlled by experimental design. As a result, subjects are almost never consulted to find out what *they* think of the experimental situation (except to ascertain, post hoc, if the experimenter's cover story really worked); rather, their mental processes are *inferred* through behavioral measures or forced-choice attitudinal responses. "Lewin insisted that experimental analysis should be undertaken only within the context of an analysis of the situation as a whole," admits one social psychologist. "Today, however . . . the emphasis is almost solely on the effects of the variable manipulation as measured by some objective means. The phenomenal meaning of the manipulation from the subject's point of view is seldom attempted."[15]

A second inconsistency is seen in the fact that when independent cognitive processing of social situations *is* acknowledged, it is still regarded as a second-rate—indeed, almost pathological—phenomenon. For example, when Leon Festinger first set forth his theory of social comparison, which suggests that persons evaluate their own opinions by comparing them with others', he distinguished between an objective "physical" reality (on which one's views should ideally be based) and a subjective "social" reality that is psychologically self-manufactured *in the absence of* adequate information from the real world.[16] The resulting processes of social comparison are thus cast in a pejorative light: they are distortions introduced by the mind when "objective" reality is inadequately apprehended. Similarly, persons who display the attitude shift inferred as cognitive dissonance are

15. Hendrick, *Perspectives on Social Psychology*, p. 38.
16. Festinger, "A Theory of Social Comparison Processes," *Human Relations* 7 (July 1954): 117–40.

really engaging in a rather contemptible process of rationalization. Not wanting to face an image of themselves as persons who said one thing while believing another, they convince themselves that they really *did* believe what they said.

Social psychologists have tended to regard their *own* thought processes—by contrast with such weak subjectivity—as quite successfully exogenic. "From the guild standpoint," writes Gergen, "they [are] attempting to map reality as accurately and systematically as possible, and to test such maps against reality in a dispassionate fashion." That they have presumed themselves largely successful in this quest for objectivity can be seen in their pointed disregard, already noted, for the concerns of the postmodern philosophy of science. As Gergen says, "People *other* than scientists were said to be dominated by cognitive constructions, motives, needs, and so on. *They* lived in a world of intrinsically generated mental processes. It is this ironic duality—the scientist employing an exogenic theory to guide his or her own conduct, while assuming an endogenic basis for others' actions—that now returns to haunt the discipline."[17]

Just what does Gergen mean when he says that social psychologists' double standard of humanness has returned to haunt them? Let us enlarge upon this comment now, for in it lies the key to the recent rebellion of a small but growing number of social psychologists against the received view.

CRACKS IN THE PARADIGMATIC EDIFICE

Much of the material in this section is given more detailed treatment in my earlier book, *The Sorcerer's Apprentice.*[18] Consequently, we will consider only briefly three factors that have converged to create a growing crisis of doubt within the positivistic paradigm of mainstream social psychology. Two of these factors—which we will label "methodological complications" and "ethical concerns"—were generated from within mainstream social psychology itself, beginning in the 1960s. To these, social psychologists have made real accommodations—but none strong enough (nor even intended) to dislodge the exogenic paradigm we have discovered to dominate the field. The

17. Gergen, *Toward Transformation in Social Knowledge*, p. 184.
18. Mary Stewart Van Leeuwen, *The Sorcerer's Apprentice: A Christian Looks at the Changing Face of Psychology* (Downers Grove, Ill.: InterVarsity Press, 1982).

third and final force, which has roots both within and outside the social psychology guild, is one that continues to gain momentum and in many ways shows promise of providing an alternative paradigm for the discipline. Although it consists of several largely independent movements, we can characterize it broadly as "the human-science reformation." Let us look at each of these three in turn.

Methodological Complications. We have already pointed out that social psychology's epistemology, methodology, and implicit theory of human nature combine to form a disciplinary edifice that is neo-behaviorist in character. According to its assumptions, human beings are largely passive respondents to external, social influences and are therefore most validly studied by controlled experimental means. However, by 1963—a scant thirty years after Lewin's inauguration of the field—some of the more thoughtful leaders in social psychology were beginning to document, with blunt honesty, just how difficult it was to obtain valid experimental results with human subjects. This did not mean they were suggesting that experimentation be eliminated as the method of choice; on the contrary, they were as anxious as ever that social psychology remain a "scientific" discipline. But for various reasons intrinsic to human social research, they concluded in effect that definitive experiments with totally reliable results were probably impossible, and that social psychologists would have to make do with various approximations of that ideal.

In Donald Campbell and Julian Stanley's landmark book, *Experimental and Quasi-Experimental Designs for Research,* [19] a crucial distinction was made between what the authors called *internal* and *external* experimental validity. Essentially, wrote Campbell and Stanley, social researchers had to choose between two opposite methodological problems. On the one hand, they could opt for laboratory experiments, with subjects assigned randomly to experimental and control conditions and independent and dependent variables carefully regulated. In this case they could be fairly confident that the manipulated stimuli had indeed been responsible for the behavioral results (i.e., the experiment would be "internally valid"). However, they could never know how far these particular results—obtained in a contrived setting at a specific time with a specific type of subject population—could be generalized to the more complex and variable world of

19. Campbell and Stanley, *Experimental and Quasi-Experimental Designs for Research* (Chicago: Rand McNally, 1963).

everyday social interaction. In other words, *internal* validity of experimental results was obtained at the cost of their *external* validity, or generalizability. Moreover, warned Campbell and Stanley, subjects may react atypically simply by virtue of *knowing* they are in an experiment, or they may be sensitized by exposure to a pretest questionnaire such that they respond nonspontaneously to its post-test version.

To increase the external validity, or "exportability," of experimental results, an opposite strategy is often used—that of covertly integrating an experimental design into the normal routines of intact groups such as classrooms, military squadrons, hospital wards, and the like. But here a threat to *internal* validity intrudes, despite the increase in external validity that comes from doing research in realistic settings. Unless there can be initial, random assignment of persons to control and experimental groups (which is usually not feasible), we cannot know if the experimental results are anything but an artifact of the particular *type* of group in which they occurred. In other words, if the control and experimental groups *begin* with overall differing characteristics (e.g., slow versus bright classes, senior versus junior officers; chronic versus acute ward-inhabitants), it may be these characteristics or their interaction with the experimental condition that really accounts for obtained differences.

Campbell and Stanley went on to suggest several rather complex research designs to overcome this problem, but these are rarely used because they involve an increase in time committed, measures taken, and/or the number of subjects used. Thus social psychologists in the 1960s were left, in practice, with the dilemma referred to earlier: were they to aim for experimental rigor at the cost of external validity, or for real-world generalizability at the cost of being unable to disambiguate the causal relationships presumed to be at work in the study?

In fact, the compromise adopted by mainstream social psychologists tried to get the best of both worlds in either one of two ways. On the one hand, there have been many attempts to *turn* the laboratory setting into a more realistic one—for example, by simulating an unexpected emergency, request, attraction, etc.—then covertly recording the subject's reactions. In these situations subjects who think they are participating in one kind of study are in reality unwitting participants in another, which is the one the researcher really cares about. On the other hand, the entire experiment may be moved to the world outside the university: emergencies may be staged with carefully randomized locations, actor profiles, and times of day, and even in the presence of randomly designated bystanders. "Lost" letters or wallets may be dropped in accordance with the variables thought to determine helping behavior, always with sufficient identification to make forwarding or return possible, and the number of arrivals at the "dummy" address counted. Existing agencies may even be approached for research cooperation. This happened when researchers replaced Salvation Army bell-ringers under predetermined conditions to see which of these was associated with more or less giving on the part of unwitting passersby. In either case (i.e., making the laboratory more realistic or the real-world situation more lab-like), the hope is that external validity will be improved without cost to internal validity, and moreover that the subjects' complete ignorance about their participation in an experiment will assure their unpremeditated reaction to the covert experimental manipulations.[20]

But with such methodological compensations came unexpected ethical considerations, the second crack in the paradigmatic edifice of social psychology.

Ethical Concerns. It is nothing new for social scientists, like medical researchers, to give incomplete information to their subjects. Persons filling out personality scales may be unaware that certain questions have been included to see to what extent they give only socially desirable responses. Students participating in studies of educational innovation are usually unaware if they are in an experimental or a control group, or even that they are in a research study at all. Subjects learning lists of nonsense syllables in a memory task have long been spared the fine details of the theory that the experimenter is trying to test.

Such *passive* omissions of information have never generated much controversy in psychology.[21] But with the advent of experi-

20. References for the kinds of studies cited in this section can be found in most introductory social psychology texts—for example, Bernard Seidenberg and Alvin Snadowsky, *Social Psychology: An Introduction* (New York: Macmillan, 1976).
21. Double-blind experiments in medicine, however, are another matter. Consider the controversial Tuskegee experiment, in which a sample of persons (from a poor rural area with few medical facilities) who had syphilis was randomly and covertly divided into two groups—one treated, the other not treated but monitored to observe the course of the disease without treatment. Years later, when this research was made more public, a debate ensued about whether it was "harmful" to withhold medical treatment, for purposes of having a control group, from persons who would ordinarily not have had it

mental social psychology, *active* deception, employed for the sake of creating believable social situations to which subjects would respond unreflectively, gradually became a routine practice. As a typical example, subjects might be told that they are merely doing a verbal learning task; but in the midst of this a "co-subject" (actually a confederate of the experimenter) simulates extreme physical distress. It is the naive subjects' unpremeditated reaction to this staged drama that constitutes the real experimental observation, and the one about which they will be told only after it is all over.

Note that there are two kinds of active deception in such a study. First of all, subjects are told that the experiment is about a topic that it is not really about at all. Second, subjects are placed in the company of others who they think are naive fellow-subjects but who are in fact trained confederates—often graduate students—of the experimenter. There are even studies in which a third and more complex form of deception has been used: subjects are falsely debriefed about the "true" purpose of the experiment (actually only one part of it) in order to prepare them for their second unwitting role in a subsequent part.

In the late 1960s some social psychologists began to question the ethicality of such deceptions and also the psychological distress that seemed to accompany them, however temporarily. It was argued that, to the extent that social psychologists were trying to unmask undesirable patterns of thought and behavior (cognitive inconsistency, failures of altruism, social conformity, etc.), subjects were being placed in situations likely to elicit such behaviors and the damage to self-esteem that might result from such "imposed insight." Moreover, it was suggested that the institutionalization of such stress and deception was giving psychologists the reputation of being untrustworthy or (equally serious) of presenting lay subjects with a recurrent message that routine lying in the cause of social science—and, by generalization, any good cause—was quite excusable. If, to avoid such problems, experiments were conducted unobtrusively in real-life settings, there arose the alternative ethical problem of secretly using persons as

anyway. Of interest is the response of Leon Festinger, one of the doyens of mainstream social psychology: "I am not so sure [that it was unethical]. These persons were not harmed by the research, in the sense that they were no worse off than if the research had not been done at all. But the judgment *of our society* was that it did violate our ethics" (Festinger, *Retrospections on Social Psychology*, p. 249).

subjects without their informed consent or proper postexperimental debriefing.[22]

It should be noted that social psychologists continue to be quite divided about the ethical seriousness of such routine deception in experiments. The majority, who are committed to an exogenic epistemology, argue strenuously that in their research, as in medical research, the knowledge gained about laws of social behavior far outweighs—and hence more than justifies—any minor stress and deception to which subjects are exposed.[23] In the words of Princeton's John Darley, "Psychologists have an ethical responsibility to do research about processes that are socially important, and to discover *clearly* what is going on—which means that sometimes they have to keep their subjects in the dark about certain aspects of the study."[24] By this account experimental research reliably yields principles of social behavior, but (as in a double-blind drug study) these can be achieved only at the cost of giving subjects incomplete or misleading information.

Nonetheless, in the wake of a decade or more of ethical debate, both the American Psychological Association (APA) and the federal agencies who supply most of the research funding for social psychologists have posted somewhat more stringent criteria for the use of deception. Proposals for any such research must now be routed through institutional review boards of interdisciplinary composition, boards who are mandated to approve the research for funding only if it involves minimal risk to subjects and cannot feasibly be carried out by any other method.[25] However, even these modest constraints have

22. Many of the debates on ethics in social psychology have been collected in books such as Arthur S. Miller, ed., *The Social Psychology of Psychological Research* (New York: The Free Press, 1972); and John G. Jung, *The Experimenter's Dilemma* (New York: Harper and Row, 1971). See also Van Leeuwen, *The Sorcerer's Apprentice;* and Irwin Silverman, *The Human Subject in the Psychological Laboratory* (New York: Pergamon Press, 1977). For recent examples of mainstream psychologists' defense of deception as a practice, see the various articles in Festinger, *Retrospections on Social Psychology.*

23. A good summary of the current state of both the ethics controversy and its accompanying legislation can be found in Morton Hunt's "Research Through Deception," *New York Times Magazine,* 12 Sept. 1982, pp. 66–67, 139–43.

24. Darley, as quoted in Hunt, "Research Through Deception," p. 143 (Darley's italics).

25. See, for example, the U.S. Department of Health, Education, and Welfare's *Health Services Regulations Governing Biomedical and Behavioral Research with Human Subjects* (1971) and the American Psychological Association's "Ethical Principles of Psychologists," *American Psychologist* 36 (June 1981): 633–38.

prompted leading social psychologists to grumble indignantly about scientific obscurantism. "Whole lines of research have been nipped in the bud," Princeton's Edward E. Jones has protested, while Columbia's Stanley Schacter, with no less than three decades of deception-buttressed research behind him, has simply stopped applying for funding to do experiments. "I simply won't go through all that [ethical interrogation]," he told one journalist. "It's a bloody bore and a waste of time."[26]

On the above account, scientific advance via social psychological experimentation has been martyred on the altar of ethical hypersensitivity. But by a quite different accounting the so-called laws of social behavior claimed by the exogenic perspective were *never* very reliable, nor can they be, because the positivistic approach is largely unsuitable for studying complex, human social interaction in the first place. The growing minority associated with this view we have earlier referred to as human-science reformers, whose concerns and arguments warrant review.

CRISIS AND REFORM IN SOCIAL PSYCHOLOGY

During the past decade the above-described ethical and methodological controversies have combined to put social psychology in what has commonly been described as a state of crisis. A number of people have attempted to explain the nature of this crisis, and the following quotations are representative of their efforts:[27]

> The need for a comprehensive theoretical treatment of social psychology and for a reformed methodology we feel to be evident from the increasing dissatisfaction with the state of social psychology, even within the citadels of the profession. The underlying reason for this state we believe to be a continued adherence to a positivist methodology, long after the theoretical justification for it, in naive behaviorism, has been repudiated.[28]

> The concern with technology and the marginal interest in theory are related to what seems to me the most critical problem we face

26. Jones and Schacter, both quoted in Hunt, "Research Through Deception," p. 142.
27. For other examples and references, see Hendrick, *Perspectives on Social Psychology*, chap. 1.
28. Rom Harré and Paul Secord, *The Explanation of Social Behavior* (Oxford: Basil Blackwell, 1972), p. 1.

today in social psychology—the continuing and growing frag-mentation of the discipline.[29]

Social psychology, as an academic and research activity, has developed as a self-contained and inward-looking discipline which has not only become separated from the phenomena it sets out to analyze, but is also sterile as a source of human understanding.[30]

I am not too happy about the clogged state of our journals, filled with the products of project-supported busyness, in which fad and fashion, methodological fetishism, and what I remember Gordon Allport to have called "itsy-bitsy empiricism" make it easy to lose direction and significance.[31]

This "state of crisis" within social psychology has been widespread enough to have become the subject of a recent master's-level thesis.[32] Based on an international survey of 230 social psychologists, A. G. Zwier's study showed that two distinct subcultures have emerged in the discipline. The reform-minded group (as the above quotations suggest) is bent upon a reexamination of the foundations and goals of social psychology, and is concerned that deeper theorizing and more critical applications replace the obsession with experimentation and control. This group is largely postmodern in its philosophy of science: "[It] tends to believe that experiments are used as implements largely to demonstrate the obvious, that fads and fashions govern research enterprises, that social knowledge is historically contingent, and that knowledge is ideologically based."[33]

The traditionally positivist group, on the other hand, is still primarily engaged in hypothesis testing—experimentally where pos-sible—and vehemently rejects the assumptions of the reformers. They are, as we have noted, convinced that positive social knowledge

---

29. David Katz, Editorial, *Journal of Personality and Social Psychology* 7 (Dec. 1967): 341.

30. M. Richards, "The Biological and the Social," in *Reconstructing Social Psychology,* ed. N. Armistead (Baltimore: Penguin Books, 1974), p. 233.

31. M. Brewster Smith, "Three Textbooks: A Special Review," *Journal of Experimental Social Psychology* 2 (Apr. 1966): 117.

32. A. G. Zwier, "The Crisis in Social Psychology: A Theoretical and Empirical Study." (master's thesis, University of Aukland, New Zealand, 1980).

33. As summarized by Gergen, *Toward Transformation in Social Knowledge,* p. 191.

is possible through application of the traditional methods, indignant about the ethical constraints placed upon their research, and according to Zwier's survey, typically "sick of hearing about a crisis in social psychology."[34] One is reminded of Thomas Kuhn's observation, quoted in Chapter One, that the proponents of competing paradigms "practice their trades in different worlds," and that the transition from one to another cannot be "forced by logic and neutral experience" but can be made only by the paradigm shift Kuhn specifically likened to a conversion.

Traditional social psychologists have accused the would-be reformers of damning the status quo without offering productive alternatives.[35] But this, according to Kenneth Gergen, is analogous to the medieval disregard of the criticisms of astrology "because the critics' capacities for prophecy failed to be superior or because the critics failed to furnish alternative pastimes." We must simply begin back at the beginning, Gergen and other reformers insist, and claim the right to enough time and resources "to establish viable end points or functions for investigation, and to examine forms of academic training, journal policies, and professional gatekeeping of more substantial promise."[36] And, indeed, there is evidence that such claims are being taken seriously, for according to Zwier's survey, the reformers as a group are having no more difficulty than their traditionalist opponents in acquiring research funds, communicating with colleagues, and publishing.

In the balance of this chapter we will look at two specific kinds of reforms that have been suggested for social psychology. It should be noted that other reform movements with overlapping goals are gaining strength in other areas of psychology or with respect to the paradigm of the discipline as a whole. These we will refer to again in Chapter Ten. The two that are described below are the most specific to social psychology and are currently the best-developed in terms of epistemology and theory.

HARRÉ AND SECORD'S "ETHOGENY"

At the heart of social psychology's crisis is the debate about the adequacy of the positivistic approach for the study of human social

34. Zwier, "The Crisis in Social Psychology."
35. Festinger, *Retrospections*, p. 253.
36. Gergen, *Toward Transformation in Social Knowledge*, p. 192.

behavior. What alternatives have been proposed as possible replacements for the positivistic paradigm? One contender is the field of *ethology*—the study of whole patterns of animal behavior under natural conditions. Most readers will know of Karl von Frisch's famous studies of bees and how he showed that they communicate the location and amount of nectar by means of complex "dances" in the air.[37] Konrad Lorenz, another pioneering ethologist, is well-known for demonstrating the mechanisms behind imprinting—the habit newly hatched birds have of following their mothers in a seemingly automatic fashion.[38] Because ethology concentrates on whole patterns of naturally occuring behavior as opposed to the contrived experimental operations of mainstream social psychology, some variation of it has frequently been suggested as a replacement for social psychology's current paradigm. For example, in his *On Human Nature*,[39] Harvard's Edward O. Wilson maintains that sociobiology—by which he means the extension of population biology and evolutionary theory to human social organization—is a perfectly adequate paradigm for the exploration (and the explanation) of seemingly unique human behaviors. In such a scheme, social behavior is simply an example of "genetically prepared learning": despite its diversity of expression among individuals and cultures, social behavior is understood as a collection of varying means toward the same single end—namely, the biological survival and reproduction of one's own kind.

Other reformers, however, have rightly perceived that ethology and sociobiology are still too reductionistic for the satisfactory study of uniquely human social interaction. While approving of both ethology's natural-observation approach and its respect for careful theorizing, British philosopher Rom Harré and American psychologist Paul Secord have looked for a system that can do justice to what in their eyes are the most *unique* features of human social intercourse—namely, the use of language, the understanding and voluntary following of social rules, and the capacity to monitor (and hence manage) one's own social performances. The result is what they have called *ethog-*

37. Von Frisch, *The Dancing Bees* (New York: Harcourt Brace Jovanovich, 1955).

38. Lorenz, *On Aggression* (New York: Harcourt Brace Jovanovich, 1963).

39. Wilson, *On Human Nature* (Cambridge: Harvard University Press, 1978).

eny, "a form of social psychology which makes essential use of actor-based understandings and construals of situations."[40] Although ethogeny is rightly characterized as part of the human-science reform movement in psychology, it should be noted that Harré and Secord (unlike other reformers to be considered later) do not castigate mainstream social psychologists for following too much the lead of the natural sciences. On the contrary, they maintain that social psychologists have looked too *little* at the *actual* conduct of modern science in their rigid adherence to a positivistic notion of science as laid down by philosophers earlier in this century. Ethogeny, like any other science, aims to explain nonrandom patterns that are observed in nature. But according to Harré and Secord, researchers in the advanced sciences (unlike social psychologists) have as much respect for precise, naturalistic observations as they do for experimentation as a methodology. Moreover, although interested in causal explanations, advanced scientists realize that the most fruitful understanding of causal mechanisms comes from a disciplined use of the imagination, and especially from the use of analogy. Borrowing from the example of physics, Harré and Secord point out that while earlier physics relied heavily on the rather passive notions of substance and quality, modern physics has made more headway since it turned its attention to concepts such as power, potentiality, agency, and spontaneity—concepts that they hold must properly be ascribed to persons as well as physical objects.

Considering persons especially in light of their linguistic powers Harré and Secord "undertake a logical analysis to identify those features that individuals must have for them to be language users. The most unique feature of a potential language user is the capacity to monitor control of one's own actions. In [our] anthropomorphic model, the person is not only an agent, but a watcher, commentator, and critic as well."[41] This, of course, is a radical departure from the paradigm of mainstream social psychology—which for all its apparent interest in cognition attributes virtually no real agency to human thought and behavior, and which, moreover, tries to evade or cancel out human reflexivity (Harré and Secord's "watcher, commentator, and critic" functions) by the wholesale use of surprise and deception

40. Harré and Secord, *The Explanation of Social Behavior,* p. 152.
41. Harré and Secord, *The Explanation of Social Behavior,* p. 6.

in its experimental designs. Harré and Secord would agree with Gergen that, in doing so, social psychologists have implicitly endorsed a double standard of humanness: functions essential to the very conduct of social science are taken for granted in themselves while denied or trivialized in their subjects. That is why, with a touch of black humor, they speak of their "anthropomorphic model of man" as the basic principle of ethogeny: "For scientific purposes, treat people as if they were human beings."[42]

Not only is ordinary language, in all its richness, the chief *example* of uniquely human powers; it is also, according to them, the ethogenist's chief tool for *understanding* and *analyzing* social interaction. "At the heart of the explanation of social behavior," they write, "is the identification of meanings which underlie it." Consequently, the ethogenist takes seriously the ordinary-language *accounts* that actors give of their behaviors—that is, "the actor's own statements about why he performed the acts in question, what social meanings he gave to the actions of himself and others."[43] Without imposing restricted technical meanings on the words elicited (as psychologists are wont to do with terms such as "reward," "drive," "achievement," "intelligence," etc.), the ethogenic social psychologist is to analyze collected accounts with the goal of discovering the rules that underlie the described behavior. In doing so, he or she is advised to draw on the detailed analyses of ordinary language produced by the Oxford School of philosophers and others in the linguistic tradition, "in which social and psychological theories implicit in ordinary speech are revealed."[44] In other words, ordinary-language accounts, if exhaustively understood, contain their own explanations of the events they portray, and rather than imposing restricted operational definitions on the episodes they observe, social psychologists should redirect their skills toward the description and understanding of such "folk psychology" and "folk sociology" theories of behavior.

This does not mean that the social psychologist now completely ceases to function as a detached observer, but the ethogenist performs this function in a very different way from that of the mainstream

42. Harré and Secord, *The Explanation of Social Behavior,* p. 151.
43. Harré and Secord, *The Explanation of Social Behavior,* p. 9.
44. Rom Harré, *Social Being: A Theory for Social Psychology* (Totowa, N. J.: Rowman and Littlefield, 1980). The classic expression of ordinary language philosophy is Gilbert Ryle, *The Concept of the Mind* (London: Hutchinson, 1949).

social psychologist. In his more recent volume Harré states that "account analyses" and "episode analyses" are complementary methods for the ethogenist. But by "episode analysis" he means the attempt to understand the dynamics of an observed social encounter by the application of a "dramaturgical metaphor."[45] While some social episodes are *formal*, having clearly stated rules and roles (games and ceremonies, for example), most are *enigmatic*: their structure and purpose are only semiconsciously apprehended, even by the participants. Consequently, the social psychologist tries to understand the enigmatic episode by comparing it to one or another formal episode. Is it most like a ceremony? Like a competitive game? Like a cooperative game?

It is quite permissible for the ethogenic social psychologist trying to answer such questions to analyze the scene, the setting, and the actors "using externally-attributed meanings and presently-existing, consciously formulated social theories."[46] He or she can also try to infer the goals of the episode—both the apparent, practical ones and the equally important but more covert social ones—such as saving face, maintaining group unity, revising a social hierarchy, and the like. However, these more detached episode analyses, done in the third person by the social psychologist, should go hand in hand with account analyses made by the persons involved in the episode. These will include the actors' own interpretations and (especially) justifications of their behavior but also, at a higher level, the "folk theories" by means of which they fit that episode into a larger world view. Only then will each participant's account be publicly compared to the researcher's third-person analysis of the episode.

When this is done, Harré and Secord note, it is quite possible that there will be discrepancies among the points of view. But it is the participant's account that has final authority in ethogenic research: "One condition for being a person is that the individual be aware (in the weak sense) of what he is doing, that is, be capable of saying what he is up to. We regard this criterion as central to any conception of the person." Nevertheless, that account may still be open to revision

---

45. Harré, *Social Being*, chap. 7. Invoking the dramaturgical model, Harré and Secord rely heavily on the earlier work of sociologist/social psychologist Erving Goffman, especially his *Presentation of Self in Everyday Life* (New York: Doubleday, 1959); *Asylums* (New York: Doubleday, 1961); and *Interaction Ritual* (New York: Doubleday, 1965).

46. Harré, *Social Being*, p. 123.

when "negotiated" with the external observer: the system "leaves room for deception and self-correction in ascribing mental attitudes. . . . Only the actor himself can give an authoritative report on the monitoring of his own behavior. [But] the fact that he is the ultimate authority does not entail that only he has access to his thoughts and feelings. Other people frequently have some access to the feelings of another and, if they speak the same language, to his thoughts as well."[47]

The prescribed methodology (and epistemology) of the ethogenist thus more resembles the modern therapeutic encounter than it does the laboratory experiment. In the negotiation of accounts, three parties are always envisaged—namely, two primary interactants and the social psychologist as observer, and all three are involved in teasing out the final meaning to be ascribed to any episode. And as in the therapeutic encounter, "there is no possibility of an absolutely objective, neutral account by which ambiguities may be resolved. Accounts can only be negotiated." Nevertheless, Harré and Secord still insist that the ethogenic approach is thoroughly within the confines of modern science:

> It is the self-monitored following of rules and plans that we believe to be the social-scientific analogue of the working of generative causal mechanisms in the processes that produce the non-random patterns studied by natural scientists. . . . [Although] accounts can only be negotiated, the open-endedness of this method of verification is no more disturbing than is the impossibility in physical science of knowing for certain if one's theoretical explanations are correct, and the never-ceasing possibility that they may have to be revised.[48]

Some Evaluative Comments. The reader may have discerned by now that the ethogenic alternative is one for which I have considerable sympathy. However, despite my attempts to summarize it as simply as possible, it is not an easy system for the student of psychology to grasp in its entirety. The reason is that it is, in fact, written in such systematic detail: combining the conceptual and analytic tools of the philosopher with a clear understanding of both the strengths and the weaknesses of mainstream social psychology, Harré and Secord have indeed tried to "begin at the beginning" and build up a

47. Harré and Secord, *The Explanation of Social Behavior,* p. 8.
48. Harré and Secord, *The Explanation of Social Behavior,* pp. 12, 17.

theoretical and epistemological edifice that can do justice to human social life. It is a system that at the moment concentrates more on a logical and structural understanding of social interactions, and the appropriate methods for understanding them, than on the empirical application of those ideas to actual social encounters. But at this point in social psychology's development, I believe that this is a strength rather than a weakness. Mainstream social psychology has indeed become unreflectively trapped in a reductionistic paradigm, the epistemology, theory, and methods of which are too behaviorist to do justice to the complexities of human social interaction. Consequently, its entire paradigm requires careful rethinking. "We all want progress," C. S. Lewis reminded his readers in Mere Christianity, "but progress means getting nearer to the place where you want to be. And if you have taken a wrong turning, then to go forward does not get you any nearer. . . . The man who turns back soonest is the most progressive man."[49]

On the ethogenic account, human beings are self-conscious producers and followers of social rules. Individuals and groups may adhere to different world views and hence justify their actions by appealing to different sets of rules. But what unites all of them in the ethogenic analysis is a concern to be perceived as "doing the right thing"—to advance what Harré has called their "moral careers." So basic is this desire that, in Harré's view, it almost always takes precedence over the mere extension of one's physical comfort. "The deepest human motive," he states, "is to seek the respect of others."[50] The Christian student can probably see that such an account has much to recommend it, even though it falls short of a fully orbed biblical anthropology. On the negative side the human impulse toward moral self-justification is one that we recognize, ultimately, as a consequence of the Fall: we are all conscious of our sin and finitude yet at the same time desperate to cover these up with evasions or rationalizations. On the positive side, having been endowed with accountable dominion, we have both the freedom and the responsibility to order our social lives by rules and rituals that are compatible with God's norms for human existence.

Because they see themselves as continuing in the tradition of mainstream science, which still separates facts from values, Harré and

49. Lewis, Mere Christianity (London: Collins-Fontana, 1955), p. 35.
50. Harré, Social Being, p. 2.

Secord have pointedly evaded the question about whether some rules have more absolute authority than others or, indeed, what is the ultimate origin of rules and rule-keeping in general. Nevertheless, their system opens up aspects of human life that are either ignored or reduced in the positivistic tradition while at the same time giving the latter credit where it is due. They willingly concede that some regularities in human behavior may be attributed to the person's responding to "the push and pull of forces exerted by the environment," while others are the result of "the person acting as an agent directing his own behavior." The challenge of social science, they maintain, is to discern which processes are most appropriately considered in one or the other of these categories or somewhere in between. They themselves have chosen to emphasize self-directed and self-monitored behavior "because it has been generally neglected in the behavioral sciences, because this is the prototype of behavior in ordinary daily living, and because we believe it to be the main factor in the production of specifically *social* behavior."[51] The result is a system that will amply repay careful study and application.

GERGEN'S "SOCIORATIONALISM"

Kenneth Gergen has already been cited a number of times in this chapter for his analysis and criticisms of the paradigm of mainstream social psychology. However, his efforts—like those of Harré and Secord—have gone beyond criticism to embrace the task of thinking about a new paradigm in some detail. Trained within the positivistic tradition and productive for many years within it,[52] Gergen suddenly began to add fuel to the disciplinary crisis in 1973, when he wrote a paper entitled "Social Psychology as History."[53] In that article Gergen argued, against the received view, that although social psychology prides itself on using scientific methods to establish general laws, both its theories and its research results are in fact little more than reflections of contemporary history. For one thing, he noted, successive generations of research subjects can differ so markedly from

51. Harré and Secord, *The Explanation of Social Behavior*, pp. 8, 9.

52. See, for example, Gergen's edited text *Social Psychology: Explorations in Understanding* (Del Mar, Calif.: Ziff-Davis, 1974), and the various references to his earlier work contained in that volume.

53. Gergen, "Social Psychology as History," *Journal of Personality and Social Psychology* 26 (May 1973): 309–20.

one another as to relativize drastically the conclusions of so-called classic studies in social psychology. Thus, for example, Solomon Asch found in the 1950s that naive subjects could easily be made to conform their judgments to those of an erroneous majority of experimental confederates.[54] But in 1980, when a team of British researchers attempted a precise replication of Asch's work (although they took pains to recruit subjects who had never heard of it), they found that in only one out of 396 trials did anyone give in to the experimentally induced social pressure. The famous "Asch effect," they suggested, may simply have been a child of its time.[55]

Not just research results but the theories that inspire or emerge from them are strongly influenced by their historical milieu, Gergen argued—drawing strongly on postmodern philosophers such as Kuhn. For example, the theory that attitude change depends heavily on communicator credibility is dependent on cultural attitudes toward authority; theories of cognitive dissonance reflect a culturally (or even subculturally) specific norm of logical consistency, and so on. Moreover, despite the official rhetoric about dispassionate scientific investigation, most social (and other) psychological theory is laden with prescriptive bias. As Gergen put it, "Most of us would feel insulted if characterized as low in self-esteem, high in approval-seeking, cognitively undifferentiated, anal compulsive, field-dependent or close-minded. . . . In their prescriptive capacity, such communications become agents of social change."[56]

But this being the case, science and society constitute a species of feedback loop in which human reflexivity is very active: told that psychologists have blacklisted (or approved of) certain social behaviors, the literate public then strives to avoid (or cultivate) the same, thus weakening the very relationships (e.g., between sex and conformity, between crowding and diffusion of responsibility) that were recorded as observed regularities in the first place. In Gergen's words, "sophistication as to psychological principles liberates one from their behavioral implications"—and this, he added, is all the more reason to regard social psychology as mainly a historical discipline rather

54. Asch, "Effects of Group Pressure upon the Modification and Distortion of Judgments," in *Groups, Leadership, and Men,* ed. Harold Guetzkow (Pittsburgh: Carnegie Press, 1951).
55. S. Perrin and C. Spencer, "The Asch Effect—A Child of Its Time?" *Bulletin of the British Psychological Society* 32 (1980): 405–6.
56. Gergen, "Social Psychology as History," p. 311.

than a scientific one. He advised his fellow social psychologists to focus more intensively on contemporary social issues and relinquish the attempt to establish transtemporal laws of social interaction. In addition, he suggested, they should aim to sensitize public behavior rather than to predict and control it—that is, they should inform people of the range of *possible* influences that might be of current significance, "thus expanding [their] sensitivities and readying [them] for more rapid accommodation to environmental change." Finally, he advocated the adoption of research methods that were more time-sensitive in order to distinguish social phenomena highly responsive to historical influences from those (more physiologically bound or more stubbornly acquired) that are relatively durable.[57]

Unlike Harré and Secord, then, Gergen does not see reformed social psychology as continuing in the natural-science tradition, however flexibly that term is defined. Ethogenists, like natural scientists, look for patterned regularities in social behavior but plead for a methodology to study these that does better justice to human volition, reflexivity, and moral consciousness. But Gergen's "sociorationalism," as he calls it, is much more historically relativist in its epistemology—although he writes with sympathy for the ethogenic alternative, considering it, along with his own, part of the same "endogenic revolt" against mainstream social psychology. Having concluded that the reality of human changeability obviates the possibility of a behavioral-science language linked strictly to observables, Gergen agrees with Harré and Secord that what is needed is a type of rationally analyzed "motivational discourse" in which we can "transcend the particulars of the ever-changing surface and treat descriptive terms [such as reading, helping, playing, etc.] as if they referred to internal tendencies or motives [which are] granted the power to originate and control the goal-directed actions of the person."[58]

In his more recent volume, *Toward Transformation in Social Knowledge*, Gergen also argues that once psychology is liberated from the pretense of having to link hypothetical constructs to external observations, it may experience a revitalization of the role of theory. He points out that the most far-ranging and significant theories of our time—those of Darwin, Freud, Marx, and Keynes, for example—do not submit to falsification in the Popperian sense but are no less

57. Gergen, "Social Psychology as History," pp. 313, 317.
58. Gergen, *Toward Transformation in Social Knowledge*, pp. 84–85.

influential for all that (and let us recall from Chapter One that precisely the same can be said of Christianity as a world view). Theoretical work, he insists, is itself a form of praxis, an activity with far-reaching social consequences of a sort that psychologists (apart from those in the therapeutic domain) ignore because, in their misguided allegiance to positivism, they are afraid to theorize boldly or with pointed value concerns. But provided that such values are both explicit and continually subject to the scrutiny of a well-nurtured "critical wing . . . whose chief concern is with the broad consequences of various theoretical viewpoints and the elaboration of alternatives," then there is no need to fear their routine inclusion in the discipline—indeed, we should encourage it.[59]

It is precisely on this point that Gergen supplies the Christian reader with something that is missing in Harré and Secord's system. While the latter show the traditional scientific hesitation to integrate specific value concerns into their theorizing, Gergen follows the lead of the German critical theorists in seeing as part of the task of social science the exposure of ideological bias (however masked by the rhetoric of neutrality) and the design of alternative perspectives for shaping a more just society in the future.[60] It is not totally clear in his writings how he proposes to reconcile his strong sense of historical relativism with this passion for justice and all that it implies—but in the long run, it is the latter that seems to be the stronger theme in his system:

> In a broad sense, [this] orientation invites conflict, favoring as it does the existence of multiple groups with varying investments. However, it simultaneously eschews hierarchies in society; it stands as a rationale against the domination of certain subcultures by others. Finally [it] grants the individual the fundamental capacity for choice. It invites one to suspend belief in the past as a prison . . . and to consider oneself as inherently free to change the trajectory of one's life. And, by granting choice, [this account] restores the concept of personal responsibility to the repertoire of evaluative terms. Because there is choice people may be properly praised or condemned for their conduct.[61]

59. Gergen, *Toward Transformation in Social Knowledge*, p. 99.
60. See particularly Jürgen Habermas, *Knowledge and Human Interest* (Boston: Beacon Press, 1971); and M. Horkheimer, *Critical Theory* (New York: Seabury Press, 1972).
61. Gergen, *Toward Transformation in Social Knowledge*, p. 172.

Thus, although all of the implications for social psychology have not been developed, Gergen's insistent rejection of the traditional fact-value dichotomy, his openness to value pluralism, and his determination to align the discipline with the needs of the weak rather than the strong could, if more widely adopted, make psychology a more acceptable area for explicitly Christian theorizing as well. But this, of course, remains to be seen.

Strange as it might seem, Gergen does not share Harré and Secord's conviction that the eclipse of positivism should mean the end of experimental research by social psychologists. They can continue to do experiments, he says, but warns that such research must now be reconceptualized "primarily as a rhetorical implement [whose] chief function is to lend power (persuasive impact, appeal, felicity) to the theoretical language."[62] Experiments and other empirical techniques are thus seen as something like object lessons in a sermon: they allow for the concretization and ordinary-language description of theoretical relationships that might otherwise get bogged down in ababstractions. But they do not, on Gergen's account, contribute in any unique way to either the verification or the falsification of the theories they instantiate. Again, despite his strong sense of historical relativity, Gergen does not totally reject the concept of cumulative knowledge in social science, either. Rather, he relocates its means: "Advances may be generated primarily through criticism, novel theory-generation, unsettling predictions, and new means of solving present problems within society. In this sense, advances in the sociobehavioral sciences may parallel those found in philosophy or the arts."[63]

At the beginning of this chapter I suggested that current social psychology would pose a particularly stark challenge to Christian students in the discipline. On the one hand, mainstream social psychology, for all its disclaimers to the contrary, has been largely a reductionist enterprise, treating its human subjects as just that: entities passively "subject to" the shaping and reshaping of social influences, with very little autonomy in dealing with these. On the other hand, a reform movement such as Harré and Secord's ethogeny attempts to take seriously the agency of persons in creating, following, and rejecting social rules, albeit in patterned ways. Gergen's sociora-

62. Gergen, *Toward Transformation in Social Knowledge*, pp. 102–3.
63. Gergen, *Toward Transformation in Social Knowledge*, pp. 105–6.

tionalism goes even further beyond traditional scientific neutrality by insisting on both the inevitability and the desirability of explicit value-concerns in social psychological theorizing.

My own inclination as a Christian is to pay close attention to these emerging reform movements—not because we as Christians reject the existence of events that shape us without our knowledge or consent, but because social psychology has clearly become stuck in its overemphasis on the latter. However, we have also seen that ethogenists study only the process and patterns of rule-keeping while evading important questions about the comparative merits of any given rules. Moreover, Gergen's forthright adherence to a set of value priorities is not easily reconciled with his strong sense of historical relativity. Still, I suggest that there is much in these reform movements for thoughtful Christians to digest and work with, even while not necessarily abandoning the more traditional approach. The closing years of the twentieth century should see this mainstream tradition yielding—either gracefully or reluctantly—much of its hegemony as it necessarily shares its resources and training procedures with those of reformers who are determined to do greater justice to the whole person in his or her role as both the researcher and the researched.

CHAPTER 10

PERSONALITY PSYCHOLOGY:
An Ambiguous Ally

The "whole man" is an elusive creature; there doesn't seem to be much that science can do with him.

—Gordon W. Allport[1]

[It is] the personality psychologist's conviction that an adequate understanding of human behavior will evolve only from the study of the whole person. . . . While psychologists in general have shown increased specialization, leading to the complaint that they were learning more and more about less and less, the personality theorist has accepted at least partial responsibility for bringing together and organizing the diverse findings of the specialists.

—Calvin Hall and Gardner Lindzey[2]

In the last chapter I pointed out that social psychology can be regarded as a kind of bridge between the natural-science and the human-science paradigms in Anglo-American psychology, and we saw that not a few social psychologists, originally trained and long active in the former tradition, are now arguing that it be supplanted or at least supplemented by the latter. In this chapter on personality psychology, the last topic of the contemporary psychological scene to be considered, we will find that this paradigmatic ambivalence is even

---

1. Allport, "European and American Theories of Personality," in *Perspectives in Personality Theory*, ed. Henry P. David and Helmut von Bracken (New York: Basic Books, 1957), p. 8.

2. Hall and Lindzey, *Theories of Personality*, 2nd ed. (New York: John Wiley, 1970), p. 6.

more striking. Indeed, if anything, the balance of forces in this field is the reverse of that in social psychology. For it is safe to say that personality (or the field of "personology" as it is also called) is the one area of academic psychology in which the freedom to theorize boldly with relevance to the real-life concerns of persons has continually overshadowed the preoccupation with empirical rigor that characterizes psychology as a whole. It is a field over which, in the words of Hall and Lindzey, "the stiffening brush of positivism has spread much more lightly" than it has over the other areas of psychology we have considered: "Personality theorists in their own times have been rebels. Rebels in medicine and in experimental science, rebels against conventional ideas and usual practices, rebels against typical methods and respected techniques of research, and most of all rebels against accepted theory and normative problems."[3]

It is generally admitted that, because of its maverick stance vis-à-vis traditional positivism, the field of personality study has been more tolerated than welcomed in the mainstream of academic psychology. Yet even its sharpest critics seem willing to admit that personology, for all its marginal status, supplies some essential correctives to the narrow theorizing and causally oriented empiricism that characterize the rest of the discipline. "This catholicity and lack of skepticism has not made personologists popular and respected among psychologists," concedes Salvatore Maddi, a personality theorist at the University of Chicago, "but it has permitted a vigor of conceptualization and a willingness to tackle complex problems."[4] Hall and Lindzey, best known as authors of texts on both general psychology and personality, agree: "The fact that personality theory has never been deeply embedded in the mainstream of academic psychology has . . . tended to free [it] from the deadly grip of conventional modes of thought and preconceptions concerning human behavior. By being relatively uninvolved in the ongoing institution of psychology it was easier for personality theorists to question or reject assumptions which were widely accepted by psychologists."[5]

It must also be said that this independence from mainstream psychology has often resulted in a lack of discipline in the work of personologists. With some exceptions they have tended to scatter

3. Hall and Lindzey, *Theories of Personality*, p. 4.
4. Maddi, *Personality Theories: A Comparative Analysis*, 4th ed. (Homewood, Ill.: Dorsey Press, 1980), p. 13.
5. Hall and Lindzey, *Theories of Personality*, p. 4.

their shot widely and to neglect the responsibility of thorough formulation and organized debate. Often they have yielded only reluctantly to empirical testing of their theories. But all of this appears to be changing as the field itself develops—and it must be noted that, like social psychology, personality psychology was not even formalized as a part of academic psychology until the mid-1930s.[6] Thus we should not be too surprised that it is a field still somewhat in search of its own paradigm.

My consideration of this atypical area of psychology will begin with a brief description of its contours and some reasons for its importance to the Christian student of psychology. I will then enlarge on what in my estimation is the most significant of these reasons—namely, that an understanding of personality theorizing may be of vital help in advancing the task of formulating a biblical anthropology. Finally, I will sound some precautionary notes about the pitfalls of this otherwise congenial field. For we will discover throughout this chapter that precisely *because* personology deals with the condition of whole persons in their life context, its various theories can easily become rivals—even hostile rivals—to Christian faith. It is in this respect that I refer to personality psychology as an "ambiguous ally" of the Christian.

THE IMPORTANCE OF PERSONALITY AS A FIELD OF INQUIRY

I have just noted that the study of personality did not receive a formal place in the university curriculum until the mid-1930s. This, of course, does not mean that its concerns were brand-new at that time. To the extent that personology is concerned *both* with what is generally human *and* with what makes individuals differ from one another, it is a field of inquiry that goes back to the ancients and resurfaces in different forms throughout the history of ideas.[7] Most contemporary definitions of personality continue to reflect this joint emphasis on *general* human nature and *unique* individuality, as the following examples show:

6. See John C. Burnham, "Historical Background for the Study of Personality," in *Handbook of Personality Theory and Research*, ed. Edgar F. Borgatta and William W. Lambert (Chicago: Rand McNally, 1968), pp. 3–81.
7. See Burnham, "Historical Background," for a concise survey of pre-twentieth-century thinking on personality.

Personality is the dynamic organization within the individual of those psychological systems that determine his characteristic behavior and thought.[8]

Personality consists of the distinctive patterns of behavior (including thoughts and emotions) that characterize each individual's adaptation to the situations of his or her life.[9]

Personality is an organization that exhibits some continuity even as it changes throughout the individual's life.[10]

[Personality theory affirms that] every man is in some respects (1) like all other men, (2) like some other men, (3) like no other man.[11]

Personality is a stable set of characteristics and tendencies that determine those commonalities and differences in the psychological behavior (thoughts, feelings, and actions) of people that have continuity in time and that may not easily be understood as the sole result of social and biological pressures of the moment.[12]

The study of personality is concerned with the various styles of behavior that different organisms habitually reflect.[13]

Although the above definitions of personality are generally typical of the field, we should also note that the Anglo-American attraction to operationism (which I discussed in Chapter Eight with reference to intelligence) has sometimes tempted personologists as well. Thus Hall and Lindzey refuse to define personality other than "by the empirical concepts which are a part of the theory of personality employed by the observer."[14] This comes very close to defining personality as "whatever the various personality tests measure," and no more. The impulse behind this truncated approach is in many ways understandable: it represents an attempt to limit the scope of personology to that which can be clearly and repeatedly demonstrated

8. Gordon W. Allport, *Pattern and Growth in Personality* (New York: Holt, Rinehart and Winston, 1961), p. 28.
9. Walter Mischel, *Introduction to Personality*, 2nd ed. (New York: Holt, Rinehart and Winston, 1976), p. 2.
10. Nevitt Sanford, *Issues in Personality Theory* (San Francisco: Jossey-Bass, 1970), p. 112.
11. Clyde Kluckholn and Henry A. Murray, *Personality in Nature, Society, and Culture* (New York: Knopf, 1948), p. 35.
12. Maddi, *Personality Theories*, p. 10.
13. Joseph F. Rychlak, *Introduction to Personality and Psychotherapy*, 2nd ed. (Boston: Houghton Mifflin, 1981), p. 2.
14. Hall and Lindzey, *Theories of Personality*, p. 11.

through empirical investigation, and thereby to curb reckless speculation.

But the associated problems of this approach when it becomes monolithic are twofold. First, such operationism all too easily slips into a denial—or at the very least a neglect—of the theoretical assumptions that lie beneath every test instrument (recall the discussion of intelligence tests in Chapter Eight)—a questionable practice in light of the postmodern philosophy of science. Second, the operationists' neglect of general personality theory in pursuit of reliable but limited personality measurements can very easily turn them from scientists into mere engineers, so preoccupied with the minutiae of experimental and correlational techniques that they become less and less able to contribute to the theoretical edifice that is the very grist of the research mill itself. It is this tendency that led Gordon Allport to characterize personologists of an operationist bent as "shameless borrowers [who] have created few basic ideas of their own (except for method) and have appropriated the heart of their theories [from elsewhere]."[15]

In light of these considerations, I will restrict my consideration to personality theory as embodied in the first list of definitions I quoted—that is, to systematic attempts to postulate both what is common to all human beings and what is unique to groups and individuals in terms of characteristic behavior and thought. This, of course, does not preclude the value of an appeal to the various empirical tests of such theories. The Christian reader may already be able to guess why an understanding of personology thus defined is an important undertaking: it is the area of psychology that most overlaps with the concerns of the biblical anthropologist. Or, to borrow Arthur Holmes' term, it is the area of psychology that is most "world-viewish" in its implications.[16]

The reader will recall from Chapter Four that a complete theory of human nature has four essential aspects: (1) a background theory about the nature of the universe, (2) a theory about the unique nature of human beings, (3) a theory that accounts for the problems of their present condition, and (4) a prescription for the solution of these problems. Although personality theorists seldom tackle all four of these areas, the attention they give to the last three is in striking

15. Allport, "European and American Theories of Personality," p. 19.
16. Holmes, *Contours of a World View* (Grand Rapids: Eerdmans, 1983).

contrast to the narrow specialization typical of most areas of psychology, a fact explicitly recognized by Hall and Lindzey in their standard text on theories of personality:

At a time when the experimental psychologist was engrossed with such questions as the existence of imageless thought, the speed with which nerve impulses travel [and] deciding whether there was localization of function within the brain, the personality theorist was concerned with why it was that certain individuals developed crippling neurotic symptoms in the absence of organic pathology, the role of childhood trauma in adult adjustment, the conditions under which mental health could be regained, and the major motivations that underlay human behavior. Thus, it was the personality theorist, and only the personality theorist, who in the early days of psychology dealt with questions which to the average person seem to lie at the core of a successful psychological science.[17]

This quotation also suggests a second reason for the importance of personology to the Christian: it is the one area of psychology in which theory, research, and clinical practice comfortably rub shoulders with each other. Indeed, it is not uncommon for texts in personology to deal with all three areas at once and in a fashion that at least attempts to be integrated.[18] As one might expect, this breadth of focus also has its disadvantages, for it is precisely the attempt to cover all three fronts at once that has led to the superficiality and carelessness that characterize much of the field. Yet to the Christian, the nature of whose world view *requires* an integration of belief and practice, there is something rightly appealing about the personologist's commitment to do likewise. This is true even though the mingling of theory with application in personology is more the result of historical accident than of principled planning: the early giants of personality theory (Freud, Jung, McDougall) were medical doctors and psychotherapists as well, and it is largely due to their initial example that theory and practical application have remained closely linked in personology ever since.

I have noted that personologists are interested *both* in what is unique to all human beings (as opposed to other organisms) *and* in how (and why) human beings differ from one another at the level of

17. Hall and Lindzey, *Theories of Personality*, pp. 4-5.
18. See, for example, Rychlak, *Introduction to Personality and Psychotherapy*.

personality expression. Both of these issues are also of enduring concern to the Christian. On the one hand, we affirm that human beings share certain common conditions as a result of their common participation in the biblical drama of creation, fall, common grace, and (for many) redemption. On the other hand, Christ's parable of the talents and the many apostolic references to "varieties of gifts" sensitize us to the uniqueness of individuals and the importance of recognizing and developing their strengths, and helping them to overcome—or at least cope with—their limitations.

This thoroughly biblical portrait, which sees the person both as unique and alone before God *and* as sharing (and needing) a common heritage with others, has been astutely captured by Dietrich Bonhoeffer in his *Life Together,* which was written from his experience of the Confessing Church after it was driven underground by Hitler prior to World War II:

> *Let him who cannot be alone beware of community.* He will only do harm to himself and to the community. Alone you stood before God when he called you; alone you had to answer that call; alone you had to struggle and pray; and alone you will die and give an account to God. You cannot escape from yourself; for God has singled you out. . . . But the reverse is also true: *Let him who is not in community beware of being alone.* Into community you were called, the call was not meant for you alone; in the community of the called you bear your cross, you struggle, you pray. . . . If you scorn the fellowship of the brethren, you reject the call of Jesus Christ, and thus your solitude will be hurtful to you. . . .
>
> Only in the fellowship do we learn to be rightly alone, and only in aloneness do we learn to live rightly in fellowship. It is not as though the one preceded the other; both begin at the same time, namely with the call of Jesus Christ.[19]

But although, as Bonhoeffer says, the tension between Christian aloneness and Christian solidarity is rooted in the call of Christ, the *universal* tension between human aloneness and human solidarity goes right back to the creation order, to the Fall, and to the common grace of God, which restricts the worst consequences of the Fall. It is this heritage that the Christian shares with the personality theorist who recognizes that each person is in some respects (1) like all other persons, (2) like some other persons, and (3) like no other person. Of

19. Bonhoeffer, *Life Together* (London: SCM Press, 1954), pp. 57–58.

course, the Christian personality theorist will differ with the non-Christian personality theorist about the *content* of these statements; indeed, we should expect some differences among Christians themselves regarding some of the details, given differences in theological traditions even among those who share a high view of Scripture. Nevertheless, all are working at the level of the whole person in interaction with the world, with other people, and with systems of values. To this extent, all are concerned with what it ultimately means to be a human being.

Finally, personologists usually include some kind of developmental statement in their theories—a statement about how the adult, whether ideal or pathological in his or her adjustment, emerges from the relatively undifferentiated child. I have already noted in a previous chapter that this is a concern that "comes with the territory" of biblical anthropology. Because the Scriptures speak of children as going from a nonresponsible status as dependents to one of full accountability before God and the community, the process by which this takes place and the responsibilities incumbent upon children's caretakers as a result are continuing concerns of the Christian community.

So much for our general outline of the concerns of personologists and their significance for Christian students of psychology. Let us now become more specific, and through a brief look at the general structure of personality theories try to see how we might be aided in our own task of fleshing out a biblical anthropology.

PERSONOLOGY AS ANTHROPOLOGY

In my experience it is common for students—both Christian and otherwise—to expect great things as they embark on their first course in personality, only to find themselves confused, bored, or disappointed by the end of it. Although initially drawn to personology by its unique concern with "questions . . . which seem to lie at the core of a successful psychological science" (to quote Hall and Lindzey again), many students find themselves overwhelmed by the diversity of independent theories the details of which they must assimilate, or alternately put off by the monolithic claims of a single position that is taught almost to the exclusion of any other.

Salvatore Maddi labels these two contrasting approaches "benevolent eclecticism" and "partisan zealotry" respectively, and suggests that their entrenchment is partly due to the relative newness of personology as a formal part of psychology: "People having partisan zeal ensure that the hard work of formulating, refining, selling, and defending particular viewpoints gets done. . . . [Benevolent eclectics] ensure a sufficiently open mind . . . so that there is freedom to accept or reject the arguments of zealots. [They also give] an opportunity for the difficult, heavily intuitive work of theory formulation to go forward without premature hampering by hard-headed, cynical evaluation."[20]

I think that Maddi is correct when he says that it is partly the youthfulness of personology that accounts for these opposite approaches to its organization and presentation. But there are other possibilities of which Christian students need to be aware. The partisan zealot of a particular theory is seldom offering a merely heuristic device for stimulating intellectual exchange or clinical practice; often he or she is also a "true believer" who is convinced of the metaphysical truth of that particular theory and the world view that is implied by it. As such, the theory and its company of adherents become cult-like replacements for biblical faith and the community of Christian believers. The benevolent eclectic, on the other hand, is often a thinly disguised scientific agnostic, determined to describe every theory as it comes along but claiming commitment to none of them in the absence of extensive empirical verification of a certain quality. This benign neutrality often masks a deeply rooted scientism that is no more congenial to Christianity in its apparent objectivity than is the theoretical orientation of the zealous partisan.

In searching for a third way between these two extremes, Maddi at least offers a manageable framework within which we may understand personality theorizing as an anthropological and, indeed, a covertly religious endeavor. His organizational scheme, which he calls "comparative analysis,"

> from benevolent eclecticism . . . borrows the breadth and balance involved in considering many theories of personality, and from partisan zealotry . . . borrows the conviction that one or a few theories are better than others. [It aims] . . . to discover the similarities and differences among many existing theories of personality as a starting point for determining which type of theorizing is the most fruitful.[21]

20. Maddi, *Personality Theories*, p. 3.
21. Maddi, *Personality Theories*, p. 2.

Such an approach also has its limits, for a Christian evaluation of any personality theory does not stop with an assessment of its logical coherence or its empirical demonstrability, however important these may be. Also to be considered is its compatibility with what the Bible reveals or implies about personhood. Nevertheless, Maddi's comparative framework offers a useful starting place for this task, so let us consider it briefly.

The Implicit Structure of Personality Theories. The reader is already aware that personality theories deal with both the commonalities and the differences among people. Some theorists are more concerned with the first of these; others are more concerned with the second. But a personality theory aiming at completeness will have something to say on both levels—both about human nature in general and about the nature and origin of individual differences.

When a theory refers to things that are said to be common to all people—inherent attributes of humanness that exercise a pervasive and relatively stable influence throughout life—it is making, in Maddi's terms, a *core statement* about personality. "It is in core theorizing that the personologist makes a major statement about the overall directionality, purpose, and function of life. This statement takes the form of postulating one or perhaps two *core tendencies* [for example, instinctual gratification, social acceptability, self-actualization, maintenance of consistency, etc.]"[22] that are presumed to be the basic motivators of human existence. Core theorizing also includes what Maddi calls the *core characteristics* common to all persons and implied by the core tendency. Thus, if one theory's core tendency is instinct gratification, its core characteristics will include a list of those instincts—sexual, aggressive, and the like. If the core tendency in another theory is "the need to predict and control the events of one's life," then the core characteristics will have a similarly cognitive flavor and will be cast in the language of mental constructs, classifications, and expectancies. Thus it is in the core statement of a personality theory that we come closest to the theorist's convictions about what is distinctively and universally human.

In what Maddi calls a *peripheral statement*, the theorist goes on to distinguish the concrete personality styles that differ from person to person. At the most minute level, *concrete peripheral characteristics* (sometimes called "traits") refer to isolated aspects of a person's

---

22. Maddi, *Personality Theories*, p. 14.

style—traits such as achievement motivation, timidity, generosity, stubbornness, etc. At the intermediate level, various traits are often seen as organized into "types" of people who share a common "package" of peripheral characteristics. Thus, for example, Freud speaks of oral, anal, phallic, and genital personality types, while Jung distinguishes introverted and extroverted types, and Rank speaks of artistic and neurotic types. We can now see that it is at the concrete peripheral level of multiple traits that a person is totally *unique*, at the "type" level that he or she is like *some* other persons, and at the core level that he or she is said to be like *all* other people.

Linking the core to the periphery of personality is what Maddi calls the theorist's *developmental statement*, which outlines the way in which the undifferentiated core tendency and characteristics interact with the social and physical environment to produce adult personality types. Significant here is the importance ascribed to the family by most personality theorists: the personality type displayed by the adult is almost always seen as heavily influenced by the type of family in which he or she matures. In addition, all personality theories imply or specify what Maddi calls an *ideal personality type*—one that most fully expresses what the theorist believes are the core tendency and core characteristics of human nature, and that is the result of implicitly ideal developmental conditions. Other, less-than-ideal developmental conditions are said to result in nonideal adult personality types that may in fact be pathological enough to require intervention.

A schematic summary of Maddi's structural analysis of personality theories is given in Figure 10.1. It should be noted that this is, in effect, Maddi's "ideal type" for a logically coherent and complete personality theory, and that many theories are lopsided in their stress on one or another of the core, peripheral, or developmental statements. Nor does Maddi suggest that a theory must be complete on all levels before being offered for consideration; but the most fruitful and influential theories, from both an intellectual and a practical standpoint, are those that, regardless of their starting point, continue to elaborate toward greater and greater completeness.

The elaboration of personality theories normally takes place through a variety of channels, as personologists do psychometric assessments of people, practice psychotherapy, or conduct empirical research aimed at demonstrating aspects or implications of a particular theory. All of these activities provide grist for the theoretical mill. But the opposite is also the case, as Maddi readily appreciates when he

Figure 10.1. Maddi's schematic representation of the structure of personality theories. The single solid line between the core statement and the periphery statement indicates that each theorist postulates an ideal course of postnatal development resulting in an ideal type, or character (*Personality Theories: A Comparative Analysis*, 4th ed. [Homewood, Ill.: Dorsey Press, 1980], p. 16).

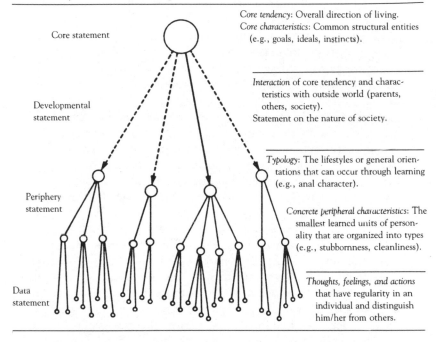

Core statement

Core tendency: Overall direction of living.
Core characteristics: Common structural entities (e.g., goals, ideals, instincts).

Developmental statement

Interaction of core tendency and characteristics with outside world (parents, others, society).
Statement on the nature of society.

Periphery statement

Typology: The lifestyles or general orientations that can occur through learning (e.g., anal character).

Concrete peripheral characteristics: The smallest learned units of personality that are organized into types (e.g., stubbornness, cleanliness).

Data statement

Thoughts, feelings, and actions that have regularity in an individual and distinguish him/her from others.

points out that personologists cannot help but conduct their research and applied activities according to their preferred theory of personality, however completely or incompletely elaborated this may be:

> When you assess a person's personality, you are working with a particular explicit or implicit sense of typology and its component, concrete peripheral characteristics. This is so because it is here that a personality theory permits pinpointing of differences among persons. . . . When you attempt to do psychotherapy, you must decide, on the basis of your view of human nature (core of personality) and the particular peripheral personality confronting you (is it ideal or not?), what is to be done. Looked at

this way, psychotherapy is a special case of development, so the therapist's view of development is also involved. [23]

Here, then, we have at least one personologist who recognizes the inevitable metaphysical underpinnings of his profession. Maddi in effect is conceding that the personologist's prescientific convictions about human nature, its ideal unfolding, and its ideal endpoint cannot help but influence his or her research and counseling activities. It is unfortunate that so few of his colleagues share this recognition or take any pains to state their orientation with any degree of clarity or frankness to prospective clients. Using the scheme I have just summarized, however, Maddi himself has done a creditable job of classifying personological orientations, so let us turn to this now.

A *Typology of Personality Theories.* It is not hard to agree with Maddi when he asserts that the field of personology has been in a state of unnecessarily prolonged infancy. For the past fifty years personality theorizing at varying levels of complexity has been done by many thinkers, most of whose names have become household words among psychologists. "We have had a set of reasonably coherent theories for some time now," writes Maddi. "[Even when] an occasional theory is added to the store already available . . . on further analysis [it] invariably seems more a rephrasing or elaboration of an earlier one than a new departure."[24] What has been lacking in all of this has been a serious and workable attempt to pinpoint the issues that *separate* various theories from each other. In Maddi's thinking (based on an analysis of twenty-two theories representative of the entire field) the presently acknowledged stock of personality theories can be divided into three basic types, with each of these three subdividing into two others.

Broadly speaking, it seems possible to classify any given personality theory as being *conflict*-oriented, *fulfillment*-oriented, or *consistency*-oriented, depending on the theorist's view of basic human nature and the social and physical realities in which it unfolds and with which it must continue to reckon in adulthood. In the first of these, *the conflict model,* human nature is seen in terms of a perpetual opposition between two great, unchanging forces, with life at best a compromising balance between the two and at worst an unsuccessful

23. Maddi, *Personality Theories,* pp. 16–17.
24. Maddi, *Personality Theories,* p. 4.

attempt to deny one or the other. Sometimes, as with Freud and his followers, the conflict is seen to be *psychosocial* in nature, with the biological instincts of the individual at war with the demands of organized society. Alternately, this conflict may be seen as occurring completely within the individual—i.e., being *intrapsychic* in nature and reflecting a profound ambivalence with which all persons are said to struggle. A classic example of an intrapsychic conflict theory is that of Otto Rank, according to which all human functioning is ultimately traceable to the tension between wanting to be unique (but at the risk of being alone) and wanting to be part of the group (but at the risk of losing one's identity).[25]

By contrast with the conflict model, the second major type of personality theory—*the fulfillment model*—assumes only one great force for human nature to respond to and locates it within each individual. Life then becomes, in its ideal unfolding, the progressively greater expression of this force. Conflict is possible within this model (the force can be thwarted in various ways), but it is not (as in the first model) inevitable. This model also subdivides into two types: in the *actualization* version the "great force" is likened to a genetic blueprint that determines the individual's capabilities and in addition urges him or her on toward complete development. Abraham Maslow is probably the best-known American theorist associated with this position; indeed, his description of the ideal type, "the self-actualizing person," has become something of a catch phrase among many readers of popular psychology.[26] Carl Rogers is another example of a fulfillment theorist of the actualization genre.[27] Alternately, the *perfection* version of the fulfillment model places less stress on innate capabilities and more on active striving toward ideals of what is noble and meaningful in life. The "great force" in this version is the motivation to strive *toward* such ideals, regardless of whether or not one's native endowments are perfectly tuned toward that end. The theories of Alfred Adler and various existential psychologists (e.g., Médard Boss, Victor Frankl, Ludwig Binswanger) are current examples of this approach; Gordon Allport and Erich Fromm are

25. Rank, *The Trauma of Birth* (New York: Harcourt, Brace, 1929); and *Will Therapy and Truth and Reality* (New York: Knopf, 1945).

26. See, for example, Abraham Maslow, "Deficiency Motivation and Growth Motivation," in *Nebraska Symposium on Motivation*, ed. M. R. Jones (Lincoln, Neb.: University of Nebraska Press, 1955).

27. See, for example, Rogers, *On Becoming a Person* (Boston: Houghton Mifflin, 1961).

primarily perfection theorists with something of an actualization orientation as well.[28]

The third and final kind of personality theory comes under what Maddi terms *the consistency model*, according to which the single most formative influence on all persons is feedback from the external world. If such feedback is consistent with what one has known before or with what one expects, a state of quiescence reigns. But if there is inconsistency, then there results a pressure to decrease this uncomfortable state of affairs. Human life is thus viewed as an endless attempt to maintain consistency. In this model the inevitable tension of the conflict model is rejected, as is the fulfillment model's presumption of either predetermined capacities or chosen ideals as blueprints for living. The *content* of beliefs or capacities is not what is important in this model but rather the *process* of balancing expectations against reality in the attempt to keep them consistent with one another.

In the *cognitive dissonance* version of this model, the inconsistency against which we are all said to struggle is always cognitive in nature: two thoughts, perceptions, or values may be experienced as "dissonant," or inconsistent, or (more often) it may be an expectation that is in conflict with the perception of an actual event. George A. Kelly and David McClelland (and in some respects social psychologist Leon Festinger, whom we met in Chapter Nine) are in this tradition.[29] In the *activation* version of the consistency model, it is not *cognitive* elements that human beings strive to keep consistent but rather a habitual and an actual level of *bodily tension*, or "activation." Broadly put, such a theory postulates that if events underexcite a person (in comparison with his or her accustomed level of activation), the resulting state of boredom will produce an impluse toward greater activation. Conversely, if events overexcite a person in comparison with habitual levels of activation, the resulting stress will be an impulse to correct downward to the accustomed level. Maddi

28. See Adler, *Individual Psychology* (New York: Basic Books, 1956); Boss, *Psychoanalysis and Daseinanalysis* (New York: Basic Books, 1963); Frankl, *Man's Search for Meaning* (New York: Simon and Schuster, 1962); Binswanger, *Being-in-the-World: Selected Papers* (New York: Basic Books, 1963); Allport, *Pattern and Growth in Personality*; and Fromm, *Man for Himself* (New York: Holt, Rinehart and Winston, 1947).

29. See Kelly, *The Psychology of Personal Constructs*, vol. 1 (New York: Norton, 1955); McClelland, *Personality* (New York: Dryden, 1957); and Festinger, *A Theory of Cognitive Dissonance* (Stanford: Stanford University Press, 1957).

himself, in conjunction with psychologist Donald Fiske, has espoused this particular type of personology[30]—but it should be recalled that it is Maddi's analysis of personality theories *in general*, and not his own preferred theory in particular, that is of primary interest and use to our present discussion. What is most significant about consistency theories as a group is that the content of beliefs and activities is deemed less important than the process of reducing inconsistency per se, which is seen to be the core tendency of human nature.

CORE STATEMENTS ABOUT PERSONALITY FROM A BIBLICAL PERSPECTIVE

Figure 10.2 presents a summary of the preceding typology of personality theories. The reader should note that I have been concentrating on the "core statements" of each of these three broad types of theory, because this is the level of discourse that most concerns the student of biblical anthropology—that is, the level at which statements are made concerning what all human personalities have in common.

This leads us to an interesting question: Is it possible to express the basic ideas of a biblical anthropology using the categories that Maddi has suggested? Can we make a statement about the "core tendency" of all human personalities and suggest an accompanying list of "core characteristics"? I believe that we can, and that such an exercise can help us to clarify what Nicholas Wolterstorff has called our Christian "control beliefs"—those basic assumptions about the world and human nature by which we are aided in understanding other theories in our discipline and in evaluating them in order to accept, reject, or possibly adapt them.[31] Bear in mind that I do not consider the following exercise the final or only possible word on the subject—especially because I am not a trained personologist myself. But in making a start on such a task, I hope to encourage others to make adjustments and refinements in an ongoing fashion.

The first question we might ask ourselves is this: Is the biblical perspective on the core of human personality best understood in terms of a conflict model, an actualization model, or a fulfillment model? But even as we ask this question, it seems that we have an additional

30. Fiske and Maddi, eds., *Functions of Varied Experience* (Homewood, Ill.: Dorsey Press, 1961); see also Maddi, *Personality Theories*, pp. 181–92.
31. Wolterstorff, *Reason Within the Bounds of Religion* (Grand Rapids: Eerdmans, 1976).

Figure 10.2. A Summary of Maddi's Typology of Personality Theories

Basic Type	Sub-Types	Representative Theorists
I. Conflict Model	A) Psychosocial Version	Sigmund Freud, Henry Murray
	B) Intrapsychic Version	Otto Rank, Carl Jung, Andras Angyal
II. Fulfillment Model	A) Actualization Version	Carl Rogers, Abraham Maslow
	B) Perfection Version	Alfred Adler, Gordon Allport, Erich Fromm, various existential theorists
III. Consistency Model	A) Cognitive Dissonance Version	George Kelly, David McClelland
	B) Activation Version	Donald Fiske, Salvatore Maddi

complication to consider. For the Bible speaks not only of the inborn personality heritage common to all human beings but also of the possibility of a *second* birth and a completely "new creation" in Christ (2 Cor. 5:17). So even as we speak of our common, human core, we must also (in distinction from all other personality theories) speak of the possibility that, through the grace of God, this very core tendency can be changed and that, moreover, this can happen at any point during the person's life span. However, I believe that there is a way of conceptualizing this without ending up with a theory that is so awkward as to leave no room for dialogue with other theoretical traditions or for acknowledgment of possible truths they may have uncovered.

Let us begin with a consideration of the common heritage of all human beings who, as the Bible puts it, have been born "in Adam." Saint Augustine wrote that God had made us for himself and that all human hearts would be restless until they found their rest in him. This is as succinct a summary of our core tendency as a Christian could ask for—if we understand that our hearts are by nature not merely restless but also rebellious. From the perspective of the Bible, the basic human tendency that we all share at birth is in the nature of a *conflict* between total loyalty to the God who created us and total loyalty to oneself and, by extension, to any of a variety of idols that we try to force into that "God-shaped void" of which Augustine wrote. But recalling that Maddi spoke of two *different* types of conflict theories, we might be led to ask whether this basic conflict is a purely *internal* one, with two parts of ourselves (the God-oriented and the self-oriented) at war with each other, or what we might call a "theo-psychic" conflict, with our inborn tendency totally at war with God until he intervenes at conversion.

Already we can see how Maddi's categories may be too simple, because the Bible seems to say that the conflict may be of *both* sorts. In writing to the Romans, Paul speaks of the wicked, who "suppress the truth. . . . What can be known about God is plain to them, because God has shown it to them. . . . [But] although they knew God they did not honor him as God" (Rom. 1:19–21). At root, Paul seems to be saying, we are at war with God and do not want to respond to *any* of the hints about his nature and Lordship that he has given us. Yet the same Paul preached to the Athenians in terms of the "unknown god" whom they *already* honored, and announced, "What therefore you worship as unknown, this I proclaim to you." He went on to explain that the deity after whom they had been so sincerely groping was "the God who made the world and everything in it . . . [the] Lord of heaven and earth . . . [who] made from one every nation of men . . . that they should seek God, in the hope that they might feel after him and find him. . . . The times of ignorance God [has] overlooked, but now he commands all men everywhere to repent" (Acts 17:22–30).

How might we conceptualize this ambivalent core tendency, which seems on the one hand to be between our own inclinations and God's call, and on the other hand to be within ourselves or between two warring halves of ourselves? Perhaps a helpful analogy would be to think of our core tendency in terms of a balance. That is, we are born with potential to recognize and even be attracted to the call of God (one side of the balance), yet *for the most part* we suppress it and cannot do otherwise in the absence of divine intervention to change our "core." In other words, the balance of this intrapsychic conflict is so decisively tipped in the direction of rebellion that neither our intuitive *knowledge* of God nor any intermittent *attraction* toward him is enough to swing the balance the other way. Yet I believe that we must still see this conflict as basically *intra*psychic, for it is hard to see how common grace could ever operate if we were *totally* against God and everything he stands for, at every moment of our lives. In such a state, as I pointed out in Chapter Five, we would be devils, not human beings, and none of the "core characteristics" by which we image God could ever by used in a creationally normative way.

What are these core characteristics? In Chapter Four I focused especially on "accountable dominion"—the potential ability and freedom to subdue the earth but in ways such that we are accountable to God. To these we would probably have to add sociability and sexuality. "It is not good that man should be alone," says God, so he creates "a helper fit for [Adam]" (Gen. 2:18). And even after the Fall the destinies of these two and their descendants remain intertwined with each other, with the nation God calls to be his particular people, with the other nations of the world, and (finally in the new covenant) with the entire body of Christian believers, both males and females. I am inclined to include dignity and self-consciousness in our list of core characteristics, and perhaps even the need for consistency. But unlike the consistency theories reviewed by Maddi, this need in human beings must be seen neither as our single core tendency nor as devoid of content. Rather, it is a core *characteristic* that we can use with utmost effectiveness to rationalize our rebellion against God. Thus, as long as our basic, intrapsychic conflict is tipped in the direction of rejecting God's total claim on us, we are busy intellectually justifying (in ways most convincing to ourselves and others) the choices we make and the idols we choose to serve.

Often these idols are extensions of our own core characteristics, and thus not so much an evil in themselves as a case of "worshipping the creation rather than the creator" (Rom. 1:25)—of elevating relative and God-given goods to a position of absolute status in our lives. Or, to put it in terms of the concepts we have been borrowing, it could be said that we try to elevate what is merely a core *characteristic* to the status of the core *tendency* that should be followed at any cost. Thus we elevate our sexuality—or our need for social recognition, logical consistency, or the control of reality through science, technology, or artistic expression—to the status of core tendency. Even our moral sense gets distorted, and we believe ourselves accountable only to our families, or our professional network, or our friends, or a certain tradition, or perhaps to an abstract goal, like the future survival of the human race on earth. We can even make an idol of our reflexive capacity, getting so caught up in self-examination that it becomes the chief end of our existence!

Thus far I have suggested that we regard humanity's common, core *tendency* as an intrapsychic conflict between worship of God and worship of self-chosen idols, with the balance of this conflict tipped decisively toward the latter at birth. I have included among our core *characteristics* accountable dominion (with the freedom that this implies), sociability, sexuality, dignity, self-consciousness, and a need for consistency. There may be others that we could argue for, but bear in mind that I am engaged not in making a final statement but in developing a preliminary exercise meant to stimulate the reader's thinking.

I suggest further that, in the image of the balance used to understand our core tendency, we also have a succinct model for understanding the process of rebirth in Christ and our subsequent maturation as believers. It is through God's intervention and our own acceptance of it that the balance of the conflict is decisively reversed, and that our desire to worship and serve God now prevails over our desire to worship self-chosen idols. There are several advantages to this image of "reversed weights." First of all, it allows room for progressive sanctification (the God-worshiping side gradually becomes heavier and heavier at the expense of the other side). But it also allows room for the struggles with sin from which Christians are not exempt (the idol-worshiping side of the balance, while in regression, still has influence). Moreover, this way of conceptualizing our changed core tendency does not alter the *structure* of our core characteristics so much as their *direction:* they are used more and more in the service of God and less and less as ends in themselves. (And yet, when Paul speaks of the fruits of the Spirit in Galatians 5:22–23, it does seem as if our core characteristics have been—if not exactly *changed*—at least *overlaid* by new ones: "love, joy, peace, patience, kindness, goodness, faithfulness, gentleness, self-control." In this sense at least, we may speak of our core characteristics as well as our core tendency changing to express more reliably that which, through common grace, shone through only fitfully in our preconversion state.)

Finally, this conceptualization also allows for the occurrence of the "great reversal" at any point in one's life span. This being the case, God's acceptance of our subsequent efforts is predicated not on the absolute amount of progress we make in the new life between conversion and death but rather on the amount of progress we make relative to our time of conversion and the abilities with which we are blessed. (Recall both the parable of the laborers in the vineyard in Matthew 20:1–16 and the parable of the talents in Matthew 25:14–30.)

It has probably not escaped the reader's attention that, once the new birth in Christ is attained, our biblically based personality theory may be better understood as an actualization theory of the perfection variety rather than as a conflict theory. Perfection theories, writes Maddi, are "expressive of idealizations."[32] The core tendencies that they posit are always cast in terms of striving for the ideal expression of something. For Adler, it is the striving to overcome real or imagined inferiorities; for Allport and Fromm, it is the striving after an idealized expression of one's human nature. All of these perfection theorists, however, deliberately avoid setting *criteria* for the "perfect" expression of superiority, or human nature, or the ideal self. Instead, they come close to reducing the core of personality to a mere set of processes, with individual preferences, whether innate or acquired, supplying most of the content of what is striven after. But in his letter to the Philippians Paul very clearly expressed his core tendency as a "new creation" and the standard for what he was striving after:

> I count everything as loss because of the surpassing worth of knowing Christ Jesus my Lord . . . [having] the righteousness from God that depends on faith; that I may know him and the power of his resurrection, and may share his sufferings, becoming like him in his death. . . . Not that I have already obtained this or am already perfect; but I press on to make it my own, because Christ Jesus has made me his own. . . . One thing I do, forgetting what lies behind and straining forward to what lies ahead, I press on toward the goal for the prize of the upward call of God in Christ Jesus. (Phil. 3:8–14)

So Paul seems to be saying that his basic motivation has decisively changed, and that the rest of his life will be a process of willing striving after the example of Christ to which God has called him. If we take this as a *locus classicus* for our biblical anthropology, then it can indeed be seen as a perfection theory rather than one of intrapsychic conflict, at least *after* we have been converted. This is so even though the same Paul, in Romans 7, seems to be writing as if he is still in a state of intense conflict. For even here the conflict is no longer a *core* conflict: he says, "I delight in the law of God, in my

32. Maddi, *Personality Theories*, p. 118.

inmost self," even while conceding "I do not do the good I want, but the evil I do not want" (vv. 15–25). He is well aware that the actual sanctification of his human capacities still lags behind his overall motivation, which is to serve God. Nevertheless, he longs for as much perfection in Christ's image as his earthly limits and his continuing struggle against the "old man" will allow.

In the final analysis, I do not think that it matters whether we use the "balance" image or the "two-stage" image (i.e., from conflict to perfection) to express our biblical anthropology. My own preference for the former is based largely on its greater theoretical simplicity. Either way, what is finally important is that our theory does justice to (1) the core *characteristics* by which all human beings image God; (2) the conflict-ridden core *tendency* (Will we be for God or for ourselves?) with which all of us are born; (3) the possibility of a very real change in this core tendency through conversion; and (4) the possibility of progressive and substantial—but in this life, never total—reorienting of our core characteristics toward the will of God during the Christian life following conversion.

Although the foregoing exercise could be seen as the beginnings of a full-blown theory of personality, its primary purpose has been to show how the Christian's "control beliefs" can interact with existing theoretical concepts in personology in a way that does justice to the latter without compromising the former. We have found that it is possible to use many of the constructs suggested by personality theorists (e.g., conflict, consistency, perfection) in developing our biblical anthropology, but that our control beliefs have led us either to reinterpret the meaning of such constructs or to assign them a different place in our own system than they have in others. Thus personality theorizing gives us an expanded vocabulary with which to think about biblical anthropology, and conversely, our biblical understanding about the nature of personhood gives us insights with which to challenge, evaluate, adapt, or reject existing theories of personality. It is this kind of mutually influential dialogue that I have tried to exemplify, working at the level of personology's concern with the core tendency and the core characteristics shared by all human beings.

In the process I have not even begun to make a developmental statement about the emergence of different "types" of personality or any statement about the nature and origin of individual differences. I believe that such a statement is worth developing, but it is beyond the scope of my present aims. Moreover, I think we must concede that there is room for controversy over such issues among Christian theorists. The Bible, while acknowledging the existence and importance of individual differences, says very little about how they are acquired—whether through nature (genetic inheritance), or nurture (socialization and learning), or both. Nor is it entirely clear, when God bestows "gifts" for the service of church and society, the extent to which he works through talents already present as opposed to empowering (perhaps this merely means motivating?) by his Spirit. But even here I think that a fruitful interaction between control beliefs and theoretical constructs in personology is possible, and I hope to see more of it.

PITFALLS FOR THE STUDENT OF PERSONOLOGY

I have spent much of this chapter trying to demonstrate how the biblical anthropologist can engage in fruitful dialogue with the personologist without compromising essential Christian control beliefs. Because both personology and biblical anthropology are concerned with what it means to be human at the level of the whole person, there is probably more room for mutual dialogue here than in any other area in psychology. Yet earlier in this chapter I also sounded a precautionary note, pointing out that because of their "world-viewish" implications, it is easy for personality theories to function almost like total belief systems and for their proponents to become single-minded zealots promoting their preferred system as the one that merits unconditional allegiance.

It is easy for the student of personology to be confused—if not swayed—by such partisan zeal, because (as we have seen) most personality theories are expressing real truths about human nature, albeit with misguided emphases from the Christian's point of view. In addition, because personology is a part of academic psychology, adherents of a particular personality theory often trade effectively on this association, implying that their particular position has the status of a scientifically verified truth.[33] The result is that the average undergraduate or lay reader of psychology (knowing neither the limits of

33. See in particular Paul C. Vitz, *Psychology as Religion: The Cult of Self-Worship* (Grand Rapids: Eerdmans, 1977), chaps. 3, 4, and 10; and also Vitz, "Christian Critique of Academic Personality Theory," *Studies in Formative Spirituality* 3 (May 1982): 263–82.

positivistic psychology nor its tenuous connection with personology) may feel overwhelmed by the claims of a particular theoretical school even while remaining vaguely uneasy about the entire thrust of the system.

Furthermore, because we live in a society that has become largely indifferent to religion (at least at the official level), many people are searching for ways to fill the resulting spiritual vacuum in their lives and also meet the need for fellowship with like-minded believers that our social and religious nature demands. All too often I have seen various "personality cults," centered on both a particular theory and its founder or chief disciples, functioning this way in the lives of sincerely searching students. For example, one of Carl Jung's most prominent students describes the Jungian path to the goal of self-realization in pointedly religious terms:

> Jungian psychotherapy is . . . a Heilsweg, in the two-fold sense of the German word: a way of healing and a way of salvation. . . . It knows the way and has the means to lead the individual to his "salvation," to the knowledge and fulfillment of his personality, which have always been the aim of spiritual striving. Jung's system of thought can be explained theoretically only up to a certain point; to understand it fully one must have experienced or better still "suffered" its living action in oneself. . . . Both ethically and intellectually [this is] an extremely difficult task which can be successfully performed only by the fortunate few, those elected and favored by grace.[34]

Here we see several aspects of false religion cleverly mixed together with some aspects that are in fact legitimate. On the positive side, the description of a faith that is both cognitive and experiential—something that involves the whole person—can be rightly attractive both to students who are disenchanted with the rationalism of their academic world and to Christians whose own church background has been distorted in either of these directions to the exclusion of the other. On the negative side—but still powerfully attractive—there are appeals to salvation through personal effort, through special knowledge granted only to a select few, and through self-understanding devoid of any radical change in the person's core motivation.

34. Jolande Jacobi, as quoted in Paul Vitz, "From a Secular to a Christian Psychology," in *Christianity Confronts Modernity*, ed. Peter Williamson and Kevin Perrotta (Ann Arbor, Mich.: Servant Publications, 1981), p. 137.

It must also be noted that adherence to various personality theories often serves as a kind of "halfway house" for Christians who are on the road to apostasy. Personologist Paul Vitz has documented numerous examples of this process in his *Psychology as Religion,*[35] showing that there is a long history of highly respected clergymen's presenting the claims of some newly espoused personality theory in conjunction with just enough selectively used references to Scripture and Christian tradition to make it seem within the bounds of orthodoxy. This too can become a trap for the unwary Christian who is looking for ways of combining religious commitment with a sincere interest in personality theory.

Vitz, who writes about personality theory from the perspective of an insider who became a Christian in midcareer, provides some additional critical guidelines for Christians who are trying to separate wheat from chaff in this area of psychology. Focusing particularly on what Maddi labeled "actualization" theories (because it is these that have dominated the academic scene in recent years),[36] Vitz mentions three assumptions, common to all such theories, with which Christians must take issue before they can hope to adapt them in any orthodox manner. The first of these is the assumption of *individualism:*

> It is most revealing that there is not one major psychological theory of personality which does not assume the isolated individual as the central unit and primary concern of its theory. Nor is there a single influential psychological theory which has any major positive theoretical terms for the important fact of human interdependence, even less of course for the concept of obedience.[37]

At the heart of such theories is the assumption that individuals can be trusted to make healthy choices, and that it is only pressure from others to conform that causes the distortions traditionally labeled as sin. Consequently, the road to individual healing is usually

35. See especially chap. 6, and also Vitz, "From a Secular to a Christian Psychology," pp. 121–49.
36. Vitz's most current interests, however, center on psychoanalysis, which has been largely an extra-university movement. The following of Vitz's writings are of particular interest in this regard: "Sigmund Freud's Attraction to Christianity," *Psychoanalysis and Contemporary Thought* 6 (1983): 73–183; "Christianity and Psychoanalysis" (two-part monograph), *Journal of Psychology and Theology* (in press); and *Sigmund Freud's Christian Unconscious* (in press).
37. Vitz, "From a Secular to a Christian Psychology," p. 125.

conceived in terms of attaining greater independence and self-assertiveness at the expense of what Vitz calls "natural groupings" embodied in family, community, and religious ties. "Today's individualistic psychology repetitively implies that the enemy is the past created by natural groupings, but not the past and present, dominated by modernist, isolated egos separated from all that is natural, with each ego being told that it is free."[38]

Some qualifiers are needed here. Earlier in this chapter I presented Bonhoeffer's perceptive understanding of the tension between our calling as individuals and our calling as interdependent beings. In emphasizing that persons have "varieties of gifts, but the same Spirit," Scripture is affirming the importance of individual differences—and we must confess that often in Christian circles these legitimate differences (which are intended for the upbuilding of the kingdom) are suppressed in the name of conformity to one or another traditional notion of the "ideal" Christian life. To chafe against such restrictions is not sin provided that the desire to develop one's own gifts is anchored firmly in a commitment to kingdom service in the context of responsibility to the church as a whole. But Vitz is correct when he notes that all too often such individual striving is motivated by a desire for total autonomy and self-indulgence that is "deeply anti-Christian." Ironically, he adds, this quest for independence is ultimately self-defeating, for "the alternative to the influence of our parents, our family, or community, and above all, of our faith is not to be free of influences, but to be controlled by the social environment of mass society. . . . Self-help psychology is the psychology of the perfect consumer. It is a theory for improving the balance sheets of gourmet restaurants, fancy hotels and casinos, Club Mediterranée, and the manufacturers of hot tubs."[39]

Related to the assumption of individualism is the assumption of moral *relativism*: the actualization of the self, whether that of fulfillment or perfection theorists, takes place largely according to self-chosen norms, which may or may not be in accord with any religious or social standards. Similarly, in consistency theories (as we have seen), the actual content of beliefs and values is not what is said to motivate human beings but rather the mere process of making sure that one's thoughts and actions are consistent with whatever beliefs

38. Vitz, "From a Secular to a Christian Psychology," p. 128.
39. Vitz, "From a Secular to a Christian Psychology," pp. 128–29.

and values are possessed. Likewise, there is a tendency for both kinds of theories to put much more emphasis on *subjective feelings* than a biblical anthropology, with its strong emphasis on our capacity to fool ourselves, would allow:

> One of the reasons for the popularity of psychotherapy is undoubtedly its ability to focus on and cultivate the subjective world of the patient and to attribute great worth to the person's feelings and opinions. . . . Now, no doubt there is a place for catharsis in psychotherapy—at least up to a point. But persistently delving into your personal emotions in private or expressing your feelings in extreme ways in public has no basis in scripture or church tradition. . . . The Christian emphasis is always on the outside reality, of God and others—there is no basis for today's almost blatantly narcissistic preoccupation with getting in touch with feelings at the expense of getting in touch with God through prayer, or getting in touch with others through charity.[40]

Finally, Vitz warns that a pervasive hostility toward religion in general has been part and parcel of almost all personality theories to date. Even the most self-consciously scientific personologists (from whom one would expect reasonable attempts to control for sampling bias) have routinely drawn their subjects from populations that are antireligious or at best nominally religious, thus guaranteeing that religion will emerge as a trivial or negative force in any resulting personality theory. Moreover, traditional Christian virtues such as humility, confession, and service are often recast in the pathology-associated language of self-abasement, masochism, and denial, while belief in the supernatural itself is all too often dismissed with clichés about weak and overdependent egos or delusional tendencies.[41]

Vitz and I are agreed that the Christian response to such distortions must not be an abandonment of this important field of psychology. Rather, the "functional atheism" of personology must have its historical roots examined and its partiality, in the guise of scientific objectivity, exposed. "Indeed," writes Vitz, "the entire claim that there is a scientific and impartial psychology needs to be exposed as the myth it is":

---

40. Vitz, "From a Secular to a Christian Psychology," p. 136.
41. Vitz, "Christian Critique of Academic Personality Theory," pp. 265–66.

At present, most secular psychologists seem to be living in a kind of intellectual time-capsule, filled with the fading air of a positivistic concept of science often uncritically imbibed during the period from 1940 to 1970. . . . The disturbing and intellectually damaging thing is not that ideology has influenced psychologists; ideology cannot but influence psychology. Rather the scandal is that no attempt has been made by psychologists to be candid about—much less to correct—this bias. Here are professors professionally trained to discover prejudice . . . who have been incapable of seeing the greater prejudice in themselves: the beam in their own eye. The result is that a generation of students has been led to believe that the ideology of secular humanism, with its assumption of atheism and its ideal of the autonomous ego, is not an ideology, but that it represents the true nature of [ideal] humankind as discovered by impartial scientific psychology.[42]

There is much here to challenge the Christian student of personology. Moreover, in addition to sharpening our critical skills in the ways suggested by Vitz, we need to be working very hard to develop alternative conceptions of the person in keeping with an ever-deepening understanding of biblical anthropology. In earlier parts of this chapter I have attempted to show one way in which such an exercise might begin. It is my hope that the common commitment of Christian personologists will extend the range and sophistication of such exercises as the character of psychology continues to change in the future.

42. Vitz, "Christian Critique of Academic Personality Theory," pp. 271-74.

PART THREE
PSYCHOLOGY AND THE AGENDA FOR THE FUTURE

CHAPTER 11

A CHALLENGE FOR US ALL

Much of psychological history can be seen as a form of scientistic role-playing which, however sophisticated, entails the trivialization, and even evasion, of significant human problems.

—Sigmund Koch[1]

The acceptance of God enlarges and enriches psychology by making religious life relevant and interpretable. . . . A Christian psychology would be both a bigger and a better psychology—that is, a broader, deeper, and truer psychology.

—Paul C. Vitz[2]

We have now come to the end of our tour of psychology's contemporary landscape. It has been a selective tour (as readers were warned it would be), constrained by certain considerations of content and method. In terms of content I have focused my attention on those areas of psychology in which the implicit or explicit image of the person looms significant for the Christian student of psychology. In terms of method I have been guided by two convictions that I suggested at the outset should condition all Christian interaction with present-day psychology. The first of these was that metaphysical world views, far from being irrelevancies or impediments to psycho-

---

1. Koch, "The Nature and Limits of Psychological Knowledge: Lessons of a Century qua Science," American Psychologist 36 (Mar. 1981): 257.
2. Vitz, "From a Secular to a Christian Psychology," in Christianity Confronts Modernity, ed. Peter Williamson and Kevin Perrotta (Ann Arbor, Mich.: Servant Publications, 1981), p. 143.

logical research and scholarship, are both inevitable and even potentially positive contributors to it. That is why I have devoted almost as much attention to the persons who *do* psychology, and their stated or unstated views of human nature, as I have to their actual studies of persons other than themselves. In this regard my philosophy of social science has been distinctly post-modern, in keeping with the work of scholars such as Thomas Kuhn and Michael Polanyi.

But my second methodological conviction has tempered the first, as it holds that acceptance of the authority of Scripture releases the Christian from the dangers (not to mention the despair) of postmodern skepticism and, in addition, supplies a set of control beliefs about human nature by which he or she can evaluate and possibly alter contemporary psychological theories that speak to the nature of personhood.

I have not been so naive as to assume that Christian readers will all agree with either my methodological assumptions or even the control beliefs I have suggested Scripture gives to us regarding the nature of personhood. Differing theological traditions interacting with differing philosophies of science and differing theoretical specializations in psychology are bound to yield differences of opinion— or at least of emphasis—among Christian psychologists, all of whom are equally committed to elucidating a portrait of personhood consistent with scriptural revelation. Thus, for example, we have seen that Christians in behavioral psychology tend to emphasize the creatureliness of human beings and their vulnerability to environmental pressures, while those in cognitive or personality psychology focus much more on the uniquely human capacities for complex problem-solving, language production, and the espousal of values around which existential choices are made.

Yet I would be dishonest if I did not admit that I hope my arguments have convinced readers of the need for change in the conduct of psychology, and it is with a consideration of such changes that I bring this volume to a close. I happen to have undertaken my task in this book at a fortuitous time. For according to the origin myth that binds psychologists together in a profession, psychology emerged as a separate and formalized discipline in Wilhelm Wundt's Leipzig laboratory in 1879. Consequently, with the recent marking of psychology's official centenary, there has been permitted a degree of historical introspection and futuristic auguring normally not tolerated in a discipline that tends to identify scientific rigor with an unrelenting presentism of outlook. So let us look at what psychologists are now saying about the past and more particularly the future of their own discipline, and consider with these some of the changes that might be urged in light of the concerns of previous chapters.

PSYCHOLOGY LOOKS AT ITSELF

Sigmund Koch, the source of this chapter's first opening quotation, has long been acknowledged as the premier philosopher-historian of psychology in the English-speaking world. His editorship of the six-volume work *Psychology: A Study of a Science*[3] crowned a twenty-five-year career devoted to exploring the prospects for and the conditions conducive to psychology's becoming a significant intellectual enterprise. Yet, when he addressed the American Psychological Association at its centenary meeting in 1979, Koch was anything but cheerful about what psychology had accomplished in its first century as a formalized discipline.[4]

To begin with, said Koch, prior to the nineteenth century there were no precedents in the history of ideas for creating new fields of knowledge by edict. Disciplines took shape and acquired an independent identity by gradually acquiring enough knowledge to become separate sciences with recognizable boundaries. Yet this is exactly what did *not* happen in psychology. On the contrary, psychology was virtually "stipulated into life" against the background of "an apparently wholesome Victorian vision: that of a totally orderly universe, totally open to the methods of science, and a totally orderly science, totally open to the stratagems and wants of man."[5] It was John Stuart Mill, among others, who argued almost a century and a half ago that the backward state of social science could be remedied only through the application of the methods of physical science, "duly extended

3. Koch, ed., *Psychology: A Study of a Science*, 6 vols. (New York: McGraw-Hill, 1959, 1962, 1963).
4. Koch, "The Nature and Limits of Psychological Knowledge." See also his "Psychology Cannot Be a Coherent Science," *Psychology Today* 3 (Sept. 1969): 14, 64–68; and "The Challenge of Ameaning in Modern Psychology: An Inquiry into the Rift Between Psychology and the Humanities," in *Science and Human Affairs*, ed. R. Farson (Palo Alto, Calif.: Science and Behavior Books, 1965).
5. Koch, "Psychology Cannot Be a Coherent Science," p. 64.

and generalized." Would-be psychologists, eager to partake of the growth and status of the natural sciences, readily agreed with Mill and in effect legislated themselves into existence as a scientific profession.

In the course of doing so, they severed the historical connection that psychological inquiry had always had with philosophical and religious questions and instead espoused what Michael Wertheimer later called a "bricks and mortar" approach, according to which controlled experimentation with the smallest conceivable bits of behavior and their smallest interrelations would gradually yield systematic understanding and total predictability and control of the person. Koch described the result:

> For close to a century now, many psychologists have seemed to suppose that the methods of natural science are totally specifiable and specified; that the applicability of these methods to social and human events is not only an established fact but that no knowledge is worth taking seriously unless it is based on inquiries saturated with the iconology of science. Thus, from the beginning, respectability held more glamor than insight, caution than curiosity, feasibility than fidelity. The stipulation that psychology be adequate to science outweighed the commitment that it be adequate to man.[6]

It must be said (as, indeed, we have discovered in preceding chapters) that this positivistic vision of a science of persons is one still held by many psychologists. In a centenary symposium entitled "Psychology and the Future," nine distinguished psychologists (Koch among them) were asked to envisage the scope and direction that they expected of psychology in the future.[7] More than half of the assembled group (two of whom had also surveyed other colleagues) still saw psychology as a coherent, scientific discipline, potentially unified by some grand theoretical scheme, perhaps of a cognitive-behavioral variety although the details were far from clear.

Yet even among these faithful adherents of the received view, there were signs of unease. For one thing, many of them predicted that the research skills of psychologists in the future would focus less on theoretical issues and more on applied problems in response to the practical needs of business, mental-health, and educational enter-

6. Koch, "Psychology Cannot Be a Coherent Science," p. 64.
7. Michael Wertheimer, ed., "Psychology and the Future," *American Psychologist* 33 (July 1978): 631–47.

prises. Now there is nothing inherently wrong with applied social science, just as there is nothing inherently wrong with applied natural science. But when a discipline begins to let the demands of the marketplace shape most of its priorities, it shows a failure of nerve—it is taking an easy escape-route from hard questions about the basic nature and scope of its subject matter.

Such an evasion is the end result of psychology's self-conscious choice of a natural-science paradigm, because (contrary to hopes and expectations) that choice has for the most part not resulted in a cumulative or progressive body of knowledge about human behavior. "Psychology's larger generalizations are not specified and refined over time and effort," Koch concluded. "They are merely replaced . . . the various phases [succeeding] each other not by virtue of differential productivity but rather because of the dawning recognition that significant problems and segments of subject-matter were being evaded—or simply because of boredom with the old paradigm."[8]

In such an atmosphere of theoretical disarray, it is hardly surprising that for many the best compromise seems to be to take one's data-gathering and analyzing skills and run with them to the security of the applied domain, where problems and goals are specified in advance by the representatives of practical life. But such a reaction, however understandable, can hardly be praised as an intellectual advance for the discipline. Besides, the realm of practical application may prove to be only a temporary haven, for if a purely natural-science approach is insufficient for teasing out answers to the problems of personhood in the university laboratory, there is no reason to suppose that it will work any better, in the long run, in the world at large. Indeed, the participants in the centennial symposium acknowledged with some unease that the massive funding that practically oriented psychological research had received in the past was decreasing so rapidly that protective legislation might be needed to keep psychology's status secure in the public eye. Koch in turn was quick to comment on the sense of self-doubt indicated by the call for such lobbying:

> Throughout the 19th century (and, indeed, before) an independent scientific psychology was vigorously invited. . . . And, as we are certainly aware, over the next 100 years, an independent, scientific psychology has been enthusiastically enacted by a bur-

8. Koch, "Psychology Cannot Be a Coherent Science," p. 66. See also his Epilogue in vol. 6 of *Psychology: A Study of a Science.*

geoning work force that now constitutes one of the largest group-ings within contemporary scholarship. But the frenetic activity of the past 100 years has apparently left the issue in doubt, [since] we are now impelled to achieve scientific legitimacy by *legislation*.[9]

But to Koch the most serious result of this century-long romance with a dubious philosophy of science has been the eclipse of "meaningful thought" within psychology (and, indeed, even within the humanities when they have tried to mimic the natural sciences by applying methods aimed at garnering "positive" knowledge).[10] To think meaningfully about something as a scholar, says Koch, is to experience a direct perception of vivid relations that seem to spring from the particularities of objects or problem situations with which one is intimately involved. It is the kind of creative insight that comes not from the application of an enshrined epistemological formula but from long and close contact with the phenomenon in question—the kind of thinking Polanyi found to be the mark of great scientific thinkers like Einstein. By contrast, "ameaningful thought," as Koch calls it,

> regards knowledge as the result of "processing" rather than of discovery. It presumes that knowledge is an almost automatic result of a gimmick, an assembly line, a methodology. It assumes that inquiring action is so rigidly and fully regulated by *rule* that . . . it often allows the rules totally to displace their human users. And objects of knowledge become caricatures, if not face-less, and thus they lose reality. The world, or any given part of it, is not felt fully or passionately, and is perceived as devoid of objective value.[11]

To summarize, then, psychology's present state of unease seems to be the compounded result of at least three factors. First, it is a discipline that legislated itself into existence on the basis of its attrac-

9. Koch, "The Nature and Limits of Psychological Knowledge," p. 257.

10. For example, literature scholar Carolyn Heilbrun describes the scientific aspirations of the "New Criticism" movement in terms of its "close attention to the text that denies the relevance of any factors outside it. . . . Its overpowering appeal was that it not only allowed but demanded separation between the personality and the intellect, between, in T. S. Eliot's words, the person who suffers and the artist who creates" (Heilbrun, *Reinventing Womanhood* [New York: Norton, 1979], p. 22). The parallel with a positivistic view of the conduct of social science is obvious.

11. Koch, "Psychology Cannot Be a Coherent Science," p. 14.

tion to a particular set of methods rather than on any passionate involvement with an enduring set of questions and problems about the nature of personhood. Second, in its wholesale pursuit of scientism, psychology has cut itself off from any help it might receive from its historical antecedents in philosophy, religion, and the other humanities, and has limited its interdisciplinary contacts almost exclusively to the biological sciences. Third, in their quest to be scientific (in the very limited sense in which they understood that term), psychologists as a group have failed to develop the capacity for meaningful thought. Standards for professional excellence have been so centered on competence in empirical research skills that theory development has remained superficial at best. In physics, the discipline with a philosophy of science that psychology has claimed to be imitating, there is a high regard for creative theorizing, with the most prestigious graduate programs reserved for students who are gifted in this regard. By contrast, it was only in the early 1970s that the American Psychological Association allowed a student in one of its accredited graduate programs to write a theoretical Ph.D. thesis as opposed to a mainly empirical one centered on hypothesis-testing and data-gathering and analysis. It is not an exaggeration to say that psychologists are in danger of becoming a collection of mere research technicians.

In his centennial reflections on psychology's future, Koch was very blunt in his prescription for change. In the past, psychology has prided itself on being an "independent, scientific discipline." In the future, he suggested, it should make no claims to being either independent *or* scientific. Institutionally independent it may remain, with its own university departments, its own journals, and its own professional organizations. But in terms of subject matter, its concerns are far too diffuse to be united under a single disciplinary rubric. Indeed, Koch suggests that to avoid such a misconception, departments of psychology be rechristened as "divisions of psychological studies," a suggestion that some universities have since acted upon. "It is now clear," Koch writes, "that no large subdivision of inquiry, including physics, can be [a theoretically unified science]. . . . As for the subject matter of psychology, anything so awesome as the total domain comprised by the functioning of all organisms can hardly be thought of as a coherent discipline."[12]

12. Koch, "Psychology Cannot Be a Coherent Science," p. 66.

Such an admonition presupposes the need for expanded inter-disciplinary contacts other than those that psychology has so carefully cultivated with the natural sciences. I agree with Koch that the place to start is with a frank expression of our conceptual dependence on philosophy—a dependence that psychologists have never escaped, however much we have tried to hide it. Most of our ideas have come from the twenty-six centuries of philosophical thought that preceded psychology's nineteenth-century bid for independence; even during the heyday of neobehaviorism, our official epistemology was ex-plicitly based on the canons of logical positivism then regnant among philosophers of science. "Psychology," in Koch's words, "is neces-sarily the most philosophy-sensitive discipline in the entire gamut of disciplines that claim empirical status":

> We cannot discriminate a so-called variable, pose a research question, choose or invent a method, project a theory, stipulate a psychotechnology, without making strong presumptions of a philosophical cast about the nature of our human subject-mat-ter—presumptions that can be ordered to age-old contexts of philosophical discussion. Even our nomenclature for the basic fields of specialized research within psychology (e.g., sensation, perception, motivation, emotion, etc.) has its origin in philoso-phy. [13]

What are these "age-old contexts of philosophical discussion" to which Koch refers and upon which psychology is so unwittingly de-pendent? Bertrand Russell summarized them in the introduction to his *History of Western Philosophy* in a way that should recall for the reader many of the issues discussed in previous chapters of this book. [14] They include questions such as these: Is the world divided into mind and matter, and if so, what is mind and what is matter? Is mind subject to matter, or is it possessed of independent powers? Has the universe any unity or purpose? Are there really laws of nature, or do we believe in them only because of our innate love of order? Are human beings what they seem to be to many astronomers, tiny collec-

13. Koch, "The Nature and Limits of Psychological Knowledge," p. 267.

14. I do not mean hereby to idealize philosophy or to rebaptize it as the queen of the sciences. I am well aware that it too has suffered from a misguided scientism in its recent history and a consequent failure of nerve in dealing with its traditional questions. But at least it has not denied its own historical involvement with them, and there are signs that they may be moving to the forefront once more.

tions of chemicals populating an insignificant planet? Or are they creatures uniquely endowed with transcendence? Or are they perhaps both at once? Is there a way of living that is noble and another that is base, or are all ways of living merely futile? If there is a nobler way, of what does it consist and how is it to be achieved? "The studying of these questions," writes Russell, "if not the answering of them, is the business of philosophy." He then adds a warning that, while not directed specifically at psychologists, could well be heeded by them: "To such questions no answer can be found in the laboratory. . . . It is not good either to forget the questions that philosophy asks, or to persuade ourselves that we have found indubitable answers to them."[15]

CHRISTIANS LOOK AT PSYCHOLOGY

It can be seen from the foregoing analysis that psychology as a discipline is ripe for reform. It would appear to be at the stage that Kuhn has called the period of "extraordinary science"—a period characterized less and less by "business as usual" according to a commonly held paradigm and more and more by debates about the theoretical and epistemological foundations that have constituted the received view. We have also seen, especially in the last two chapters, that much of this debate centers on the image of persons and, consequently, the most appropriate methods for studying them. Many perceptive and productive scholars in psychology and related disciplines are now arguing that nonhuman, "passive" models of the person have been made to carry more theoretical and empirical freight than they can bear, and that more "active" models of the person—as chooser, actor, scientist, or self-reflector—need to be elaborated and explored according to new methods that are compatible with such models. These would augment—even if they would not totally replace—the older models and methods derived from psychology's association with the natural sciences.[16]

15. Russell, A History of Western Philosophy (New York: Simon and Schuster, 1945), pp. xiii-xiv. I am aware that Russell, at one point anyway, had high hopes for a scientific behaviorism (see, for example, Chapter Seven, note 12 of this volume). I am presuming that by the time he wrote the above survey he had outgrown this phase.
16. See, for example, Ralph Ruddock, Six Approaches to the Person (London: Routledge and Kegan Paul, 1972); and John Shotter, Images of Man in Psychological Research (London: Methuen, 1975).

The reader will recall from previous chapters (especially Chapters Five through Seven) that many evangelical Christians have made their peace with the received view by means of a perspectivalist resolution. According to this view, persons are acknowledged to be related both "downward" to the rest of nonhuman creation (and, as such, subject to the same laws) and "upward" to God, created in his image and thus in many ways free, accountable, and creative. In adhering to the received view in psychology, with its stress on passive models of the person and methods for studying them derived from natural science, perspectivalists are not ruling out other models or methods; they are merely ruling them out of psychology per se on the grounds that all sciences must be unified around a single approach that stresses causal explanations of a deterministic sort.

Yet we have seen in the course of this book that there are ample grounds—both theoretical and epistemological—for expanding psychology's mandate to include models and methods that better do justice to the whole range of human functions, and not only those that most resemble the functions of machines or animals. In the last two chapters readers have seen what some of these methods might be. But that presentation has been somewhat abstract; it has not been tied to specific examples of research, let alone to any that have been undertaken by Christians. Consequently, in what follows I am going to consider an example of what some have called "new paradigm" research,[17] recently undertaken and published in Britain by Christian social psychologist Tom Kitwood, on the topic of adolescent value systems in an advanced industrial context.[18] In considering Kitwood's research I hope to both exemplify and summarize some reforms needed in psychology if it is to do justice to aspects of the person that are biblically significant yet traditionally neglected in mainstream psychology.

Disclosures to a Stranger: Psychology in the Human-Science Mode. Kitwood introduces his work on adolescent values as an exercise in the "empirical social psychology of the person: a science in which there [is] as full as possible an acknowledgement of individual human powers, the social nature of human life, and the relationship

---

17. See Peter Reason and John Rowan, *Human Inquiry: A Sourcebook of New Paradigm Research* (New York: John Wiley, 1981).

18. Kitwood, *Disclosures to a Stranger: Adolescent Values in an Advanced Industrial Society* (London: Routledge and Kegan Paul, 1980). Kitwood is also the author of *What is Human?* (London: Inter-Varsity Press, 1970).

between consciousness and the conditions of everyday existence."[19] Already there are several points we should note about this project. First of all, the topic is unusual. Psychologists have done relatively little work on values, I think largely because the passive models of personhood that have dominated the field are unable to handle the existence of values other than as environmentally determined "residues" that come to be attached to the person in a mechanical fashion. That there might be a uniquely human urge to structure one's life around a value system that is more than the result of social conditioning (however important this may be) is not a premise that sits easily with the positivistic mode of psychology.[20]

Second, it should be noted that the project is an empirical one in terms of method. Many social scientists, both Christian and otherwise, have assumed that in order for an investigation to qualify as empirical and scientific it must have all of the trappings of a positivistic methodology: reductionism, operationalization and quantification of what is being investigated, impersonal detachment of the investigator from the persons being studied, and (wherever possible) controlled experimentation.[21] Anything other than this is often simply assumed to be in the realm of the humanities, or at best proto-scientific. But as we saw in Chapter Nine, it is increasingly common for workers in the advanced sciences to use careful, naturalistic observation, combined with a disciplined use of imagination and cognition, to arrive at an understanding of a particular phenomenon. So it is hardly a sign of regression for psychologists to do likewise, and Kitwood is fully justified in calling his approach a scientific one.

Finally, in terms of biblical anthropology, Kitwood's approach acknowledges three vital features of personhood that are still largely neglected in mainstream psychology. The first of these—"an ac-

19. Kitwood, *Disclosures to a Stranger*, p. 1.
20. Some exceptions to the general neglect of values research in psychology include Milton Rokeach, *The Nature of Human Values* (New York: The Free Press, 1973); and Gordon W. Allport, Peter E. Vernon, and Gardner Lindzey, *A Study of Values*, 3rd ed. (Boston: Houghton Mifflin, 1960). See also Al Shoemaker and Martin Bolt, "The Rokeach Value Survey and Perceived Christian Values," *Journal of Psychology and Theology* 5 (Spring 1977): 139–42. All of these, however, are examples of psychology in the naturalistic, positivistic mode.
21. See Mary Stewart Van Leeuwen, *The Sorcerer's Apprentice: A Christian Looks at the Changing Face of Psychology* (Downers Grove, Ill.: InterVarsity Press, 1982), chap. 2, for an elaboration of these positivistic research criteria.

knowledgement of individual human powers"—touches on what I have previously referred to as creativity and dominion in contrast to the passivity assumed by traditional models of the person. The second—"the social nature of human life"—acknowledges that individuals are what they are in the context of *mutual* interaction with others, in contrast to the one-way relationships of influence assumed and studied in the standard paradigm of social psychology. The third—"the relationship between consciousness and the conditions of everyday existence"—acknowledges the presence and power of human reflexivity, which allows persons to monitor themselves and their situations critically and thus take part in changing their perceived and even actual character. Moreover, Kitwood's study of the conditions of adolescent existence is what he calls "psychology in the realist mode." In contrast to the naturalist *and* the rationalist approaches that have jointly characterized psychology (see Chapter Three), Kitwood shares with Rom Harré and Paul Secord (Chapter Nine) the conviction that ordinary human life, as perceived and expressed in ordinary language, is both significant and researchable. In all of these ways Kitwood helps to realize the goal put forth by Paul Vitz in one of the opening quotations of this chapter: that of Christian participation in the construction of a "broader, deeper, and truer psychology."

Let us now look a little more closely at Kitwood's project. In the little research on individual values that has been done in the positivistic mode, the most common approach has been to give persons a finite list of values and ask them to rank these in order of their importance to the respondent. Thus, for example, the Rokeach Value Survey includes a list of eighteen possible "end values" (e.g., a world at peace, national security, self-respect, salvation, pleasure, etc.) and another list of eighteen possible "means values," or preferred ways of arriving at one's valued end-states (e.g., through honesty, ambition, competence, imagination, loving-kindness, etc.). The average ranking of the various values for various subcultures (students, church members, middle-class homemakers, etc.) is then computed and compared.

Already such a methodology is something of a departure from psychology's positivistic ideals in that it does not involve experimental manipulation or the interval-scale quantification of the test items or the responses to them. Yet it seemed to Kitwood that still more adjustments were needed. For one thing his pilot testing of adolescents of various ages and social classes showed them to be not nearly as capable of formal operational thought in their way of dealing with life—and especially with personal and interpersonal values—as Piaget's work had suggested they would be. That is to say, they were rarely able or willing to reflect upon their own lives in terms of abstract value principles cut loose from actual experiences, as is required in the more traditional research mode. Consequently, Kitwood adopted a more indirect approach, giving to each of the 150 young people making up his sample a set of fifteen common "situations" derived through pilot work and discussion with other young people. Given to all the adolescents a day or two before the interview, the list was accompanied by instructions asking them to try to remember situations such as the following: "When you got on really well with people"; "When you made a serious mistake"; "When you discovered something new about yourself"; "When you did what was expected of you"; "When you had to make an important decision"— and ten others. The young people were asked to choose ten of the fifteen situations to talk about during a tape-recorded "chat" (the word "interview" was deliberately avoided because of its evaluative associations). Thus the adolescents, rather than being forced to search for abstract value-labels to characterize themselves, were asked to reflect on concrete, critical incidents in their lives, through an analysis of which a value profile of adolescents as a group and in their various subgroups (determined by sex, class, age, etc.) might be derived.

A second significant change from mainstream research approaches can be seen in the care with which the actual interaction with the teenagers was structured. In previous chapters I have referred to the importance of human reflexivity, and in Chapter Eight especially we saw how research in the positivistic mode tries to neutralize the impact of this uniquely human process by deceiving participants about the true nature of the research. Kitwood's methodology was carefully designed to reverse this practice, for to him it would have been inconsistent to study uniquely human processes in a manner that at the same time tried to circumvent some of them.

This methodology gave the adolescents an opportunity to reflect ahead of time on the "situations" and to choose which ones to respond to. It also established a number of other research guidelines to which each interviewer carefully adhered. Respondents were assured of the confidentiality of their comments; care was taken with seating arrangements during the interaction, so as to avoid any impression of confrontation or difference in status. The researchers took no notes during the interview, as this (they came to understand) conjured up associations of interrogation by principals, police officers, and caseworkers. "Why" questions were kept to a minimum, and when asked they were always begun "Do you know why . . ." so that no participant would feel compelled to come up with an answer. The participants were even permitted to bring a friend to sit by if they thought they would feel too uncomfortable talking to the researcher alone. Of course, as a result of using all these procedures to enlist the trust of the participants, the research process proceeded more slowly than most: each interview took about half a day, and each one demanded a great deal of concentration and imaginative understanding on the part of the researcher.

Kitwood's aim in all of this was partly methodological: he was determined to enlist the participants' reflexive processes *on behalf of* the task at hand rather than trying to fight in an adversarial fashion against such reflexivity by using incomplete or misleading information. But his own "morality of persons" is evident in his methodological choices as well. As he himself puts it,

> The concept of *person* itself has come to be, in part, an ethical one; it has descriptive meaning, but also perhaps contains some latent imperatives. For to talk of persons is to imply that they should be treated with respect and consideration; that they should not be reduced to the level of an object. Those who participate in experiments or surveys are often designated by some other term ("subject," "respondent," "organism"), thus implicitly relieving the social psychologist of certain human obligations. In this inquiry there has been an attempt to work out the practical as well as the theoretical implications of dealing with persons. . . . In fact, had this not been done it is very unlikely that this piece of research could have been carried out at all, because adolescents are extremely sensitive to whether they are being given the status of persons. Where this is not the case, they have their own means of ensuring that nothing is extracted from them against their will.[22]

It is of interest to note that follow-up letters, which an unusually high number of participants answered (anonymously) confirmed both the methodological and the ethical success of Kitwood's approach.

22. Kitwood, *Disclosures to a Stranger*, p. 42.

The participants uniformly stated that they *had* spoken of their experiences in a sincere and spontaneous manner—often surprising themselves in the process.[23] This is in striking contrast to the vexatious "guinea-pig effect" that is known to plague traditional research and lead to countermanipulation by participants who often feel indifferent—if not downright hostile or anxious—about the task that confronts them.[24] This is not to say that no artificiality whatsoever pervades the human-science research setting. Indeed, the title of Kitwood's book, *Disclosures to a Stranger*, is a deliberate attempt to keep the reader aware of the fact that the research setting, however carefully constructed to promote trust and involvement, is still a unique social situation that elicits unique roles. What one discloses in the role of "stranger meeting stranger" is generally different from what one discloses to better-known others.

Yet this does not necessarily work *against* self-revelation. We are all acquainted with the "stranger on the bus" type of incident in which a person we have never met before starts telling us his or her most intimate problems. Sometimes the very neutrality of the stranger creates an atmosphere of safety. As one of Kitwood's participants put it, "I didn't feel there was any need for pretences at all— unlike talking to someone who knows you and expects a certain reaction."[25] In addition, a stranger who takes time to make one feel comfortable and accepted may be rewarded with greater sincerity than a better-known person who is rushed or completely inattentive.

The methodological point in all of this is significant: although there is a certain reliability and replicability to be gained from the narrow operationalizations and rigidly standardized procedures of traditional psychology, the "fallout" or side effects of such an approach, based on the assumption that participants have been rendered effectively passive, makes the generalizability of any findings extremely suspect. By contrast, the more open procedures of researchers like Kitwood gain in holistic, realistic understanding of persons what they may have lost in operational precision. "It is," in Kitwood's words, "an invitation to the social psychologist to be ambitious, and to try to

23. Kitwood, *Disclosures to a Stranger*, pp. 85–87.
24. See, for example, Sidney Jourard, *Disclosing Man to Himself* (New York: Van Nostrand, 1968); Arthur G. Miller, ed., *The Social Psychology of Psychological Research* (New York: The Free Press, 1972); or Irwin Silverman, *The Human Subject in the Psychological Laboratory* (New York: Pergamon Press, 1977).
25. Kitwood, *Disclosures to a Stranger*, p. 86.

understand the person holistically, risking the censure of those who would say that the concepts have an inadequate empirical grounding, or that their range of applicability is not clearly demarcated."[26] At the very least, we may insist that research in such a realistic mode be conducted as often and accorded as much legitimacy as more traditional, positivistic research on the same topics. Since both approaches have weaknesses, it would seem that only through a combination of the two will we be able to "heterogenize the irrelevancies" (in Donald Campbell's striking phrase)[27] and arrive at a clearer understanding of the phenomenon being studied.

This view of social scientists as tentative and fallible contrasts with Koch's assessment of psychologists generally, whom he characterized as having an "assembly-line" mentality in their assumption that knowledge is the automatic product of a particular set of methods. But, as Kitwood recognizes, it is rarely this simple: "As often occurs in the physical and biological sciences, it may be necessary [for psychologists] to obtain data by whatever methods are feasible, and to compensate by as careful and critical an interpretation as one can make":

> To go through a one-hour interview thoroughly, making adequate notes and a few verbatim transcripts, might require three hours or more, and for some purposes it would be necessary to listen to parts of the tapes a number of times. Moreover [our] data were not of a kind that could be atomized, transferred to cards, and later stored in a computer. *It quickly became evident that for the handling of such apparently unstructured material the main apparatus for data-processing would have to be the human mind, attending to the meaning of each person's discourse with the utmost concentration.*[28]

Kitwood and his colleagues are thus aiming to apply what Koch labeled "meaningful thought" to their immense body of qualitative data, in contrast to the assembly-line mentality that Koch deplored. One example of this is their attempt to extract verbatim transcripts of all anecdotes about physical conflict in the interviews, and to analyze these in order to see if some "code" of conduct seems to regulate this aspect of adolescent life. This indeed turned out to be the case, at

---

26. Kitwood, *Disclosures to a Stranger*, p. 42.
27. Donald T. Campbell, Personal Communication, Dept. of Psychology, Northwestern University, April 1968.
28. Kitwood, *Disclosures to a Stranger*, pp. 52–53 (italics mine).

least among working-class boys, whose implicit code about aggression seemed to comprise the following rules:

1. If one's dignity, status, or rights are seriously violated, one ought to fight.
2. If one is attacked physically, one ought to fight back.
3. There are some circumstances where a largely ritual conflict will suffice instead of a genuine fight.
4. If the odds against one are very strong, it is wiser to avoid a fight.
5. If a fight is becoming more serious than its "occasion" merits, it is right to intervene to try to stop it.
6. Some people are so despicable that they "deserve" to be beaten up.
7. It is wise to adopt a general manner of a kind that will enable one to avoid being a case under rule 6.[29]

It is apparent that the results of this kind of analysis have a richness that escapes the coarser screen of the traditional approach to values research.

In the foregoing consideration of this piece of research in the realistic mode, the reader may have noted a final positive feature—namely, that the methodological barriers between psychology's "two cultures" (academic and clinical counseling) are slowly being broken down. "In general 'tone,' and in the attempt to achieve an empathetic understanding, [the research method] is not unlike some methods of psychotherapy, such as that of Rogers and his followers," Kitwood has noted. "It sets out to understand consciousness in relation to the person's life-situation, and to view existence not as a set of separate phenomena, but as an interconnected whole."[30]

This too is a change to be welcomed. The reader may recall that in Chapter Five I mentioned that dissatisfaction with the anthropological and epistemological assumptions of mainstream academic psychology has led the majority of Christian students to pursue clinical or counseling careers instead of academic careers. Although this is an understandable reaction, one of its results has been that the very persons who are most motivated toward an understanding of the uniquely human are kept so busy in their practices that they have neither the time nor the support for the kind of organized research in the mode that Kitwood has demonstrated. But with the increasing

29. Kitwood, *Disclosures to a Stranger*, pp. 175–86.
30. Kitwood, *Disclosures to a Stranger*, p. 51.

acceptability and value accorded to research in the realistic mode, it is my hope that more Christian students will be motivated to stay in the academic setting and help to develop modes of inquiry that are more adequate to their control beliefs about the person, and that, moreover, can both revitalize mainstream psychology and add resources to the clinician's and counselor's store of knowledge for applied ends.

A SUMMARY CHALLENGE

Throughout this volume and particularly in this final chapter I have suggested that because psychology is becoming more open to the development of a human-science paradigm, Christians should be challenged to greater activity in the field. I have pointed out that our acceptance of scriptural authority should be an advantage, not an impediment, to such a task—but not because Scripture gives us a complete anthropology that can substitute for a systematic psychology; Scripture does not do this, although some Christians have tried to force this kind of systematic completeness into their reading of it. But Scripture does tell us enough about the ultimate origin, nature, and destiny of human beings to give us a set of control beliefs by which we can critically evaluate existing psychological theories and help to formulate more adequate ones.

In Chapter Ten I tried to develop the implications of the phrase "made in God's image" in terms of a preliminary model of personality that could be contrasted with existing models in psychology. In assuming an irreducible core *tendency* to order life around allegiance to God or to some self-chosen substitute, as well as core *characteristics* such as sociability, sexuality, dignity, and reflexivity, I tried to view human personality through the lens of those control beliefs that appear to me to be strongly implied in a reading of Scripture. This is not to say that other analyses are impossible; indeed, it should be our ongoing task to struggle toward a scriptural hermeneutic that can clarify and correct such modest beginnings. But it does imply that, in Paul Vitz's phrase, we must be "constructionist" rather than "reductionist" in our psychology of the person:

> The secular modernist assumes that all so-called "higher things," especially religious experience and related ideals, are to be understood as really caused by underlying lower phenomena. Examples: Love is reduced to sex and sex is reduced to physiology. . . . Spiritual life is reduced to sublimated sex, as in Freud. . . . In contrast, the Christian is a constructionist who sees higher

meaning and divine significance in psychological experiences. Sex is seen [in the context of] love, love as sacred, marriage as a sacrament.[31]

Similarly, social life should never be studied merely as if it were one more environmental influence shaping the individual's behavior in a mechanistic way. It must be studied as a mutual dynamic among persons, as a forum in which various roles are both learned and chosen, and ultimately as an imperfect yet sacred and divinely normed reflection of the fellowship that God desires *with* his people and *for* them in the company of the saints.

Thus, as constructionists we agree with Koch that psychologists must struggle to think in meaningful, human categories about the human significance of human behavior. But as *Christian* constructionists, bound to Christ by the grace of God, we are uniquely aware of human themes that are still considered puzzling or irrelevant to psychology as a whole—themes such as pride, guilt, the search for an object of worship, and the transcendent origins of human creativity. Yet to say that we are "uniquely aware" of such themes does not mean that we are *adequately* aware of them—and this brings us to a final and very serious challenge.

I have already referred positively to Koch's suggestion that psychologists see themselves as involved in an inherently interdisciplinary enterprise. I have also echoed his call for psychologists to become better acquainted with the philosophical underpinnings of their discipline. But obviously there is a further challenge for Christians as well. In a sense, Christians in psychology are by definition interdisciplinary, for whenever we speak in terms of "the integration of faith and learning" we are already acknowledging that we see our discipline through the lens of our study of Scripture and theology as well as vice versa. Yet I think we must admit that for most of us the study of Scripture and theology has rarely proceeded much past the Sunday School level.

Historian Mark Noll, writing about evangelicals and the study of the Bible, put it quite succinctly when he said that "theologically conservative American Protestants have always nurtured a deep at-

---

31. Vitz, "From a Secular to a Christian Psychology," p. 123. Note that in calling marriage a sacrament, Vitz is consistent with his adopted tradition of Roman Catholicism; but Protestants, even if they do not view marriage as a sacrament on a par with baptism and communion, can still agree with the spirit of his remarks.

tachment to the Bible [but] it has not always been a particularly academic attachment." And yet, he points out, "a reinvigorated evangelical Bible scholarship has been continuing now in North America for more than a generation"—characterized by a rise in high-level professional certification among evangelical Bible scholars, by their participation *as evangelicals* in the professional societies of their discipline, by the growth of adjunct, evangelically based professional societies, and by the tremendous growth of evangelical biblical scholarship in published form.[32]

What this revival of orthodox biblical scholarship is telling us is that we can and should be pursuing our understanding of Scripture on an intellectual as well as a confessional level if we want to mine its resources effectively for psychology. But as yet there is little evidence that Christians in psychology have found effective ways to do this. The pattern of our training is still largely secular—certainly on the graduate level where the contours of our professional identity are shaped. As a result, any subsequent attempts at integration take place between two unequally trained halves of our intellectual selves: that of the psychologist trained for years in a secular environment, and that of the biblical student, trained mostly in Sunday School and perhaps in a couple of compulsory religion courses if we attended Christian liberal arts colleges.

I believe it is time we acknowledged that this is not enough and took advantage of the present mood of reform in psychology to mount training (and continuing education) programs more adequate to our own needs as Christian professionals and academics. Granted, we have a couple of boldly innovative programs from which to learn: there is the doctoral program in psychology at Fuller Seminary, the graduates of which are also required to have earned an M.A. in theology. There is also the program of the Psychological Studies Institute, which provides biblical and theological training for students enrolled in the graduate psychology program at Georgia State University. Finally, there are master's-level programs in Christian studies, mounted by schools such as Regent College in Vancouver and New College in Berkeley, specifically aimed at adding a Christian dimension to the intellectual lives of graduates from secular universities. But as yet no long-term evaluations of such programs have

---

32. Noll, "Evangelicals and the Study of the Bible," *Reformed Journal* 34 (Apr. 1984): 11, 12.

emerged to give us suggestions for future schemes; moreover, those programs with a concentration in psychology are geared toward the training of counselors and clinicians only, and not toward the shaping of academic psychologists who can go on to grapple with psychology's paradigm where it originates and also dominates the field—in the university setting.

Such programs are far from inexpensive; Fuller's doctoral students in psychology, for example, often take on the burden of heavy, long-term debts to complete their training. But if we are serious about being Christian *scholars* in our conduct of psychology, we must find ways both to multiply and diversify such programs, and to make them accessible to qualified and motivated students without undue financial burden. For if it is true, as Koch put it, that psychology is necessarily the most philosophy-sensitive of all the disciplines, it is equally true that it is the discipline that is most affected by religious world view considerations. Indeed, much of this volume has been intended as a demonstration of this very point. Thus, in my view, the Christian community has a special responsibility for the future conduct of psychology, both academic and applied, and for the training of Christians within it. It is my hope that both Christian professionals and Christian laity and students will have been aided in that task by this consideration of the person in psychology.

INDEX

Abelson, Robert, 152–56
Adler, Alfred, 221–22
Allport, Gordon, 178, 208, 211,
    212, 221–22
Aristotle, 29–30, 36–40, 42–43
Aronson, Elliot, 181
Artificial Intelligence (AI): Chris-
    tian responses to, 158–60, 172–
    73; and human intelligence,
    165–66; research examples of,
    152–56, 157, 164–65; "strong
    AI position," 152, 156–58;
    "weak AI position," 152–56
Asch, Solomon, 203
Atthowe, John M., Jr., 124–25
Augustine, Saint, 37, 52, 72, 74–
    75

Bandura, Albert, 125
Bannister, Donald, 71
Behavioral psychology: Christian
    response to, 136–40; counter-
    control in, 122–27; history of,
    4–5; operant conditioning in,
    112–14, 119; resistance to cog-
    nitivists to, 144–51; respondent
    conditioning in, 110–12, 119;
    self-control techniques in, 128–
    30
Behaviorism: metaphysical, 114–
    15, 120, 138–40; meth-
    odological, 114–15, 138–40
Behavior modification: applied,
    115–16; ethics of, 132–35
Bergson, Henri, 144–45
Binet, Alfred, 160–61
Black, Max, 123–25

Bonhoeffer, Dietrich, 214
Boring, Edwin G., 6, 84, 85, 161
Boss, Médard, 221–22
Brain: and biofeedback, 97; and
    effects of damage to it on person-
    hood, 94–97; history of research
    on, 81–82
Buck-Morss, Susan, 167
Buddha (Siddhārtha Gautama),
    22–28
Bufford, Rodger, 109, 138, 139
Buss, Allan R., 3, 8, 167

Campbell, Donald T., 188–89,
    254
Chomsky, Noam, 147–51, 158
Cognition: in Aristotle, 38–39; in
    behavioral psychology, 122–23;
    cross-cultural research on, 166–
    68; developmental aspects of,
    144–51, 163–64; neglect of in
    psychology, 4; in personality the-
    ory, 222–23; and philosophy of
    science, 32–33; in Plato, 32–33;
    revival of interest in, 143–58; in
    social psychology, 181–82
Collingwood, R. G., 73
Common grace, 60–61
Comte, Auguste, 6–7
Cooper, John, 88, 102–3
Cosmology, biblical, 46–47

Darley, John, 192
Darwin, Charles, 43–44
Democritus, 31–32, 36, 42–43, 45
Dennett, Daniel C., 156–58, 165
Descartes, René, 83–85, 94

261